SHAPING THE POST-SOVIET SPACE?

Shaping the Post-Soviet Space?
EU Policies and Approaches to Region-Building

LAURE DELCOUR
*Institut de Relations Internationales et Stratégiques, Paris, France
and Ecole Nationale d'Administration, Strasbourg, France*

LONDON AND NEW YORK

First published 2011 by Ashgate Publishing

2 Park Square, Milton Park, Abingdon, Oxon OX14 4RN
711 Third Avenue, New York, NY 10017, USA

Routledge is an imprint of the Taylor & Francis Group, an informa business

First issued in paperback 2016

British Library Cataloguing in Publication Data
Delcour, Laure.
  Shaping the post-Soviet space? : EU policies and approaches
  to region-building.
  1. European Union--Russia (Federation)
  I. Title
  341.2'422'0947'09049-dc22

Library of Congress Cataloging-in-Publication Data
Delcour, Laure.
  Shaping the post-Soviet space? : EU policies and approaches to region-building / by
  Laure Delcour.
      p. cm.
  Includes bibliographical references and index.
  ISBN 978-1-4094-0224-4 (hardback)
  1. European Union countries--Foreign relations--Former Soviet republics. 2. Former
Soviet republics--Foreign relations--European Union countries. 3. European Union--
Former Soviet republics. 4. Regionalism--European Union countries. I. Title.

  JZ1570.A57D45 2011
  341.242'20947--dc22

                                                                    2010048801

  ISBN 978-1-4094-0224-4 (hbk)
  ISBN 978-1-138-25775-7 (pbk)

Contents

List of Abbreviations

BOMCA	Border Management Programme in Central Asia
BSEC	Black Sea Economic Cooperation Organization
BSS	Black Sea Synergy
CABSI	Central Asia Border Initiative
CADAP	Central Asia Drug Assistance Programme
CBSS	Council of the Baltic Sea States
CDC	Community of Democratic Choice
CEEC	Central and East European Countries
CEPOL	European Police College
CIS	Commonwealth of Independent States
COEST	Working Party on Eastern Europe and Central Asia within the Council of the EU
COMECON	Council of Mutual Economic Assistance
CFSP	Common Foreign and Security Policy
CIB	Comprehensive Institution-Building
CSTO	Collective Security Treaty Organisation
DCFTA	Deep and Comprehensive Free Trade Area
EaP	Eastern Partnership
EC	European Community
EDF	European Development Fund
EEAS	European External Action Service
EMCDDA	European Monitoring Centre for Drugs and Drug Addiction
ENP	European Neighbourhood Policy
ENPI	European Neighbourhood and Partnership Instrument
EPA	Economic Partnership Agreements
ESDP	European Security and Defence Policy
EU	European Union
EUBAM	European Union Border Assistance Mission
EUMM	European Union Monitoring Mission
EurAsEC	Eurasian Economic Community
EUROJUST	European Union's Judicial Cooperation Unit
EUROPOL	European Police Office
FRONTEX	European Agency for the Management of Operational Cooperation at the External Borders
GAERC	General Affairs and External Relations Council
GUAM	Georgia Ukraine Azerbaijan Moldova Organisation for Democracy and Economic Development

IMEMO	Institute of World Economy and International Relations
INOGATE	Inter-State Oil and Gas to Europe
NATO	North Atlantic Treaty Organization
NGO	Non-governmental Organisation
OECD	Organization for Economic Co-operation and Development
OSCE	Organization for Security and Co-operation in Europe
PCA	Partnership and Cooperation Agreement
PfM	Partnership for Modernisation
NIS	New Independent States
PHARE	Pologne Hongrie Assistance à la Restructuration Economique
SCO	Shanghai Co-operation Organisation
TACIS	Technical Assistance to the Commonwealth of Independent States
TRACECA	Transport Corridor Europe Caucasus Central Asia
UND	United Nations Development Programme
USSR	Union of Soviet Socialist Republics

Foreword

This book is important for three reasons.

First, the post-Soviet space is the most important neighbouring region of the European Union. Economic, political and societal interdependence has been growing steadily over the past 20 years. Since the 2004 enlargement, several EU member states share borders with former Soviet republics. Those countries are of tremendous importance for the Union's energy security – be it as producers of oil and gas or as transit countries. Most importantly, however, most countries in the post-Soviet space are neighbours *in* Europe. Therefore, for the EU the question is not only about how to build up diplomatic relations with them, but about how to integrate them. It is essentially about the future of the European continent.

Secondly, the European Union has advanced to become one of the key players in the post-Soviet space. It is a central economic and trade partner and the biggest provider of economic support, technical assistance and humanitarian aid in the region. Through the various policy instruments it has deployed in the past few years it supports political and economic reform processes, civil society and conflict resolution. Some of the eastern neighbours nurture the hope of becoming EU members in the foreseeable future. For them, but also for less ambitious regional players, the Union has become an alternative political model and also a counterweight to Russia's overpowering influence.

And yet, the Union often finds itself overwhelmed by the complex dynamics in its eastern neighbourhood. As Laure Delcour rightly points out in her introduction, this is a *terra incognita* in every sense of the word: 12 countries (15 post-Soviet republics minus the three Baltic countries which are now members of the EU), which share certain characteristics that are the legacy of their Soviet past, but which nevertheless have taken very different development trajectories since the demise of the Soviet Union. A host of factors – state weakness, political and economic instability, corruption, constant tensions over energy trade issues, socio-economic and environmental problems – undermine their sustainable development. Unresolved conflicts and disagreements over borders, resources and many other issues make it questionable, to say the least, if the post-Soviet space can be called a region at all. Last but not least there is Russia, who considers the post-Soviet space her 'sphere of privileged interests' and external actors such as the EU as competitors for influence.

Finally, the Union's foreign and security policy itself is a 'moving target.' Internal decision-making processes affecting political strategies and instruments are not always transparent and easily understandable from the outside. Often they reflect delicate internal compromise rather than the most effective response to the realities on the ground in the respective countries or regions. EU rhetoric tends to be self-affirmative which sometimes makes it difficult for the Union to have an objective and critical perspective on the way in which its foreign policy impacts on its eastern neighbourhood. Now the Lisbon Treaty promises to streamline and rationalise decision-making and to make EU foreign policy more efficient and comprehensible for third countries. It will take some time, however, before the treaty is implemented and before its effects become visible.

Clearly, misunderstandings abound between the EU and its eastern neighbours. When people do not understand each other they need translation. What Laure Delcour offers in her study is a translation that works both ways: On the one hand, she explains the internal dynamics and key drivers of EU policy towards the post-Soviet space. On the other hand she examines the conditions EU policy meets in that space and explains the reasons for its success or failure on the ground. Thanks to her dual expertise in European foreign policy *and* in post-Soviet affairs she provides the reader with a unique perspective. Last but not least, the political reorganisation of the post-Soviet space is an extraordinarily topical issue that is, high up on the agenda of all relevant actors. Therefore, it is most apt that Laure Delcour chooses the prism of regionalisation for her analysis of the interaction between the European Union and its eastern neighbours.

I hope that this important volume will gain a wide readership both inside the European Union and in the post-Soviet space – and beyond.

Sabine Fischer
European Union Institute for Security Studies

Acknowledgements

The idea of this book originates in the observation of EU policies during trips and stays in various post-Soviet countries over the last fifteen years, first in Russia starting in the mid-1990s and then also in other new independent States during the following decade. The picture that gradually emerged from these observations in the field was manifold. It highlighted a European Union which was gaining influence and striving more and more to shape an area which was *terra incognita* in the EU's external relations two decades ago, which the EU discovered only very gradually and which became crucial to the EU's foreign policy agenda. It also reflected a European Union increasingly differentiating – and possibly compartmentalising – its policy framework between several sub-areas within the post-Soviet space, closely integrating with some of them while trying to protect itself from potential threats originating in others. This book intends to explore the connection between the multiple aspects of this picture, and in particular the way in which the EU has envisioned, used, or induced region-building in its policies in the post-Soviet area.

A number of persons played a role in making this book possible; while only some of them can be mentioned here, I owe a considerable debt to all of them.

I want first to thank my editor, Natalja Mortensen, for her support and her patience through the drafting and production processes of this book. I am also grateful to Véronique Charléty, at ENA, for her understanding and encouragement.

My warmest and special thanks to Sabine Fischer for agreeing to write the foreword of this book and for all the interesting discussions we had about the EU and the post-Soviet area.

I am most grateful to Benoît Challand, Benjamin Demière, Hélène Naudet, Florent Parmentier, Elsa Tulmets and Kataryna Wolczuk for their insightful comments on draft chapters of the present volume.

A book is about testing ideas, confronting them with facts and, in light of those facts, refining these ideas with the intent of either elaborating on some facets or adjusting other concepts. Presenting my research at various conferences and exchanging ideas with colleagues has been more than useful in this experimental process. I have benefitted considerably from my participation in conferences organised by CERI/Sciences-Po, the EU Institute for Security Studies, GARNET, the Centre for Russian and East European Studies of Birmingham University and the Slovak Foreign Policy Association.

Last but certainly not least, I am most indebted to Chad Steponik for the wonderful job he did during the editing phase of this work and for his valuable comments; *un immense merci*, Chad!

Laure Delcour

Chapter 1
Analytical Framework

Following the end of the Cold War and the overthrow of communist regimes, the European Economic Community (EEC) emerged as both a pole of attraction and a strategic anchor for the stabilisation of the whole continent. Yet, whereas the Community's answer to the upheavals in Central and Eastern Europe was quickly designed and ushered in through the enlargement process, more time was needed to build a strategy *vis-à-vis* the former Soviet Union. Arguably, the Community was overwhelmed by the pace and the depth of changes affecting the former USSR. When the Soviet Union[1] collapsed, a major issue for the EEC was clearly identified as the preservation of regional links among New Independent States (NIS) replacing the USSR, as summarised by Jacques Delors, then president of the European Commission, who described the post-Soviet challenges faced by the EC as follows (Delors 1992: 173):

> In the former Soviet Empire, everything will depend upon what the peoples will decide for themselves. Will they follow the path of anarchy ...? Or will they note that, even though independent, they have for economic or even political reasons to work together in the framework of a kind of confederation, or maybe even of a federation modelled after the Community, since they quote this example more and more often? Will Russia, remembering the pre-communist period, gather its forces to aggregate the ensemble and act as a tutor or as a monitor? There is an additional difficulty: where should Russia or this post-Soviet Union, which belong altogether to Europe and to another world, be placed?[2]

The post-Soviet area thus emerged as a two-fold enigma for the European Community. First, the question of the links to be developed between the Community and the independent states arose suddenly in the early 1990s as one of the tasks to be dealt with by the nascent European foreign policy. Indeed, owing to the lack of official relations between the USSR and the EEC until the end of the 1980s, the whole area was a *terra incognita* to Brussels. Second, the USSR's collapse posed a major challenge to the EEC in light of its traditional approach encouraging regional cooperation in its foreign policy. A possible evolution towards other forms

---

1 The Union of Soviet Socialist Republics (USSR, also known as the Soviet Union) consisted of 15 republics which became sovereign states in 1991: Armenia, Azerbaijan, Belarus, Estonia, Georgia, Kazakhstan, Kyrgyzstan, Latvia, Lithuania, Moldova, Russia, Tajikistan, Turkmenistan, Ukraine, Uzbekistan.

2 Translated from the French by the author.

of cooperation or integration between the new sovereign states was therefore of great interest to the European Community. To sum up, the EC had to design in the former USSR a policy framework starting from scratch and with limited possibilities to apply its preferred region-building approach. Moreover, it had to cope with an environment undergoing drastic changes at a time when it was itself building new stages of its own integration process.

Because of these specific features, the former USSR is a stimulating field for studying what the European Union does and how it acts in the international arena. How has the EEC, subsequently transformed into a Union,[3] tackled this post-Soviet puzzle and the disintegration dynamics affecting this area, at a time when it was itself undergoing in-depth changes while giving a decisive impetus to the building of a political and economic Union? To what extent has the EU influenced and directly contributed to shaping the post-Soviet region?

This book will analyse the EU policies designed for and implemented in the former Soviet Union as a test of Europe's capacity to promote one of its core foreign policy objectives – support to regional cooperation – and to raise a distinctive profile in the international arena.

Understanding an International Actor in the Making: The Case for a Bottom-up Research Perspective

Since the early 1990s, the EU has undoubtedly emerged as a 'global actor' (Bretherton and Vogler 1999) displaying a 'new assertiveness' (Rummel 1990) in the international arena. By prompting new and wide-ranging EC policies in the former Eastern block, the end of the Cold War radically transformed the EC's international role and its external action. Two main processes can be identified in this regard.

The first one is well known and relates to the *institutionalisation* of a European foreign policy. The term 'foreign policy' is used widely here. It refers to the management of relationships between the EU (including its Member States) and the outside world.[4] In this respect, institutional changes that have occurred since the 1990s include the creation of a Common Foreign and Security Policy (CFSP) representing the second pillar of the European Union which came into being with the entry into force of the Maastricht Treaty, the creation of the position of High Representative for CFSP in the Amsterdam Treaty, the launching of a

---

3   The European Community became the European Union following the entry into force of the Maastricht Treaty in 1993. For greater convenience both names are used indifferently in this book.

4   This definition is similar to the one adopted by Karen E. Smith, who defines foreign policy as 'the activity of developing and managing relationships between the state (or, in our case, the EU) and other international actors, which promotes the domestic values and interests of the state or actor in question.' See Karen Smith 2008: 2.

European Security and Defence Policy (ESDP), and the changes introduced by the Lisbon Treaty, particularly in the position of the High Representative of the Union for Foreign Affairs and Security Policy. Other important institutional changes, although less visible, have also affected the Communities pillar,[5] namely the growing number and importance of Directorate Generals in charge of external relations within the European Commission. These changes gradually turned the EU into a foreign policy *actor* alongside the member states (albeit, for a long period of time, a decidedly 'divided' actor with three different pillars and miscellaneous decision-making procedures). This evolution is not over, and the entry into force of the Lisbon Treaty is a preliminary step toward the development of a renewed institutional framework for foreign policy. The creation of a European External Action Service (EEAS) is another major development in this respect.

The second remarkable process at stake is the universalisation of the EU's external action.[6] In the 1990s, the EU concluded new agreements and launched new aid programmes for a number of third countries or regional groupings, including in areas where it previously had no policy. Its network of policies and programmes now spans the globe. Moreover, both the scope and the content of the Union's foreign policy have also deeply been altered and broadened. Once limited to trade and development cooperation (the main components of the previously-named European Community's external relations), the EU's activities have expanded along with its competencies. Conflicts in the Balkans were instrumental in initiating a European policy in an area which had remained sensitive and therefore neglected since the rejection of the European Defence Community in the 1950s. For the first time in 2003, the European Union drafted a security strategy, a document which reflected a growing engagement as a security actor (Council of the European Union 2003). Migration, conflict prevention and management, and energy security have emerged as core issues on the European foreign agenda (Council of the European Union 2008; Vasconcelos 2009). Hence, the EU's foreign policy has gained a global dimension, spanning the world and encompassing most policy areas.

The point here, however, is not to describe at length the landscape of the EU's foreign affairs; it is rather to highlight the deep transformations those affairs have undergone and their constantly evolving character, resulting from both external and internal pressures. Changes in European foreign policy occur not only as a result of external events, as obvious in the case of the end of the Cold War. They are also tightly connected to internal developments in the European integration process. As a result of this combination of a changing external environment and a constantly

---

5   The pillar structure was introduced with the Maastricht Treaty on 1 November 1993 and abandoned with the entry into force of the Lisbon Treaty on 1 December 2009. The Communities pillar formed the first pillar of the Union.

6   On this issue, see the analysis of Franck Petiteville on EU cooperation activities (Petiteville 2001).

evolving integration process, the European Union is still an international actor in the making (Delcour and Tulmets 2007: 3–8).

European Foreign Policy's Status as a 'Very Fast-Moving Target' (Carlsnaes 2004: 3) Creates a Major Analytical Challenge for Scholars

Over the past two decades, increasing attention has been dedicated to the objectives pursued by the EU in its foreign policies, to the assessment of the EU's influence in the international arena and to the way this influence is exerted. The external developments of European integration have given rise to a number of publications, which Franck Petiteville (Petiteville 2006) divides into three strands based upon their core theme. The first group of publications, he argues, focuses on the institutionalisation of a European foreign policy. The second strand analyses key policies developed abroad by the EU and their impact. Finally, a third group of scholars have strived to theorise the EU's international actions (Petiteville 2006: 15–18).

Crossing these strands and topics studied by scholars, the issue of the EU's specificity as an international actor has been at the core of academic discussions. This specificity is widely explained through the historical developments of the EU integration process (for example, the long-standing lack of military capabilities following the failure of the European Defence Community in the 1950s) and its *sui generis* polity combining supranational and intergovernmental elements. Concepts such as 'civilian power',[7] 'soft power',[8] and 'normative power'[9] have been used to illustrate the EU's uniqueness as an international actor. For some authors, the EU's distinctiveness in the international arena stems from the promotion of normative objectives in its foreign policy. Other scholars instead point to the uniqueness of the EU's tools and instruments and emphasise the specific ways in which it pursues its foreign policy objectives. More specifically, they stress the EU's reliance on persuasion and diplomacy rather than on coercion (K. Smith 2008: 233). Given the fast-changing environment of the EU's foreign policy, a key issue for academics has been to assess the persistence of the EU's distinctive profile, especially in view of the development of military capabilities which the Union had lacked until the end of the 1990s. For some of them (K. Smith 2005), the development of a European Security and Defence Policy is expected to affect the nature of the EU as an

---

7   The concept was originally coined by François Duchêne in 1973 (Duchêne 1973); see also Whitman 1998.

8   Joseph Nye defines soft power as 'the ability to get what you want through attraction rather than coercion or payments … Hard power, the ability to coerce, grows out of a country's military and economic might. Soft power arises from the attractiveness of a country's culture, political ideals and policies' (Nye 2004: 256). For a comparison of US and EU soft powers and an analysis of their differences, see Tulmets 2007.

9   See in particular Manners 2002 and 2006; Sjursen 2006; Laïdi 2008.

international actor and to undermine the EU's civilian power. Yet, as convincingly pointed out by academics conducting research on the EU use of sanctions (de Wilde d'Estmaël 1998, Portela 2005), civilian tools can also be used in a coercive manner.

The above-mentioned literature has undoubtedly contributed to defining *what the European Union is* in the international arena and how it distinguishes itself from other international actors. Nevertheless, several conceptual gaps have been identified in the analysis of the EU's foreign policy. Those stem primarily from an analytical focus on the EU's specificity as a complex international actor. Christopher Hill and Michael Smith deplore the tendency to concentrate on the EU's *sui generis* qualities, combined with a reliance on the tools of comparative politics. They call for bringing back international relations theories in the study of EU foreign policy (Hill and Smith 2005: 4). Brian White highlights two limits in what he calls 'the EU-as-actor-approach' (White 2004: 17–18). First, this approach relies on the assumption that the EU can be analysed as a single actor in the international arena and therefore misses its pluralist and multi-level character. Second, it focuses on the outcomes of European foreign policy rather than on its processes, thus missing key elements such as the factors, conditions, context and/or actors leading to the construction of a foreign policy.

While there is certainly scope for exploring other theoretical approaches,[10] it can also be argued that *another major analytical gap lies in the connection between the conceptual approaches used so far and empirical research conducted.* Many of the policies analysed in the literature have been examined in a deductive manner, as case studies to illustrate the already elaborated conceptual approaches on the EU as a civilian or normative power (see for instance Tocci 2007a; Laïdi 2008).[11] Yet, as convincingly put by Karen Smith, studying *what the EU does* in the international arena also allows one to feed the findings back into the larger debate about the EU's international actorness (K. Smith 2008: 2). In other words, in a reversed perspective, focusing on selected policy fields and their design and implementation can help elucidate the nature of the EU's external governance and, conceptualising further, the EU as an international actor (Delcour and Tulmets 2008: 11–12). Such an approach supported by field research also allows to better take into account the processes leading to the construction of EU foreign policy and its various levels.

The Case for Selecting Region-building and Interregionalism as a Policy Field for Analysing EU Foreign Policy

The present book will adopt such an analytical perspective. To that purpose, it intends to focus on a specific policy field, namely to explore the policies designed and implemented by the European Union to support regional cooperation in the former USSR. Regional cooperation here is understood primarily as cooperation

---

10   See the discussion hereafter on the analytical framework of this book.

11   This argument was developed in Delcour and Tulmets 2008: 11–12.

among the former Soviet Union republics; but it also refers to schemes designed both for EU Member States and former Soviet countries around a common border. In other words, the present book will examine *EU approaches to regional cooperation both with and between post-Soviet countries as well as EU attempts to foster interregionalism.*

Emphasis will be put on *processes* leading to increased cooperation and integration, in other words on region-building. Such an emphasis indeed allows to account for the role played by both internal and external actors, in other words to examine the way in which the EU has supported regional cooperation in the former Soviet Union and the degree to which such support has been hindered by local developments. Specific attention will be paid to the factors fostering regionalism or, on the contrary, to those hindering region-building and thus provide an explanation for the prevalence of bilateralism in EU policies implemented in the former Soviet Union. Interregionalism relates to the relationships (whatever their degree of institutionalisation may be) between regional groupings, in the present case between the European Union, on the one hand, and regional or subregional organisations and forums grouping several NIS on the other.

The EU is not only frequently quoted as the first attempt at regional cooperation after World War II but also as the most accomplished system of integration. It is still widely perceived or represented by the majority of academics seeking to conceptualise regionalism as the prototype for regional integration. Neo-functionalist approaches (Haas 1964) have shed light on the processes guiding neighbouring states and regions in fostering integration in specific sectors. Two points are salient in their argument: the role of supranational institutions (for example, the High Authority in the European Coal and Steel Community) and the spill-over process described by Ernst Haas as encouraging countries to expand existing cooperation to adjacent areas (Haas 1968). Functionalist and neo-functionalist approaches have been criticised – by intergovernmentalists,[12] among others – for downplaying the role of national governments and thus failing to explain important political developments in the European integration process. However, in attempting to conceptualise EU regionalism, intergovernmentalists and neo-functionalists have mainly concentrated on the internal integration project. Thus, while the mechanisms underpinning the EU system have been described at length, less attention has been paid to the external aspects of such a model.

Yet, there is clearly a strong link between the EU internal regional integration process and its foreign policy objectives. As far as European foreign policy is concerned, the EU contributes to fostering interregionalism and to supporting regional cooperation outside its borders. These two objectives have been pursued unevenly across the globe.

---

12   See in particular the publications by Andrew Moravcsik (Moravcsik 1993; Moravcsik 2005).

The former, that is, the links and dialogues developed by the EU with other regional groupings, has increasingly raised the attention of scholars over the past few years. While a convincing theory of interregionalism is still considered to be lacking (Hänggi, Roloff and Rüland 2006: 10), a number of publications have analysed the wide network of interregional arrangements concluded by the EU worldwide and they have shown the way in which *interregionalism has become a major component of the EU's foreign policy since the end of the Cold War.*[13] This growing importance can be explained through both internal and external factors. On the one hand, a new wave of regional cooperation, concurrent with globalisation processes, emerged at the end of the 1980s and in the 1990s, leading to the creation of groupings and organisations such as the Mercado Común del Sur (MERCOSUR), the North American Free Trade Agreement (NAFTA), South Asian Association for Regional Cooperation (SAARC), the Southern African Development Community (SADC) and a number of others. This 'new regionalism'[14] coincided, on the other hand, with the worldwide expansion of EU foreign policies. Against that background, promoting region-to-region relations is considered by the EU as a foundation for its external policies as far as it enhances its international actorness and efficiency.[15] When it comes to empirical case studies, publications have mainly focused on the interregional links between the EU and a few areas or their regional groupings, mainly East Asia[16] and South America (EU–MERCOSUR links),[17] and also Africa.[18] *As far as EU support for*

13   See in particular, Söderbaum and van Langenhove, 2006; Hänggi, Roloff and Rüland 2006; Telò 2007.

14   The term was coined to distinguish these new regional groupings from the 'old' regionalism embodied by the EU. In contrast to older cooperation schemes, new forms of regional cooperation take place in a globalised and multipolar world and they result from the states' willingness to cope with global transformations. See Hettne, Inotai and Sunkel 1999.

15   This argument is developed by Fredrik Söderbaum and Luk van Langenhove (Söderbaum and van Langenhove 2006: 3). Interregional links help the EU promote the liberal internationalist agenda, build its own identity as a global actor and strengthen its power (Söderbaum and van Langenhove 2006: 120–9).

16   See for example, Gilson, J. 'New Interregionalism? The EU and East Asia', in Söderbaum and van Langenhove 2006: 59–78; Dent, C.M. 'The Asia–Europe meeting process: beyond the triadic political economy?' in: Hänggi, Roloff and Rüland 2006: 113–27.

17   See for example, Vasconcelos, A. 'European Union and MERCOSUR', in: Telò 2007: 165–84; Santander, S., 'The European Partnership with Mercorsur: A Relationship Based on Strategic and Neo-liberal Principles', in: Söderbaum and van Langenhove 2006: 37–58; Faust, J, 'The European Union's relations with MERCOSUR: the issue of regional trade liberalization', in: Hänggi, Roloff and Rüland 2006: 155–67.

18   See for example, Söderbaum, F. 'African Regionalism and EU–African Interregionalism', in: Telò 2007: 185–202; Farrell, M. 'A Triumph of Realism over Idealism? Cooperation between the European Union and Africa', in: Söderbaum and van Langenhove 2006: 15–36.

regional cooperation is concerned, as demonstrated by Karen Smith, it is one of the oldest goals, one of the core norms promoted and one of the core objectives pursued by the Union in the international arena (Karen Smith 2008: 2). Therefore, as stressed by De Lombaerde and Schulz (2009: 1), through its direct and indirect contributions the EU is expected to have an impact on regionalisation elsewhere.

The EU has promoted regional cooperation in other parts of the world using several tools, for example, through the conclusion of similar types of agreements with countries belonging to a single area, through the design of regional strategies and aid programmes rather than bilateral ones, through the encouragement of neighbouring countries to cooperate with one another and, on an exceptional basis, through the use of conditionality.[19] The European Development Fund (EDF) benefiting the Africa–Caribbean–Pacific (ACP) countries is the most famous example of a regionally-designed cooperation programme; all agreements regulating cooperation (the Yaoundé convention, the successive Lomé conventions and the Cotonou agreement) were concluded with ACP countries as a whole. Africa is also the continent where the EU has systematically tried to foster regional subgroupings, including the negotiation of Economic Partnership Agreements (EPAs) (Farrell 2009). Another major region-building initiative is the Euro-Med partnership. This partnership identifies the regional level as the most appropriate one to tackle problems which are deemed common to Southern Mediterranean countries and in particular to promote democratisation and security.

Not surprisingly, in carrying out empirical research on EU support to regional cooperation, academics have focused their attention on the above examples,[20] either because of the centrality of a regional dimension in the EU's foreign policy in the area concerned (for example, in Africa) or because of the flagship character granted to the regional initiatives (for example, the Euro-Med partnership). The EU's quest for region-building as well as for interregionalism has been considered an expression of its 'civilian power',[21] thus feeding back into the conceptual debate on the nature of the EU as an international actor. When it comes to the content and objectives of the EU's foreign policy, scholars have shown for instance that the regional dimension embedded in the Barcelona process is a means for the EU to promote its own norms in the South Mediterranean countries,[22] yet it can also be considered a policy instrument for improving geopolitical stability in the region

---

19   This applies to the Western Balkans area. The political and economic conditions linked to EU cooperation aid, contractual relations and trade policy are defined in the framework of the regional approach proposed by the European Commission in 1997. See the conclusions of the General Affairs Council, 29 April 1997, http://www.consilium. europa.eu/ueDocs/cms_Data/docs/pressdata/en/gena/028a0057.htm.

20   De Lombaerde and Schulz (2009: 1) note however that few systematic studies have been conducted on the EU's contribution to regionalisation worldwide; they aim at bridging this gap in their comparative research (2009).

21   This is the argument developed by Mario Telò (Telò 2006).

22   See for example, Bicchi 2006.

and reducing migration to Europe (Farrell 2009: 1172). In other words, the EU's emphasis on region-building is either explained through a rational cost-benefit analysis of issues and possible solutions or through an 'attempt to promote its own model' (Bicchi 2006: 287). *Support for regional cooperation as a foreign policy objective and promotion of interregional dialogues are thus tightly interconnected with the EU's own experience of integration.*

Following this argument, regional cooperation is therefore constitutive both of the EU's internal and external identities. As a result, EU policies and initiatives to foster regional links in the world offer a fruitful ground to study the EU's self-perceptions, its instruments and its influence on the international arena. They also allow for highlighting the interconnection between various policy actors and levels in the conduct of the EU's foreign policy. The core questions here are the following: To what extent does the EU's foreign policy convey a message promoting regional cooperation and interregionalism? How deeply is this message linked to its own internal model of integration, that is, to its core norms and values? To what extent does it reflect EU institutions or member states' interests? To what extent have EU region-building discourse and initiatives triggered effective cooperation, thus substantiating the hypothesis of an exogenous regional cooperation and enabling the EU to raise its profile in the region concerned?

Explaining Exceptions in the EU's Foreign Policy: The Former Soviet Union as a Non-existent Region, or as a Merely Forgotten One?

While the case for defining region-building as a core EU foreign policy objective is strong, the present book finds its root in the observation of a gap in the picture of the EU as widely promoting interregionalism and regional cooperation worldwide. It argues that the former Soviet Union stands as an exception in this respect.

Following the collapse of the USSR, the EU has based its policies *vis-à-vis* former Soviet Republics on a bilateral approach; it later (and even quite recently) introduced subregional initiatives that are nonetheless considered merely complementary to the prevailing bilateral dimension. A few publications have already noted the absence of any regional dimension in the EU policies *vis-à-vis* Central and Eastern Europe. Karen Smith has shown how policies focused on EU enlargement have superseded the promotion of regionalism/inter-regionalism in this part of the world (Karen Smith 2006: 99). However, the former Soviet Union has until recently remained marginal in the academic literature concerning EU foreign policy, especially with regard to the analyses of region-building and interregionalism. Except for a few publications (for example, Hillion 1998; Raux 1998; Delcour 2002), EU policies in the post-Soviet area were largely neglected by academics in the 1990s and early 2000s. Though research on EU policies in the former USSR has developed considerably over the past five years (parallel to the design of new policies and instruments *vis-à-vis* the New Independent States), it leaves questions unexplored and conceptual gaps unfilled.

Among EU policies in the former Soviet Union, the European Neighbourhood Policy (ENP) launched in 2003–2004 has, from its very beginning, received unprecedented interest from the academic community. The number of conferences, papers, seminars, books and articles dedicated to the neighbourhood policy over the past five years make it the first external EU policy to attract such large attention from scholars within a very short timeframe.[23] In the wide array of publications dedicated to the ENP, many proceeded from a comparison with the 1990s enlargement process, arguing for instance that although methods were similar in both policies, incentives differed (Kelley 2006). The analysis of connections between the EU's integration process/internal policy and external policies such as the ENP also led other scholars to favour an analytical framework based upon the external governance approach which seeks to grasp the way in which the EU expands its rules abroad (Lavenex 2004, Lavenex and Schimmelfennig 2009). Apart from the ENP, the EU's strategic partnership with Russia has also been extensively analysed,[24] quite often with a view to pointing out the diverging natures of these two international actors and Russia's specificity in the picture of an increasingly Europeanised Eastern Europe. Less attention has been paid to the EU's policies and instruments in Central Asia,[25] which are also linked to the recent impetus given to that partnership.[26]

Furthermore, issues pertaining to regionalism and interregionalism between the EU and the NIS have not been at the core of academic research, though they have been touched upon. Exceptions include regional and cross-border cooperation involving Russia and the EU or its member states – which have been studied in-depth – as well as case studies ranging from Kaliningrad or Karelia to the Baltic Sea region (see for example, Engelen 2004). More specifically, the Northern Dimension launched by the European Union in 1997 has triggered a wide interest in EU region-building initiatives involving former Soviet countries (see for example, Haukkala 2005; Aalto, Blakkisrud and Smith 2009). Regional cooperation in the other sea basin shared with the former USSR (the Black Sea) has also been widely analysed; nevertheless, until the EU enlarged to Romania and Bulgaria and launched Black Sea Synergy in 2007, academic research did not focus on the NIS concerned, but rather on the Balkans or EU candidate countries (see for example, Bechev 2006). To sum up, scholars have concentrated either on EU-NIS bilateral relations or on specific EU initiatives. *Owing also to their*

---

23   See among many others, Cremona and Hillion 2006; Kelley 2006; Koopmann and Lequesne 2007; Rupnik 2007; Delcour and Tulmets 2008.

24   See, for example Averre 2005; Emerson 2005; Antonenko and Pinnick 2005; Allison, Light and White 2006; Kempe and Smith 2006; Friedrich Ebert Stiftung 2006; Leonard and Popescu 2006; Bordachev 2010.

25   On EU policies in Central Asia, see Matveeva 2006; Melvin 2008; Emerson et al. 2010.

26   The 'New Partnership with Central Asia' was endorsed by the European Council in June 2007.

theoretical and analytical focuses, they have scarcely questioned the EU vision of the entire post-Soviet space, in particular the presence (or the absence) of a coherent EU regional vision for what was once a State. As a consequence, issues such as EU regional initiatives involving a number of NIS or interactions with post-Soviet regional or subregional organisations remain largely unexplored. Whereas some academics seem to have taken for granted, as a basis for their analysis, the fragmentation of the post-Soviet space, other scholars have often treated EU and NIS region-building processes as parallel (Malfliet, Verpoest and Vinokurov 2007), without studying in-depth the influence EU policies may have on regionalism and region-building in the former USSR.

Starting from the opposite side, the present book argues that there is a strong case for questioning the exception represented by the post-Soviet space in the picture of EU foreign policy with respect to region-building. It is based upon the assumption that such a lack of interregionalism and support for regional cooperation is also revealing and meaningful. A public policy can indeed be defined as 'what governmental actors decide to do or not to do' (Mény and Thoenig 1989: 134). The absence or the belated and limited character of EU-backed region-building initiatives in the former Soviet Union are therefore expected to shed new light on the nature of the EU as an international actor.

Research Questions, Hypotheses and Variables

This book intends to explore the policies designed and implemented by the European Union in the former Soviet Union from the angle of region-building. Through analysing the main policies that have been implemented by the EU since the 1990s in the post-Soviet area, it will explore the way in which and the degree to which the European Union relies upon either bilateral or regional tools, develops a regional vision in the post-Soviet area and contributes to regionalism and to interregionalism. As far as the promotion of regionalism has been identified as a distinctive EU feature in the international arena, these issues will be analysed in light of the EU capacity to behave as both an effective and a distinctive international actor.

The central argument of the book is that the post-Soviet area stands as an exception in EU external action in that the EU does not appear to be trying to strengthen regional cooperation or to develop interregional links in this area. This assertion stands for the period following the collapse of the Soviet Union as well as for new policies designed in the early 2000s, especially for the European Neighbourhood Policy. It is thus argued that a bilateral dimension has always prevailed in the EU's approach to the former Soviet Union, even though the policy framework has evolved.

Given the context in which EU policies *vis-à-vis* the NIS were designed in the early 1990s, a first hypothesis will be tested: whereas the EU initially reacted to the dissolution of the USSR by stressing the need for regional cooperation,

*disintegration processes at stake in the former Soviet Union have prevented
the EU from developing its traditional regional approach.* In other words,
exogenous factors prevail over endogenous ones to account for the weakness
of norms promoting region-building and the primacy of a bilateral EU policy
framework in the 1990s as well as the 2000s after the EU strategy *vis-à-vis* NIS
was thoroughly reviewed in the context of EU 2004 enlargement.

At the same time, the review of EU strategies in the post-Soviet area that
has taken place since the early 2000s has led to a growing differentiation in EU
policies in the post-Soviet space, in other words to a subregionalisation between
three main areas, namely the Western NIS and South Caucasus countries
included in the ENP, Russia and Central Asia. This trend needs to be explained
and further explored, especially with a view toward determining whether the EU
is currently trying to promote its traditional region-building objectives within
the subregional policy frameworks. The second hypothesis to be tested assumes
that *the growing subregionalisation of EU policies stems from the enlarged EU's
interests, especially regarding security.* Security will be simply defined here as
'the condition of being protected from or not exposed to danger; [....] a feeling
of safety or freedom from or absence of danger' (Oxford English Dictionary,
quoted in Biscop 2004: 3). This definition usefully points to the subjectivity of
security, that is, to its being constructed by agents. Following this argument,
there is no danger *per se*, but a perception of danger which differs across time
and space and among policy actors. Consequently, a prerequisite to analyse the
EU's approaches and role in the former Soviet Union is to unravel what, for the
EU, is to be secured in this area and how the EU proposes to secure it. Indeed,
according to Buzan and Wæver (2003: 71), 'the very act of labelling something a
security issue – or a threat – transforms this issue and it is therefore in the political
process of securitisation that distinct security dynamics originate.' The broad
definition of security adopted here therefore mirrors the EU's own inclusive
approach. The EU policy documents on security (Council of the European Union
2003 and 2008) indeed target a number of levels and of sectors (for example,
conflicts, but also migration, energy-related issues and various traffics), and
the Union increasingly puts the emphasis on soft security threats (Vasconcelos
2009). This validates the argument of a distinctive EU security approach (Biscop
2004) favouring human security (Ellner 2008). To sum up, the second hypothesis
assumes that the EU either pursues different policy objectives, supports difficult
norms or uses different policy tools in the three above-mentioned areas subject
to its perception of threats. *The dependent variable of the research is thus defined
as the support to regional cooperation and interregionalism in EU policies in
the former Soviet Union and their contribution to region-building in this area.*
Three sets of explanations can account for the EU's promotion of regionalism
(or lack thereof).

A first explanation draws upon institutionalist approaches and focuses on
the institutional framework and arrangements within the EU decision-making
system. The present book will largely draw upon these approaches, as far as they

are best suited to highlight the organisational processes leading to policy design and decision. More specifically, historical institutionalism[27] shows how institutions structure actors' incentives and thus influence the distribution of power as well as the cultural context. In other words, historical institutionalist approaches are useful to assess the degree to which institutions shape EU policies, either in the agenda-setting or in the implementation and evaluation/lesson-drawing phases. As far as the promotion of regional cooperation is concerned, focusing on the institutional conditions of EU foreign policy foregrounds the role of specific institutions and actors that open windows of opportunity to act as policy entrepreneurs for defining region-wide solutions. The European Commission, for instance, has been a major actor in favouring regionalism in EU policies worldwide.

Besides the role played by specific EU actors and institutions in the making of the Union's foreign policy, historical institutionalism also allows for assessment of the degree of coherence in policy implementation. Initiatives supporting regional cooperation may be put forward by different EU actors;[28] each EU Member State indeed develops its own policies in a given region, and these may favour such or such partner countries for historical, economic or political reasons. At the same time, the promotion of regional integration does not appear as a topic for divergences among EU actors as far as it draws upon a shared model and a common past; it can therefore be considered 'a way [for the EU] to validate its own internal coherence' (Farrell 2009: 1179).

Finally, historical institutionalism also sheds light on EU institutions' organisational culture, practices and memory. This approach is particularly useful for assessing the degree to which the EU tends to export its norms and its foreign policy objectives in a reflexive manner. Unlike realists, institutionalists do not consider norms and foreign policy objectives to be exported because they are more efficient or because they increase the exporter's influence. Institutionalists focus on the causes and roots of the export process rather than on its outcomes. For instance, they put the emphasis on learning processes (Rose 1993), on the experience gained in previous policies and on evaluations of previous instruments (Farrell 2009). Yet, other approaches grant policy-makers less rationality. In this context, the concept of institutional isomorphism[29] is helpful

---

27 Historical institutionalism is a political science approach placing the emphasis on institutional dynamics (Saurugger 2009: 213). More specifically, historical institutionalism highlights the role of institutions in transforming actors' preferences and structuring decision-making processes, and the importance of the historical context to account for change within institutions.

28 EC support for region-building can also be favoured by member states to answer specific national interests, for example, either to avoid a marginal situation on the continent, or to increase their role in the EU policy process. Among others, such arguments have been used to study the role played by some member states in the design of the ENP or in its developments. See for example, Natorski 2008; Lang 2008; Liberti 2008.

29 That is, 'the homogeneity of organizational forms and practices' (Di Maggio and Powell 1983: 148).

in grasping the EU's support for regional integration and interregionalism. Following this concept, the EU (particularly the European Commission) would seek to shape other countries and regions after its own model. As for the role of memory, historical institutionalism employs an important concept called 'path dependence',[30] which puts the emphasis on organisational memories in explaining the recurrence of a policy pattern.

A second set of explanations pays specific attention to the processes leading to the social construction of region-building (Adler 1997). The social constructivist approaches[31] are relevant for the purposes of our analysis because of their emphasis on processes and on interactions. 'Constructivism sees the world as a project under construction, as becoming rather than being' (Adler 2002: 195). It looks at the intersection of structures and agents and points to the 'identity-forming role' (Checkel 1999: 545) played by institutions and neglected by institutionalist approaches. In other words, social constructivism examines the interaction between material capabilities, discourse, norms and ideas. This approach is suitable both to the study of EU integration[32] and European foreign policy, as far as EFP itself is under construction (White 2004: 22), and to that of region-building. More specifically, two major aspects of constructivist approaches are valuable under the present research.

First, publications building upon constructivist approaches allow to test the second hypothesis selected in the analytical framework and to explain the conditions under which an issue is securitised. According to Buzan and Wæver (2003: 71), 'the very act of labelling something a security issue – or a threat – transforms this issue and it is therefore in the political process of securitisation that distinct security dynamics originate.' Such an approach points to the subjectivity of security, that is, to its being constructed by agents. Following this argument, there is no danger *per se*, but a perception of danger which differs across time and space and among policy actors. This approach is useful to unravel what, for the EU, is to be secured in its eastern vicinity and further east in the post-Soviet area, and how the EU proposes to secure it (for example, through fostering regional cooperation). In other words, constructivist approaches will inform on the connections between securitisation and regionalisation.

---

30   See in particular, Mahoney 2000.

31   Constructivist approaches analyse reality as a social construction and results from the interactions between social agents. See Wendt 1999. As noted by Steve Smith, 'there is no such thing as a social constructivist approach or theory' (Smith 1999: 682). To reflect the variety of approaches used by constructivists, Smith refers to 'social constructivisms'; Adler (1997: 335–6) distinguishes between modernist, rule-based, narrative-knowing and postmodernist constructivism.

32   See in particular, Checkel 1999 and 2001. In his critique of 'social constructivisms', Smith also notes that 'social constructivist approaches have much to offer the study of European governance' (Smith 1999: 684).

Second, presupposing that regions are social constructs as much as territories (Adler 1997), constructivism pays specific attention to the processes leading to the social construction of region-building in European foreign policy. This approach is valuable in that it considers regionalisation in a dynamic perspective in which interdependence and convergence processes are at stake.[33] Constructivist approaches also emphasise the need to take into account the interactions between the EU and external actors, as far as 'actorness is constructed through the interplay of internal political factors and the perceptions and expectations of outsiders' (Bretherton and Vogler 1999: 1). According to constructivist explanations, EU support for region-building would thus reflect interactions with the actors of the region concerned, as well as the perceptions of the EU against those of other region-builders. The hypothesis here is that social, political, cultural, and economic interaction among players (that is, states, local entities, NGOs, private businesses) located in contiguous geographical space help creating a common regional identity. However, following this argument, in the reversed situation the lack of a regional dimension in EU policies in the former Soviet Union would also stem from partner countries' lack of interactions among themselves and from their preferences for bilateralism. In other words, does the prevalence of bilateralism in EU policies reflect disintegration processes in the former Soviet Union and the dominant belief in partner countries that the Soviet Union no longer constitutes a region?

In a third set of explanations, region-building may be analysed through a grid privileging power, in line with realist approaches. The assumption here is that the EU seeks to strengthen its influence in the international arena and its identity as a global player. According to the realist view, regions are seen either as a means of domination or as an alliance aimed at increasing the power of the region-builder. For instance, the Euro-Mediterranean partnership has been described as a means for the EC to exert direct influence on partner countries (Attinà 2003). According to the realist grid of analysis, recent region-building attempts in the Eastern neighbourhood should be seen as first and foremost serving the EU's own interests, for example, securing energy supplies or enhancing security in unstable areas. Conversely, the lack of support for regional cooperation in the 1990s should be explained by the attainment of better gains through a bilateral approach. This could also be the case for the ENP: the predominance of bilateral tools (for example, the Action Plan, the main ENP instruments) would enable the EU to maximise its influence over partner countries. Such an explanation will be used to a very marginal extent to account for EU policies in the present book, as far as it considers the EU both as a unitary and as a rationale actor. Specifically, realist approaches will be used to analyse the degree to which other region-builders may act as competitors with the EU. This appears to be the case for Russia in particular, which considers NIS as the top priority on its foreign policy agenda and sees the EU as a region-builder from outside (K. Smith 2006).

---

33   See also Vasilyan 2009: 206.

Stemming from these explanations, three independent variables will therefore be used to analyse the regional dimension in the policies implemented by the European Union in the post-Soviet area:

- the selection by the EU of the regional framework to defend its policy objectives in the post-Soviet area;
- the existence of endogenous regional initiatives, mechanisms and structures fostering cooperation among former Soviet countries, and
- the presence and influence of other region-builders (insiders, for example, Russia and Kazakhstan, and outsiders, for example, China and the United States) in the post-Soviet area.

Sources and Methodology

This book relies upon the following sources:

- Policy documents issued by EU actors (the European Commission, the Council of Ministers, the European Parliament and when relevant, other institutions and actors, for example, the Committee of Regions, the Court of Auditors, and Member States' governments and national parliaments). The methodology used for analysing these sources is based upon critical discourse analysis,[34] which includes three stages: an examination of documents' structure and emphases, a comparison of documents over time to highlight possible changes in the major themes identified in the first phase of analysis, and an analysis of the social and political context to identify possible gaps and inconsistencies. To that purpose, sources issued by various EU actors will be crossed, and they will also be compared, when relevant, to NIS' policy documents.
- Empirical material gathered during field research, that is, semi-qualitative interviews and data collected during participation in EU-funded cooperation projects in four New Independent States, representative of each of the policies currently implemented by the EU: Russia; Ukraine and Georgia for the European Neighbourhood Policy; Kazakhstan for the New Partnership with Central Asia. The limits of this material are the following: First, these data were not collected in the framework of a funded research project; rather, they result from the author's opportunity to travel in the field and to participate in EC cooperation projects. As a consequence, even though similar questions were asked and similar documents examined in all countries, the corpus displays some gaps that

---

34   See in particular, the publications by Van Dijk (2001 and 2007). For an analysis of the role of language in the EU integration process, see Diez 1999. For an application of discourse analysis methods to the ENP, see Kratochvíl 2008.

do not in any case hinder a well-grounded comparative analysis. Second, the information has been collected through different time periods. While field research on EU policies was undertaken as early as the mid-1990s in Russia, it was carried out after the launching of the ENP in Georgia and in Ukraine, and in Kazakhstan after the design of a new EU strategy for Central Asia. For these countries, the emphasis will therefore be put on the most recent EU initiatives.

- The existing literature will contribute to fulfilling the gaps in the empirical material gathered for this book.

Structure of the Book

Chapter 2 traces back to the roots of the EU's policy *vis-à-vis* the New Independent States and its developments in the 1990s. It sheds light on a paradox. On the one hand, the EU's initial policy following the collapse of the USSR was embedded in the vision of the post-Soviet area as still having a common identity and thus requiring a regional approach. On the other hand, while it designed and developed in the 1990s one of its major region-building initiatives for the Southern Mediterranean countries (that is, the Barcelona process), the EU seems to have barely promoted regionalism in the former USSR. The overall policy framework and policy discourse largely focused on bilateral relations with each of the former Soviet Republics.

Chapter 3 analyses the growing differentiation and the subregionalisation process that have prevailed in EU policies since the early 2000s. The 2004 and 2007 waves of enlargement had far-reaching implications for the interactions between the EU and the post-Soviet area. They have resulted in an increased political, economic and security interdependence with neighbouring countries, that is, Western NIS and Russia. This third chapter will argue that security issues have played a crucial role in reframing the EU vision for the former Soviet Union. The high priority gained by those countries on the EU external agenda and the renovation of EU policies can also be explained by the role played by specific EU member states and institutions that have pushed forward new initiatives.

Chapter 4 focuses on the strategic partnership developed with Russia. The chapter argues that in spite of different leverages (conditionality in the case of ENP countries, selective adaptation in the case of Russia), the objectives promoted by the EU (security and stability) do not significantly differ from the ones asserted in the neighbourhood policy. However, the strategic partnership developed with Russia raises a number of challenges to the EU's foreign policy. Through its insistence on developing an equal partnership and through its renewed international assertiveness, Russia does not only defy the coherence between EU member states, it also questions the EU's soft power and disrupts its vision of the continent's architecture.

The neighbourhood policy, which is widely presented as a flagship policy by the EU, will be examined in more detail in Chapter 5. The Union promotes, through the ENP, an unprecedented example of policy export which potentially involves neighbouring countries in a wide process of Europeanisation. The chapter explores policy implementation in the field and highlights several tensions undermining the EU's attempt to export its norms. The first one is well-known and relates to the discrepancy between neighbours' expectations *vis-à-vis* the EU and the lack of accession perspective in the ENP; the case of Ukraine is examined in detail. The second source of tension stems from the effects of Russian policies *vis-à-vis* Western NIS, especially those who have chosen a pro-Western path after the 'colour revolutions'; the case of unresolved conflicts in Moldova and the South Caucasus is analysed in-depth, with a focus on the 2008 war in Georgia. The chapter also looks at the more recent EU initiative aiming at developing a regional dimension in the ENP, that is, the Eastern Partnership, and assesses the degree to which this initiative is likely to reduce the tensions present in policy implementation.

Central Asia has traditionally lacked priority on the EU foreign policy agenda when compared to other post-Soviet countries; however, the relations of the EU with the five Central Asian Republics received an unprecedented impetus in 2007 with the design of a political strategy reflecting the growing importance of the region, especially for energy supplies. Chapter 6 will argue that in developing in the area its traditional approach supporting regional cooperation and interregionalism, the EU is strongly constrained by the growing differentiation among Central Asia republics and by competing region-builders, mainly by Russia.

Chapter 7 analyses the consistency between current EU policies in the post-Soviet area, understood as the extent to which various EU policies within a given geographical framework are compatible with one another. Based upon examples drawn from transversal issues (for example, visas and migration, energy), it points to existing gaps between EU policies stemming from their increasing compartmentalisation. It shows how these gaps are explored and exploited by other region-builders, first of all by Russia, which still perceives the former USSR as its own sphere of influence. More specifically, the chapter argues that Russia has so far thwarted all EU attempts to link its various geographical policies and to promote a trans-regional approach, especially with respect to energy.

As a consequence of gaps noted in Chapter 7, regional cooperation has incrementally emerged as a necessary component in EU policies to complement the existing bilateral tools. Chapter 8 will examine two initiatives launched by the EU, the Northern Dimension and Black Sea Synergy. Even though they were launched within ten years of each other, these initiatives pertain to the same functional logic aiming at fostering region-building around core thematic issues. The chapter will assess the capacity of these initiatives to bridge the gaps between EU policies in the former Soviet Union, and in particular to engage Russia in a region-building process.

The conclusions will answer the research questions raised, summarise the main findings and propose a characterisation of the EU as a foreign policy actor in the former USSR.

Chapter 2

The EU and the Post-Soviet Area after the Collapse of the USSR: The Shadow of Regional Integration

On 8 December 1991, leaders of Russia, Belarus and Ukraine, meeting at Belavezha near Minsk, stated that the USSR no longer existed 'as a subject of international right and as a geopolitical reality.'[1] At the same time, they signed an agreement creating the Commonwealth of Independent States (CIS) which formed the basis of the text endorsed two weeks later by leaders of other former Republics[2] meeting in Alma-Ata.[3] Thus, whilst the breakup of the Soviet Union has been primarily considered a turning point closing a seven-decade period of communism, it did not imply *per se* dissolving the links among its former components. An overview of the few months preceding the Belavezha statement sheds light on ambivalent dynamics in this respect, as shown on the one hand by the attempts of the Baltic States to assert their national sovereignty and to leave the USSR in the first months of 1991 and on the other hand by a majority voting on a referendum held in March 1991 for the retention of the Union. The missed putsch against the president of the USSR (August 1991) was a turning point which resulted in accelerating the decay of the Soviet Union. In the wake of the putsch, the Soviet republics declared their independence one after another.[4] As a result, the agreements signed in December

---

1   Text of the Belazheva statement (also known as the Belazheva agreement), quoted in Brzezinski and Sullivan 1997: 44. Russian text available at: http://www.cis.minsk.by/main.aspx?uid=176.

2   The Declaration on the New Commonwealth signed on 8 December 1991 set up a Community consisting of the Russian Federation, Belarus and Ukraine, open to all former republics for accession. Leaders of the five Central Asian republics, meeting in Ashgabat on 13 December, were reluctant to join a Slavic-led organisation, and they stressed the need for an equal participation by all subjects of the former USSR in the design and decision-making process of the new community. This concern was taken into account in the Alma-Ata Declaration signed on 21 December 1991. Brzezinski and Sullivan 1997: 42.

3   The name of Alma-Ata, then Kazakhstan's capital city, was changed in 1993 to Almaty.

4   The Baltic States' independence was recognised by the central authorities in September. On 1 December, the referendum organised in Ukraine resulted in an overwhelming majority of voters choosing independence. From then on, the Union and all attempts by the central authorities to replace it (for example, the new economic community initiated in October) seemed doomed to fail.

1991 confirmed the dissolution of the Soviet Union and provided for a settlement of the main outstanding issues stemming from its disappearance as a subject of international right. However, the majority of former Soviet Republics[5] also agreed to join the newly created CIS, which was meant to become the successor entity to the USSR and was composed of sovereign states.

By the end of the year it was therefore not clear whether the breakup of the USSR and the creation of a new Commonwealth should be seen as discrete or as intermingled processes, as contradictory or as complementary events. The major questions raised were the following: Should the disappearance of a seven-decade old state be interpreted principally through the prism of ideology or also through the angles of empire and nation-building?[6] Did the breakup of the USSR put an end to the communist regime but not, as suggested by the creation of the CIS, to the links existing among the former Soviet republics? Or did these links die together with the ideology that sustained the Empire? The decisions made on 8–21 December 1991 left crucial questions either partially or totally unanswered with respect to the future relationships between the former Soviet Republics. This was especially true regarding the role to be played by the state, which was soon thereafter considered to be either continuing or succeeding (in any case, embodying) the former centre, Russia.[7] Questions concerning its interactions with the periphery of the former Empire remained as well.

This chapter will examine the EU's interpretation of, and reaction to, these events. In addition, an overview of the EU's subsequent policy *vis-à-vis* CIS countries in the 1990s will seek to answer the following questions: To what extent has the EU supported strong ties among former Soviet republics in its policies? How far has it relied upon the structures designed to replace the USSR to develop its traditional regional approach and to foster interregional links?

The upshot of the examination presented here will be the revelation of a paradox. On the one hand, the EU's initial policy following the collapse of the USSR was embedded in the vision of the post-Soviet area as still having a common identity and thus requiring a regional approach. On the other hand, while it designed and developed in the 1990s one of its major region-building initiatives for the Southern Mediterranean countries (that is, the Barcelona process), the EU seems to have barely promoted regionalism in the former USSR during the same period. As a result, the overall policy framework and policy discourse developed throughout

---

5   Except Georgia and the three Baltic States, Estonia, Latvia and Lithuania. All of them signed the document confirming the dissolution of the USSR, but the Baltic States refused to join the new Commonwealth. Georgia joined the CIS in 1993.

6   For a thorough analysis of the meaning of the overthrow of communist regimes (both in 1989 and 1991), see Armbruster 2008.

7   The Russian Federation continued to exercise the international rights and obligations that were previously those of the USSR. In particular, it took over the USSR seat in the United Nations Security Council. See Eisemann and Koskenniemi 2000, in particular pp. 249 s. and 781 s.; Hamant 2008.

the 1990s largely focused on bilateral relations with the New Independent States. This chapter will rely mainly upon exogenous arguments to account for the limited place of the regional level in the initial EU policy mix.

The Former Soviet Union, A Virgin Land for the European Community

The major hypothesis raised in the first chapter assumes that the post-Soviet area stands as an exception with respect to the EU's traditional objective of supporting region-building. However, whereas this book primarily focuses on the post-Soviet period, this chapter will refer back to the pre-1989 epoch and look at USSR–EC relations during that period to account for the central hypothesis. It can indeed be argued that the above-assumed peculiarity in the EC's external policy finds its roots in the Soviet era. For 40 years, the Communist bloc also stood out as an exception in the European Community's external relations insofar as it constituted a blind spot in the overall picture of an expanding network of economic and cooperation agreements, be they concluded with third countries or with regional groupings.[8] In the mid-1980s, the Community had indeed established links worldwide, except with its counterpart organisation in the Eastern bloc, the COMECON (Council of Mutual Economic Assistance).

Such mutual ignorance was primarily linked to the USSR's refusal to recognise the EEC and to its suspicion *vis-à-vis* an organisation that was above all regarded as the North Atlantic Treaty Organization (NATO)'s economic arm (Light 1988; 2006: 2). It should be pointed out, however, that the Soviet perception of the European integration did not remain monolithic[9] but evolved over time (Gautron 1997; Lipkin 2006). The initial line supported by Soviet authorities analysed the European integration process through the lens of Marxist ideology (Neumann 1996: 134) while also stressing the centripetal trends within the Eastern bloc, and thus considered the EEC as intrinsically intermingled with NATO.[10] Nevertheless, beginning in the 1960s under the impetus of the Institute of World Economy and International Relations (IMEMO, Russian Academy of Sciences),[11] European

---

8   For an excellent analysis of these networks of agreements and cooperation programmes concluded by the EEC, see Edwards and Regelsberger 1990.

9   See, among others, Pipes 1976; Adomeit 1979; Surovell 1995; Robin Hivert 2006; Robin Hivert and Soutou 2008.

10   This interpretation stems from the Soviet vision of the world as exclusively bipolar; it accounts for the USSR's refusal of any EEC enlargement to Finland or Austria because of their international status. See Gautron 1997, Light 2006.

11   IMEMO researchers published in the Institute's journal three series of analyses, called Theses, on European integration (1957, 1962 and 1988). Cf. 'O sozdanii obshchegorynka i Evratoma' [On the creation of the common market and Euratom], *Mirovaya Ekonomika i Mezhdunarodnye Otnoshenya (MEiMO)* no. 1, July 1957; 'Ob imperyalisticheskoy 'integratsii' v Zapadnoy Evrope' [On imperialist 'integration' in Western Europe], *MEiMO*, no. 9, September 1962; 'Evropeyskoe soobshchestvo segodnya.

integration started to be seen both as a reality and as reflecting divergences among capitalist states. This paved the way for limited openings in the 1970s.[12] However, it was only with *perestroika* that the 'dialogue of the deaf'[13] ended. A joint declaration between the EEC and the COMECON was signed in June 1988 (Council 1988), followed by their mutual recognition in August 1988. These developments reflected a major shift in Soviet thinking on European integration.[14]

This brief insight into EC–Soviet relations thus highlights parallel processes of economic integration in the Eastern and Western parts of Europe until the end of the 1980s. It is argued here that four decades of mutual ignorance during the Cold War, combined with the crisis affecting the Soviet Union in the mid-1980s and its disintegration, considerably affected the subsequent links to be developed between the USSR and the EC, as well as the EC's policy in the former Soviet Union. Soon after the establishment of official relations with the COMECON, as argued by Lippert (1993: 134), the EC sketched a differentiation between the USSR and Central Europe and dedicated more attention the latter in connection to political upheavals affecting especially Poland and Hungary in the first half of 1989. In the wake of 1989 events, the Community further developed relations with Central European countries, thus outlining a dual regional vision of the Eastern bloc.

It took, however, much more time to give an impetus to its newly established links with the Soviet Union. The deliquescence of the USSR indeed hampered both the familiarisation of the European Community with what was still a virgin land in its external relations and the design of a European strategy for its Soviet policy. A brief insight into the chronology of EC–Soviet relations highlights the limits with which the Community was confronted in designing its policy *vis-à-vis* the USSR. The first political and national upheavals in the USSR[15] took place at a

---

Tezisy Instituta Mirovoy Ekonomiki i Mezhdunarodnykh Otnoshenii AN SSSR' [European Community today. Theses of the Institute of world economy and international relations of the Academy of Sciences of the USSR.], *MEiMO*, no. 2, 1988, 5–18.

12   Since 1974 (after bilateral agreements between EC member states and COMECON countries had expired), the common trade policy has applied to state economies. See Maresceau 1989: 3.

13   The expression is used by Barbara Lippert (1990: 120). John Pinder refers to a 'stubborn diplomacy' (Pinder 1991).

14   The third and last set of IMEMO theses, published in December 1988, highlighted this shift in Soviet thinking on European integration. Even though limits were stressed regarding the Community's political and security capacities, they explicitly promoted a positive vision of the EEC through connecting peace on the continent after World War II and the European integration process. See Neumann 1996: 164.

15   1988 constitutes a watershed as far as the expression of nationalism within the Soviet Union is concerned, be it inter-ethnic or directed against the center, be it expressed violently or through political organisations. In February 1988, violence was perpetrated against Azerbaijanis after a resolution called for the unification of Nagorno-Karabakh with Armenia; this was followed in Azerbaijan by massacres of Armenians. In June, a pro-independence movement, Sąjūdis, was created in the Lithuanian Soviet Socialist Republic.

time when the EC was just establishing links with the country. A year later, the EC signed a trade and cooperation agreement with the USSR (18 December 1989, see European Communities 1990), which entered into force in April 1990 just after the Baltic States adopted the first measures to assert their sovereignty over the centre.[16] The principle of a European assistance programme to an economically devastated Soviet Union was agreed upon at the Dublin European Council in June 1990,[17] and the Commission presented the corresponding proposals in December 1990 (European Commission 1991) at a time when the centre had lost control over the economic system. Finally, the European Commission opened a delegation to the USSR in February 1991, about one month after the bloody intervention of Soviet troops in Vilnius.

This overview of the two processes, the Soviet deliquescence and the nascent European presence in the USSR, sheds light on clashing temporalities. In this respect, for two main reasons, the dissolution of the Soviet Union confronted the European Community with a number of specific policy challenges and questions. First, the absence of a relationship with the USSR until the end of the 1980s was specific to the EC since, unlike other international actors (and unlike its own Member States), the Community as such had no contact with Moscow. Second, the collapse of the Union disrupted the EC's own rhythm of construction at a time when it decided to deepen its own integration.[18] The Belazheva statement declaring the dissolution of the Soviet Union was indeed drafted on the eve of the EC head of states and governments' meeting in Maastricht to close the intergovernmental conferences on political union and economic and monetary union. The European Community was therefore faced with the task of building a strategic vision for an unknown region, the post-Soviet area, while its own agenda was overloaded with issues pertaining either to the deepening of its own integration or to enlargement to Central and Eastern European countries.[19]

---

16   Lithuania was the frontrunner in the efforts to reestablish the Baltic States' independence. In March 1990, Lithuania declared the restoration of its independence, lost during the Second World War. Almost simultaneously, the Estonian Supreme Council denounced Soviet occupation since 1940 as illegal. Latvia followed in May with the planning of a transition period before recovering independence.

17   Less than a year before, in July 1989, the EC had launched a similar programme for Poland and Hungary (PHARE, from the French Pologne Hongrie Assistance à la Restructuration Economique) and had been appointed as the coordinator for international assistance to Central Europe. The principle of assisting the Soviet Union raised much more issues and triggered reluctance on the part of some EC Member States, *inter alia* the United Kingdom.

18   Steven Smith uses the expression 'twin revolutions' to point out both the simultaneity and the interconnection between the end of the Cold War and the impetus given to the European integration process (Smith 1994: 2).

19   The first paragraph on the conclusions of the Maastricht European Council is devoted to the Treaty on the European Union and the second one to enlargement.

Designing an EU Approach after the Breakdown of the USSR: Hoping for Regional Integration, Coping with Disintegration Dynamics

The USSR collapsed at a time when the EC was practically designing a policy *ex nihilo*. As a result, the early 1990s offer a fruitful ground to grasp the EU's emerging vision of the post-Soviet space and to study the formulation of EU policies from the perspective of region-building. To what extent did the EC advocate for the preservation of ties between former Soviet Republics following the dissolution of the USSR? To what extent did it contribute to promoting new cooperation projects between the independent states? How did it interact with the regional organisations succeeding the USSR?

An insight into the design of European policies sheds light on a fragile balance and ambivalence between two approaches, the first one resorting to the traditional EC objective of supporting regional cooperation and the second one promoting differentiation between the former Soviet Republics. Both approaches are combined in the EC's initial reactions after the dissolution of the Soviet Union.

On the one hand, as clearly expressed in the Statements under European Political Cooperation[20] released from 1991 through early 1992, the EU's initial policy following the collapse of the USSR was embedded in a vision of the post-Soviet area as still having, if not a common identity, at least similar problems and thus requiring a regional approach. While announcing immediately after the Belazheva statement its willingness to develop relations with each of the New Independent States (NIS), EC initial reactions also stressed the need for preserving a degree of regional cooperation among the former Soviet Republics (European Council 1991; Delcour 2002). This emphasis on the links uniting the new countries is also reflected in the design of a single approach[21] for their recognition, which for the EC had to be based upon a set of political criteria to be fulfilled by the NIS.[22] Similarly, the technical assistance programme that had been launched the year before to support the Soviet Union was kept under a single framework for all NIS (and Mongolia). The name it was given in 1992, Technical Assistance to the Commonwealth of Independent States (TACIS), further confirms the EC's

---

Developments in the former Soviet Union are touched upon in a declaration included in annex. See European Council 1991.

20   From the 1970s onwards, European Political Cooperation introduced foreign policy consultations between EC member states. It was superseded by the Common Foreign and Security Policy when the Treaty on the European Union entered into force in 1993.

21   Namely, their commitment to abide by the provisions of international treaties (United Nations Charter, Final Act of the Helsinki Conference, Charter of Paris), to respect the inviolability of borders and to ensure the continuity of the Soviet Union's commitments regarding disarmament and non-proliferation. See European Political Cooperation 1991.

22   These criteria were considered to be fulfilled in January 1992. See European Political Cooperation 1992.

willingness to foster interregional links with the organisation created to replace the USSR.

However, as early as February 1992, the European Commission proposed to base the EC's strategy on differentiation between the former Soviet Republics (European Commission 1992a). The differentiation principle was first targeted at the three Baltic States, which were quickly integrated into the EC's policy framework for Central Europe. For those countries that had been incorporated belatedly and by force into the Soviet Union (in 1940 as a consequence of the Molotov–Ribbentrop pact), the return to Europe, the recovering of sovereignty and the nation-building process were tightly interwoven processes. By extending European identity to the three Baltic countries and by developing 'politics of inclusion' (Wennestern 1999) *vis-à-vis* Lithuania, Latvia and Estonia, the EC/EU contributed to their self-identifying as European and to their drifting away from other former Soviet republics. This approach obviously coincided with the preferences of all three countries, which had asserted the continuity of their new states with the pre-1940 entities and had refused to sign the document creating the CIS in December 1991.

Beyond the example of the three Baltic States, the differentiation principle was also promoted in the overall EC approach *vis-à-vis* the post-Soviet area. The introduction of this principle, quite unusual in an external policy preferring links with other regional groupings, stemmed from an analysis of the CIS as being 'largely ineffective' (European Commission 1992b) only two months after its creation. This negative assessment can be better understood by recalling the circumstances that led to the creation of the CIS and by explaining the diverging perceptions of former Soviet republics' leaders. While the heads of republics who signed the Belazheva statement shared a common interest in deciding the dissolution of the USSR, they implicitly had different motivations for initiating a new regional organisation.[23] The CIS served both Russia's preferences for preserving remaining links between republics and retaining a central role once the USSR was dissolved and for President Yeltsin's political interests in his struggle with the Soviet Union President, Mikhail Gorbachev. Belarus considered the newly launched organisation as a way to maximise its influence *vis-à-vis* other former republics whereas to Ukraine, the CIS could only be seen as a temporary arrangement on the way to independence. Moreover, the incentives of other republics for joining the CIS both deviated from those of the three Slavic countries and diverged among themselves. The Commonwealth as envisaged in the Belavezha statement was considered by Centrasiatic republics to be a restricted Slavic club excluding other former republics.[24] Through the Ashgabat declaration, all five Central Asian

---

23   This paragraph is based upon the analysis by Brzezinski and Sullivan (1997: 41).

24   It particularly triggered Kazakh President Nazarbaev's bitterness. The Ashgabat declaration signed on 13 December by the five Central Asian countries stated: 'One should take into account in [CIS] documents, decisions and agreements the historic and socio-economic realities of the republics of Central Asia and Kazakhstan, which, unfortunately,

countries requested a status equal to that of Russia, Belarus and Ukraine within the new organisation; at the same time, while leaders Nazarbaev of Kazakhstan and Akaev of Kyrgyzstan favoured the preservation of links between the former republics, more specifically among Central Asian countries, regional integration did not rank among the top priorities of other Central Asian states.[25] Finally, while Armenia from its independence onwards considered its participation in the CIS as a cornerstone of its foreign policy, neighbouring Georgia initially refused to join the Commonwealth. In other words, the creation of the CIS was grounded in different or even competing visions of integration.

Centrifugal trends among NIS were therefore deemed unavoidable by the Commission, but at the same time they were certainly not desirable for the EC. Regional cooperation was identified as an objective to be encouraged by the EC with a view to fostering stability in the post-Soviet area (European Commission 1992b: 2). The pursuit of this objective was based upon a willingness to diffuse the EC's successful model of integration. Indeed, whereas the EC was still poorly known by the general public across the New Independent States, this example found resonance in the early 1990s in academic circles and among policy-makers in various former Soviet republics. On a number of occasions, the organisation formerly considered as NATO's economic arm was thus presented, in the light of its successes and of its growing attractiveness, as a pattern to reproduce for developing regional integration schemes between former Soviet republics.[26]

A detailed analysis of policy documents thus highlights a binary position, reproducing the patterns experienced by the EC in its relations with third countries through support of regional cooperation which was in turn altered by a realist analysis of the situation prevailing in the former Soviet Union.

Such a duality is reflected in the policy framework developed in the early 1990s based upon the Commission's proposals. The cornerstone of this framework is the negotiation of new agreements to replace the trade and cooperation agreement signed with the USSR. The latter was deemed outdated not only because one of the contracting parties was dissolved, but also because it did not match the level of relations that the EU intended to develop with the NIS (European Commission 1992b: 2). Three aspects are salient in the EU's proposal for a new type of agreement with the former Soviet republics, later called partnership and cooperation agreements (PCA). First, the former Soviet Union is differentiated further from

---

were not considered during the preparation of the agreement on a commonwealth…The Commonwealth of Independent States cannot take shape on an ethnic, religious or any other basis infringing on the rights of individuals or peoples.' Quoted in Brzezinski and Sullivan 1997: 47.

25   See Chapter 6.

26   See references by Kazakh president Nazarbaev to the European Currency Unit (ECU) and to other steps of the European Economic Union as a road to follow by CIS countries; interview to Interfax, 26 November 1993, quoted in Brzezinski and Sullivan 1997: 179. For academic analyses, see Korovkin 1992; Shishkov 1997.

Central European countries (CEECs) as well as from the Baltic States, a feature that had been present ever since the EC had established links with the Eastern bloc and that had become prevalent after the overthrow of the communist regimes in 1989. At a time when most Central European countries had signed association agreements (also called 'Europe agreements') and were engaged in a process of accession into the Union, the NIS were offered non-preferential agreements. These agreements were framed around wide-ranging economic cooperation and political dialogue, thus bringing EU relations with the NIS to an unprecedented level, but they remained below the association proposed to CEECs, *inter alia* regarding the free movement of goods. The new type of agreement designed exclusively for the former Soviet republics was therefore conceived as an 'intermediary model' (European Commission 1992b: 9–10) between trade and cooperation agreements on the one hand, and association agreements on the other hand. In other words, whereas the choice of two different types of agreements for CEECs and for NIS stemmed from the progressively divergent paths followed by the former USSR and by Central Europe (Maresceau 1997: 4), the EU's increasingly distinct legal framework also contributed to widening the gap and was perceived as such in Russia and other NIS. [27]

The second important aspect in the design and the negotiation of PCAs relates to differentiation *among the former Soviet republics*. Such a differentiation is primarily linked to the EC political priorities in the region and to the relative importance of the countries concerned. As early as January–February 1992, the Commission singled out three countries with which exploratory talks for the future agreement should be launched as soon as possible: Russia, Ukraine and Kazakhstan.[28] To the EC, Russia in particular deserved special attention: the unique statement referring to the former Soviet Union in the Commission's work programme for 1992 mentioned the need to define 'a new framework for cooperation with the Russian Federation' (quoted in Delcour 2002). Ukraine and Russia were in fact the first two NIS to sign the PCA in June 1994 (European Communities 1994 a and b), whereas negotiations took a bit more time for the Caucasus and Central Asian countries. Nevertheless, and this is the third important aspect of the EC's proposals for designing a policy framework with NIS, the type of agreement foreseen is *similar for all former Soviet republics*. The Commission clearly conceived the EU's policy in the post-Soviet area as combining differentiation and congruence, as taking into account 'specific features within a common framework' (European Commission 1992b: 9). Such a common framework was linked to the EC's willingness to contribute to the former USSR's political and economic stability, *inter alia* through encouragement of regional cooperation.[29] Considered the heir to

---

27   This was noted *inter alia* by Vladimir Shemiatenkov, the Russian head of negotiations for the EU–Russia partnership and cooperation agreement. See Shemiatenkov 1997: 281.

28   *Europe* no. 5677, 27/02/1992.

29   Conclusions of the General Council, 2 March 1992; European Commission 1992b: 9.

the former centre, Russia was supposed to act as a locomotive in this process;[30] as indicated by Jacques Delors in a visit to Moscow, it was expected to become one of the two poles (together with the Community) of the European continent, able to aggregate CIS countries and to put forward regional cooperation or integration projects.[31] Such expectations partly explain the place assigned to Russia in the Union's post-Soviet policy.[32]

To sum up, the legal and political framework designed by the EU for its relations with the NIS in the early 1990s left the door open for region-building. This was possible because of the combination of a bilateral approach (for example, in the negotiation of PCAs as well as in the programming and the implementation of TACIS national programmes) with a common framework (for example, similar type of agreement and mechanisms of assistance). As a result, support for regional cooperation was neither explicitly claimed nor excluded from the EC's initial policy framework.

The EU's Policy Framework and Instruments in the 1990s: Bilateralism as a Rule, Regionalism as an Exception?

Throughout the 1990s, however, the policies implemented by the Union in the former Soviet Union largely focused on bilateral relations with NIS and remained void of any clear regional strategy. Whereas the EU policy framework designed for the former Soviet Union in the early 1990s did not *per se* reflect a clear strategic choice between a differentiated and a common approach, the EU increasingly developed its relations on a bilateral basis with each NIS. Though similar in their main features, PCAs were negotiated bilaterally, thus highlighting differences in the pace of reforms and in relations with the EU. As far as technical assistance is concerned, the national programmes agreed upon with the authorities of each NIS

---

30 See the questions raised by Jacques Delors on the future links between former Soviet republics after the collapse of the USSR: the first option would be anarchy with no organised relations, in the second one cooperation could take the form of a confederation or of a federation modelled after the European Community, the third one would be a grouping tutored by Russia. Delors 1992: 273.

31 *Europe* no. 5741, 1–2/06/1992.

32 The expression 'Russia-first policy' has been used by academics to describe the EU policy in the former Soviet Union in the 1990s (see for example, Vahl 2006: 9). This expression overlooks important facts or EU motivations. A closer look at the PCAs signed with CIS countries and EU funds committed through TACIS indicates that the priority given to Russia was in no way exclusive. For instance, the PCAs signed with Ukraine and Moldova also included a provision for a future free-trade area. Moreover, while Russia received almost half of the funds committed through TACIS in the 1990s, Ukraine has equally benefited from EC assistance if one considers funds committed per capita (European Commission 1999). This clearly shows that Western NIS, rather than Russia alone, mattered to the EU.

accounted for over 70 per cent of the funds committed by the EC under TACIS (European Commission 1999: 52).

However, the EU developed noteworthy initiatives to support region-building. This section will explore these policy measures and propose explanations for their introduction.

In the 1990s a regional dimension was *de facto* present in the EC policy, but only under specific conditions and to achieve specific purposes. According to the EC discourse, the Community only backed regional cooperation in the former USSR in two cases: first, in order to mitigate disruptive effects stemming from the collapse of the Union and second, when the regional level proved the most appropriate to tackle common problems (European Commission 1992b: 11). The regional dimension was mainly present in EU policy through the technical assistance programme which was managed from the European Commission headquarters, TACIS.

Because it quickly became operational (as opposed to the longer time-span usually needed to negotiate new agreements), TACIS was the first instrument to play a major role in attempts to preserve links between the former Soviet republics, a priority that both the Council and the Commission had identified immediately after the dissolution of the USSR to limit turmoil. Since it states that '[cooperation between former Soviet republics] will be stimulated as much as possible' (European Commission 1992c), the TACIS indicative programme for 1992 reflects both the EC's traditional support for region-building and its realistic analysis of the situation prevailing in the post-Soviet area. Projects were thus identified either to restore inter-state trade in agriculture or to assist the Russian government in rethinking its economic relations with other former republics.

After 1992, when the situation stabilised and while the bulk of TACIS funds was committed bilaterally for each NIS, EC support was principally channelled through programmes specifically designed at a regional level for some specific sectors. An insight into these programmes illuminates the Community's motivations and methods to support regional cooperation and points to incentives not expressed in the EC discourse. In the early 1990s, inter-state programmes were developed in those sectors in which cooperation between NIS was deemed necessary.[33] This was the case, for instance, in the environmental protection sector. In the TACIS programme, the environment was dealt with both at a national level and through a dedicated inter-state programme, the latter providing an overarching framework to the former. The importance devoted to inter-state cooperation in environmental issues stemmed from an analysis of the challenges faced by the NIS as being similar. For instance, one of the projects launched under the TACIS inter-state programme derived from the reported lack of awareness in the former Soviet Union regarding environmental issues (European Commission 1996: 84–5). The

---

33   Like PHARE initially, TACIS was conceived as a demand-driven programme. The request of at least two NIS was therefore necessary for the Commission to launch inter-state projects. Such a low ceiling favoured regional activities.

inter-state programme also acted as a policy toolbox for the formulation of national environmental policies in the NIS, *inter alia* through setting legal standards, designing a framework for policy implementation and developing management and evaluation tools.[34] In other words, while the NIS undoubtedly showed analogous signs of neglect toward the environment and presented similarly devastated areas that prompted the use of regional tools, EC support to inter-state projects also contributed to upholding similar features in their ways of managing environmental issues. Energy and transport also provide interesting sectoral examples of EC support to inter-state cooperation[35] with a view to tackling common challenges. As far as transports are concerned, the TRACECA programme (Transport Corridor Europe Caucasus Central Asia) launched in 1993 was created to support regional cooperation among NIS in order to eliminate transport bottlenecks and with the broader objective of creating transport corridors throughout the European continent.[36] The programme concept derives from the huge difficulties experienced by the EC in conveying humanitarian aid to the Caucasus and Central Asia countries through Russia in the early 1990s; it is thus aimed primarily at mitigating disruptive consequences linked to the USSR collapse of NIS transport infrastructures. Through the INOGATE (Inter-State Oil and Gas to Europe) programme initiated in 1999, the EC supported the modernisation of oil and gas distribution systems within a difficult economic context after the collapse of the Soviet Union. This entailed large-scale regional projects, for instance those aimed at rehabilitating inter-state pipelines in the NIS and rationalising their use, in compliance with international standards as provided for in the Energy Charter.[37]

However, examples drawn both from energy and transport projects as well as other sectors also indicate that EC support for inter-state projects cannot be explained only through the traditional Community support for region-building (considered at that time as the best way to tackle common problems in the context of economic and political transition). It can be argued that those sectors in which the EC channelled its assistance regionally were also crucial areas for its own interests and that the way in which the EC designed inter-state TACIS projects answered these interests. This is quite clear in the case of nuclear safety, a major EC concern after the USSR's collapse as indicated by the Council in various

---

34   These were among the main objectives of an inter-state TACIS project called 'Development of common New Independent States environmental policies', in which the EC committed €4 million (European Commission 1996a).

35   In her analysis of the EU's efforts to foster regional cooperation in the South Caucasus, Vasilyan (2009) prefers the term 'regionalization' which, she argues, connotes both internal and external impulses. She thus refers to TRACECA and INOGATE as part of this regionalisation process (2009: 208).

36   Nine such corridors were identified in March 1994. For instance, corridor nine was designed with a view to linking the Baltic, Mediterranean and Black Seas.

37   Such a project was implemented from 1996 to 1999 for a budget of €12 million. European Commission 1998: 59–60.

European Political Cooperation Declarations (for example, European Political Cooperation 1991). A few years after the Chernobyl catastrophe, enhancing nuclear safety in the former Soviet Union was obviously a major EC objective that could best be managed at an inter-state level. The importance of this objective to the EC is demonstrated by a series of facts. Nuclear safety in the 1990s turned out to be both the main sector for which the EC adopted an inter-state approach and a cornerstone of EC assistance in Central Europe and the former Soviet Union. It accounted for nearly 20 per cent of the funds committed by the EC through the TACIS programme in the 1990s[38] and it was managed by a specific unit within the European Commission.[39] Moreover, it was one of the few technical assistance sectors to be covered by an in-depth investigation of the Court of Auditors of the European Union (Court of Auditors of the European Union 1999) and to be included by the Committee of independent experts in the *Report on Allegations regarding Fraud, Mismanagement and Nepotism in the European Commission* (Committee of independent experts 1999). Clearly, in the case of nuclear safety, developing assistance activities at an inter-state level was prompted by efficiency requirements with a view toward preventing possible threats after the USSR collapse, thus contributing to the Union's security objectives.

Other examples show that inter-state activities also have been used to enhance the Union's influence in the region and to reach its political objectives. For instance, the TRACECA programme does not only aim at modernising Southern NIS's transport infrastructures. In this framework, European norms and standards have been providing, since the early 1990s, the milestones for modernising or integrating transport and energy sectors, thus increasing the EU's visibility at a time when it had a low profile in an unknown area. Moreover, the design of corridors, like the rehabilitation of pipelines in the framework of INOGATE, was also meant to connect regions with huge energy reserves to Europe while steering clear of Russia and Iran (Radvanyi 1998). Therefore, TRACECA and INOGATE activities had region-building effects on the NIS: to some extent, as shown by Jean Radvanyi (1998), they resulted in the drifting away of Southern and Eastern NIS from Russia and contributed to the development of a new Great Game around the Caucasus countries and the Caspian Sea. EC programmes to support inter-state cooperation thus reflected a European regional vision (albeit roughly sketched and not explicit in the EU discourse) of the post-Soviet area and of its relationship to the Union.

The interconnection between the EU's security interests and the development of a regional vision is even clearer in the case of the Northern Dimension, an initiative tightly linked to the fourth EU enlargement, after which Russia shared

---

38   These figures include support to nuclear safety and to the environment which were merged in one priority sector. European Commission 2000.

39   Unit C5 within DG1A managed nuclear safety projects for both TACIS and PHARE programmes. This merging of PHARE and TACIS management also confirms the prevalence of EU security interests in launching nuclear safety programmes.

a border with the Union for the first time. Proposed by Finland at the Luxemburg European Council in December 1997 and launched during the Finnish Presidency in 1999, the Northern Dimension aims at strengthening security and increasing prosperity around the Baltic Sea region, especially through the creation of favourable preconditions for private investment in sectors of strategic importance.[40] Fostering regional cooperation is thus justified through the need for ensuring political stability and avoiding conflicts – a justification which is reminiscent of the EU's own experience, after which the Northern Dimension is partly modelled.

Conclusion

At a time when the EU launched one of its major region-building initiatives, the Euro-Med partnership, regionalism and inter-regionalism remained marginal in its policy *vis-à-vis* the former Soviet Union. While the EU emphasised the similarity of challenges faced by the NIS in their transition process, it did not initiate an inter-regional forum to discuss these issues as it did in the case of Southern Mediterranean partners.

Yet EU initial reactions to the collapse of the Soviet Union were deeply rooted in the vision of the former republics as still forming a region and in its self-perception as a model of integration. The EU's insistence on the need to preserve regional links among the new sovereign countries and its design of similar types of agreements for all NIS confirm the EU's tendency to 'reproduce itself' (Bretherton and Vogler 1999: 249) through 'making it regional' (Bicchi 2006: 287) in its relations with third countries. The policy framework designed in the early 1990s should thus be seen as part of a pattern of behaviour, especially since the EU at that time had a poor knowledge of CIS countries stemming from several decades of mutual ignorance between itself and the USSR. With hardly any specialists of the former Soviet Union staffing its external service, the EU experienced difficulties in building up a strategy for each country and thus initially relied upon familiar procedures. This was even more the case as the Commission, well-known for its regionalist ideology, increasingly emerged as the main actor in formulating the first policy steps *vis-à-vis* the NIS. Moreover, the coincidence between disintegration processes in the East of the continent and further integration in the West was interpreted, both within the EC and in the former USSR, as an opportunity for the European Community to diffuse its experience of regional integration to the other part of the continent. Both the EC discourse and the toolbox developed for the NIS thus formed the basis for a possible subsequent regional policy.

However, the limited scope of EU initiatives taken to support regional cooperation throughout the 1990s can be better explained by taking into account the role of internal and intra-regional developments within the new sovereign

---

40 The Northern Dimension is analysed in more detail in Chapter 8.

States, namely the prevalence of centrifugal trends. On the one hand, the former Soviet republics underwent an accelerated disintegration process throughout the 1990s. After the collapse of the USSR and the introduction of economic reforms in the NIS, intra-CIS trade decreased[41] and these dynamics were not offset by the various multilateral projects put forward to restore links. Furthermore, the former Soviet Union experienced a time of political instability and wars: conflicts burst out in Moldova, Georgia and Tajikistan, and between Armenia and Azerbaijan, worsening the dislocation process of the former Union.

On the other hand, the construction of new States and sometimes of national identities hardly seemed compatible with regional cooperation, not to mention integration. Many among the former republics (Georgia, but also Ukraine)[42] were reluctant to accept, or simply rejected, the idea of regionalism after the collapse of the USSR. A few others, for example, Russia and Kazakhstan, were proponents of new unions that might also serve their regional ambitions. In other words, there was no agreement on regional cooperation or on the role of the organisation launched in December 1991 to 'replace' the USSR. The alternative patterns of regional cooperation which were designed in the first part of the 1990s to make up for its perceived shortcomings also proved ineffective to various degrees;[43] the question of their compatibility with the CIS rarely was raised (and then only half-heartedly). As a result and in spite of further steps to integrate, the CIS remained largely an empty shell. Two factors explain its failure. First, the CIS lacked cementing principles or common objectives which would replace ideology. Second, when the CIS was launched the post-Soviet area lacked a leader: contrary to many expectations, Russia in the early 1990s was not strong enough to act as an engine for new integration processes. At the same time, it kept sufficient control on the area, which was conceptualised as the 'near abroad', to prevent any competing region-building project. EU policies were thus strongly affected by the disintegration dynamics taking place in the 1990s. While the EU still considered these countries as part of a single area, these dynamics prevented the deployment of traditional methods for supporting further regional cooperation (for example, region-to-region agreements). Regional tools were thus initially conceived as correcting the potential negative effects of centripetal trends. This 'negative regionalism', however, was increasingly combined with initiatives serving the EU's interests once the Union had familiarised itself with the post-Soviet area.

---

41   As noted by economists, intra-USSR trade was already unbalanced between those republics benefiting from the Soviet Union and those being disadvantaged, *inter alia* Russia. Once the political reasons for maintaining the Soviet Union had disappeared, a decline in trade between republics was therefore likely. See for example, Duchêne 1994.

42   Zbigniew Brzezinski and Paige Sullivan show how Ukraine has opposed further integration through evasion of implementation or through outright refusal to take part in regional cooperation, Brzezinski and Sullivan 1997, Chapter 5.

43   For instance, the Slavic Union discussed in the years 1993–4 or the Eurasian Union presented by President Nazarbaev in 1994.

Chapter 3

Shaping a Regional Security Order? The EU and the Creation of a 'Security Complex'[1] at its Periphery

In the years following the dissolution of the Soviet Union, the post-Soviet area remained outside of the EU's major foreign policy preoccupations. Overall, the EU kept a low profile in the region as EU policies were strongly constrained by the hectic transformation processes at stake. On the whole, the EU's involvement came in reaction to the region's political, economic and social developments which it sought either to support or to mitigate, rather than as the result of a far-reaching strategy. In this process, the European Commission appeared as a major actor for proposing a new contractual framework for the New Independent States and for managing instruments (for example, technical assistance) which derived to a large extent from its experience in other parts of the world. In other words, the EU's approach in the post-Soviet area throughout the 1990s was both experimental, in that it tested in an unknown area various tools imported from other policies,[2] and technical in that it was not sustained by a strategic vision of either EU interests in the area or the way in which the EU envisaged its own interactions with these countries.[3]

The picture which emerges from the following decade is drastically different and offers two critically distinct features when compared to the 1990s. By the end of the 2000s, the EU appears to have gained substantial influence in all parts of the former Soviet area, more specifically in the Western countries which became its neighbours as the result of the last waves of enlargement. The EU now deploys a number of new policies and instruments in the former Soviet Union. At the same

---

1   Buzan 1991. Buzan's definition of a security complex is given hereafter.

2   More specifically, when it comes to technical assistance programmes.

3   This does not mean however that the EU had no political objectives in the former Soviet Union. Certainly, support to the political and economic transformation processes initiated by New Independent States as well as to smooth relations between these countries could be defined as the major goal pursued by the Union, as evidenced by various EU policy documents in the 1990s. Yet, these objectives did not entail a high political profile, but rather a role of reform supporter; hence the central role of technical assistance in the EU's policy. The TACIS programme was both the first policy tool to be implemented in the former Soviet area and the cornerstone of the EU approach at a time when agreements providing for the overall contractual framework of relations required a lengthy process of ratification (Delcour 2002).

time, the post-Soviet space[4] is no longer an object of EU foreign policy. Instead, the EU has introduced a differentiation between several sub-areas according to the policies it pursues, that is, the strategic partnership with Russia, the European Neighbourhood Policy with Western NIS and South Caucasus countries, and the more recent partnership with Central Asia. While each of these policies will be studied in more detail in the following chapters, the present chapter will examine the processes through which the Union reframed its policies in the former Soviet Union and differentiated among sub-areas. Quite oddly, the latter dimension is underresearched. Whereas the various policies developed by the Union in the early 2000s attracted the attention of scholars, there has been little questioning of the dynamics which led to the EU's growing distinction between several zones. Rather, the policy frameworks defined by the Union seem to be taken for granted by scholars and what is more, they seem to be considered implicitly as corresponding to objective geographical regions.

The present chapter will question that presupposed correspondence. It will focus on the processes which resulted in the EU's revision of its policies in the former Soviet area in order to account for the current differentiation between three sub-areas. The analytical framework presented in Chapter 1 proposed two possible explanations elucidating EU policies and approaches to region-building. The first one is exogenous and suggests that the renovation of EU policies would have occurred principally as the result of developments in the New Independent States. In line with this hypothesis, the EU's delineation of subregions within the former Soviet Union would be justified, on the one hand, by the persistence or the emergence of common identities, shared interests and schemes of cooperation within each of these sub-areas and, on the other hand, by opposite dynamics (that is, disintegration) between various sub-areas which ten years before were part of the same state. If one follows this argument, the EU's reassessment of its policies would stem from its having taken stock of regional developments since the demise of the Soviet Union. The other hypothesis, on the contrary, is endogenous and claims that the main reason for this overhaul process lies within the EU. Following this hypothesis, the revision of EU policies is connected to developments in the Union's foreign and security policy, more specifically to its emergence as a security actor and to its definition of threats.

The present chapter will argue that the EU's reassessment of its policies in the post-Soviet area originates both in endogenous and exogenous processes, yet to different degrees. It will highlight the increasing importance of security in the EU's discourse with and agenda for the former Soviet Union. The chapter will draw upon

---

4   'Post-Soviet space' refers here to 12 of the 15 former Soviet republics. As shown in Chapter 2, immediately after the collapse of the Soviet Union the three Baltic States refused to join post-Soviet regional organisations and instead chose to follow a European path. As early as 1992, the European Union had disconnected the three Baltic states from the rest of the USSR in its policy framework. Estonia's, Latvia's and Lithuania's accession to the EU in May 2004 is a major step confirming the disconnection from the other post-Soviet republics.

constructivist approaches to security, in particular the research conducted by Adler (1997), Adler and Barnett (1998), Buzan (1991), Buzan, Wæver and de Wilde (1998), and Buzan and Wæver (2003) to identify the way in which the interplay between various EU actors has contributed to defining the EU's interests in the former Soviet Union at the turn of the century and to comprehend the processes through which the Union has constructed threats at its periphery. It is argued that the Union has stepped up the promotion of its norms and practices in its vicinity with a view to shaping a regional security order. The concept of 'security complex' defined by Buzan (1991: 190) as 'a group of states whose primary security concerns link together sufficiently closely that their national securities cannot realistically be considered apart from one another' will be central to grasp the evolution of EU policies in the former Soviet Union at the turn of the century.

The present chapter will maintain that the new policy frameworks proposed by the EU in the post-Soviet area arise from a multifaceted construction by the Union, including a construction of its role as a global actor, of the security challenges by which it is confronted on the international stage and of its relation to its geographical environment. Such a construction is consubstantial of deep changes that have taken place at the end of the 1990s and in the early 2000s in the European integration process, principally in the EU's foreign policy and in the area which was then called 'Justice and Home Affairs.'

Security at the Roots of the EU's New Attention Paid to its Vicinity

The reframing of EU policies in the former Soviet Union in 2003–4 and more specifically the creation of the European Neighbourhood Policy have primarily been analysed in light of the EU's enlargement to Central and Eastern European countries. Academic attention has focused on the formulation phase of the new policies, emphasising both the respective role played by EU actors and the transfer from the enlargement experience to the new policy. Yet, in the analyses conducted on the new policies developed by the EU in the post-Soviet area (especially on the ENP, for example, Kelley 2006), little has been said of the pre-existing EU frameworks in the region. The analytical emphasis put on the formulation of new policies in connection with the enlargement process suggests that the EU either built new policy frameworks starting from scratch in the former Soviet Union or that it proceeded through 'tabula rasa', that is, that it took the opportunity of Central European countries' accession to the Union in order to 'reboot' relationships with the New Independent States. The present section maintains that the reframing of EU policies in the post-Soviet space should be placed both in a broader focus and in a longer temporality. It argues that the review of EU policy frameworks is an incremental process which cannot be adequately summarised by the enlargement moment alone; substantial changes in EU policies *vis-à-vis* some of the Western NIS indeed occurred well before the enlargement process to Central and East European countries was finalised. Moreover, while the EU's enlargement is undoubtedly of utmost importance for explaining the increased attention to the Western New Independent States, this section argues that the rise of these countries on the EU's agenda should also be investigated in connection to the EU's changing perceptions of threats and of its role as an international actor.

This broader focus allows for the observation of shifts in the EU policy framework in the former USSR as early as the mid-1990s. Throughout the end of the decade, Russia and Ukraine became the subjects of increasing EU attention, with EU discourse and new initiatives focusing on political, economic and security challenges. True, the strengthening of the EU's relationship with these countries was to some extent predictable in light of the contractual framework which was put in place in the mid-1990s and which became effective a few years later. The EU's relations with Western NIS gained a new impetus as a result of the entry into force, after a lengthy ratification process, of the first Partnership and Cooperation Agreements with Russia in December 1997, followed by Moldova and Ukraine in July 1998. This paved the way for the institutionalisation of a regular political dialogue between the EU and these countries, for enhanced economic cooperation and for increased synergy with EU assistance programmes.[5] At the same time, the end of the ratification process also induced a major shift in the EU policy-making process as far as the role of EU actors is concerned. As indicated by Christophe Hillion (2000: 8), while the EU Member States had already played a major role in the elaboration and in the conclusion of the agreements, the entry into force of the PCAs ushered in an increased influence for the then 15 countries of the EU. This was primarily connected to legal aspects of the agreements, namely to their mixed character. Beyond their legal foundations, the PCAs were given 'a strong political dimension' (Hillion 2000: 8), *inter alia* through the political principles referred to in their preambles and through the introduction of conditionality. Such developments induced a greater involvement of EU Member States in EU–NIS relations. In other words, the entry into force of the PCAs initiated a shift from a relationship centred on assistance and economic cooperation to a broader political agenda, a development which occurred to some extent at the expense of the European Commission.

What is more, a few months after the PCAs came into force this emerging political agenda was fleshed out further by the next steps undertaken by the Union in the framework of the Common Security and Foreign Policy (CFSP), the then second pillar of the EU. More specifically, the EU sought to step up its engagement by designing a political strategy specifying its overall objectives in the countries concerned. It is in this context that the two major Western countries of the former USSR, Russia and Ukraine, gained specific salience within the Union's foreign

---

5   Following the entry into force of the PCA, TACIS was more tightly linked to the broader political framework of relations. The programme was used as a channel to serve the purposes of the agreements and conditionality foreseen under the PCA was applied under TACIS, for instance, in 2000 following Russian military intervention in Chechnya (Delcour 2002).

policy agenda. EU Member States (in various formations) emerged again as the major actors in the agenda-setting process, in the formulation of draft strategies, in their adoption and in their implementation. In December 1998, the European Council called the Council to 'continue its work on a comprehensive EU policy' *vis-à-vis* Russia, thus implicitly acknowledging the absence of an EU strategy in this country (European Council 1998, point 1.3.98) and inviting the Council to close this gap by drafting a common strategy. As explained in detail by Hiski Haukkala (2000: 24–7), the drafting of the strategy for Russia (an unprecedented exercise, since common strategies were a new instrument provided for by the Amsterdam Treaty) primarily involved as early as the end of 1998[6] a small number of Member States including Germany, Finland, France and Great Britain – in other words, three large Member States (including the forthcoming Presidency, Germany) and a small country, Finland, which was, however, the only neighbour of Russia within the EU. After being endorsed by the Council, the common strategies were adopted for Russia at the European Council meeting in Cologne in June 1999, and for Ukraine at the European Council meeting in Helsinki in December 1999 (European Council 1999a and 1999b). While these common strategies do not create new instruments in the EU toolbox both in Ukraine and in Russia, and as such do not offer substantial added value (Haukkala 2000: 4), they are significant in that they bring a clear signal of an increased EU political commitment *vis-à-vis* these countries. The fact that these are the first common strategies ever adopted by the Union gives Russia and Ukraine a high priority in the EU's foreign policy.

Arguably, developments within these countries are relevant for explaining the EU's new attention. The economic crisis which hit Russia in 1998, with its potential for social and political disruptions in the Union's biggest neighbour, alarmed the EU and triggered a reflection on the response to be delivered:

> It [The European Council] reaffirms Russia's importance as a strategic partner to the Union ... It stresses the Union's solidarity with Russia and its people during the present economic crisis. That crisis is multifaceted. So too must be the response of the EU ... (European Council 1998, point I22).

As far as Ukraine is concerned, the country expressed its aspirations in 1998 for EU membership (President of Ukraine 1998). The Helsinki European Council held in 1999 did not recognise Ukraine as a candidate country (while at the same time such status was granted to Turkey); instead, the common strategy adopted in Helsinki was presented as a first response to Ukraine's aspirations:

> The European Council underlines the importance it attaches to the emergence of a democratic, stable, open and economically successful Ukraine as a prominent actor in the new Europe. The common strategy takes account of Ukraine's

---

6   That is, even before the European Council of Vienna formally decided to draft the common strategy and also before the Amsterdam Treaty came into force.

European aspirations and pro-European choice (European Council 1999c point I19.56).

However, while the common strategies should be considered elements of the EU's interaction with Russia and Ukraine[7] and as responses either to crises threatening their stability or to partner countries' preferences, they are primarily inward-looking exercises. They reflect the growing EU security concerns at its periphery[8] and the emergence of the EU as a security actor.

Turning to the content of these common strategies allows for the identification of interests shared by EU Member States *vis-à-vis* Ukraine and Russia. What is new in both strategies is the emergence of security issues as a core EU concern in its relationship to Ukraine and Russia. The EU strategies encompass a broad range of security issues going well beyond military threats and including, to use Buzan's classification, economic, political, societal and environmental threats. Economic and political issues, which had traditionally been at the core of EU policy documents in the former USSR, are considered in the common strategies through a security angle insofar as the consolidation of democracy and the integration of Western NIS in the world economy are presented as tightly connected to stability in these countries. The strategic objectives pursued by the EU in both countries thus include contributions 'to the emergence of a stable, open and pluralistic democracy [in Ukraine and in Russia], governed by the rule of law and underpinning a stable functioning market economy' (European Council 1999a and b).[9] While further democratisation and economic reforms are implicitly seen as prerequisites for stability, EU common strategies (in particular the strategy for Russia) also present a broad list of challenges to stability and security on the European continent, including nuclear safety, environmental degradation, security of energy supplies, organised crime, money-laundering, human trafficking and drug smuggling (European Council 1999a: 3).[10] Conflict prevention and arms control are also mentioned as objectives of EU–Russia cooperation. Yet, none of these challenges correspond to new threats; some of them (for example, nuclear safety) had figured prominently in EU policies since the demise of the Soviet

---

7   Christophe Hillion (2000: 12) mentions that although this was not an obligation, the EU presented its draft common strategies to Russian and Ukrainian authorities during the bilateral summits with partner countries foreseen under the PCA, that is, in February 1999 for Russia and in July 1999 for Ukraine. Interestingly, the common strategy was considered by Russia as a two-way exercise: the Russian Federation issued a few months later its mid-term strategy (2000–2010) for relations with the European Union.

8   The growing importance of the periphery is confirmed by the fact that another common strategy was prepared in 1999 for the Southern Mediterranean partners.

9   The statement is similar in both strategies.

10   Such a broad vision of security challenges is confirmed in the EU's latest security documents (Council of the European Union 2008) which put the emphasis *inter alia* on energy security. See also Chapter 7.

Union, others (such as organised crime and various traffics) had been identified as widespread scourges in former Soviet republics in the early 1990s.

At this point, it may be instructive to consider the nature of threat identification, especially in light of the following definition from Wæver: 'Something is a security problem when the elites declare it to be so' (Wæver 1995: 54). Arguably, the emergence of these challenges on the EU–Russia and EU–Ukraine political agendas therefore results from a threat vision constructed by the EU in light of its own specific concerns and interests. Issues such as possible shortages in energy supplies, potential disasters in nuclear plants and the extension to the EU of Russian or Ukrainian criminal network activities were increasingly identified as threats to the EU's model at the end of the 1990s.

Following the constructivist approach, the securitisation of EU discourse in its common strategies for Russia and Ukraine raises two main questions.

First, what are its implications for EU policies *vis-à-vis* Russia and Ukraine? In developing a strategic vision for Russia and for Ukraine, the EU focuses on the 'relational' character of security (Buzan 1991). In the EU's rhetoric, what transforms these transnational challenges into a risk to the stability of the whole continent is the new proximity with countries of the former Soviet Union:

> Geographical proximity, as well as the deepening of relations and the development of exchanges between the Union and Russia, [is] leading to growing interdependence in a large number of areas. Only through common responses will it be possible to find solutions to challenges which are more and more often common to both parties (European Council 1999a).

As a consequence, stability and security within these countries cannot be disentangled from the Union's own stability and security. The EU's discourse in the common strategy reflects the emergence of Europe as an 'ontological referent for where things happen', to use Buzan's and Wæver's words (2003: 5). This calls for enhancing cooperation with both countries to address security issues. The EU thus indicates its interests in an enhanced dialogue on environment, energy, conflict prevention and non-proliferation of weapon of mass destruction with both countries. In light of such dialogue, Ukraine and Russia are considered through slightly different lenses: while the regional scale is privileged as far as Ukraine is concerned, Russia is seen as a strategic partner on the European continent.[11]

Yet, overall the EU's vision meant to manage its growing interdependence with both countries is ambiguous. On the one hand, the EU's discourse highlights a construction of European security around two poles, the Union and Russia. Such

---

11   The EU clearly pictures Ukraine as a potential regional leader, implicitly around the Black Sea: 'The geopolitical situation of Ukraine, situated along the North–South and East–West axes gives Ukraine a unique position in Europe. The EU recognises Ukraine's regional importance' and further 'The EU supports Ukraine's efforts to promote cooperation and stability in its region.' European Council 1999b.

a discourse is inspired from the approach developed by EU leaders (for example, Jacques Delors) after the collapse of the Soviet Union, according to which the European Community and an independent Russia (capable of aggregating the newly sovereign states around her) would act as the two pillars of the continent's architecture. In this approach, Russia is implicitly 'otherised' as far as it is deemed to be complementary to the EU to ensure the continent's security: 'The issues which the whole continent faces can be resolved only through ever closer cooperation between Russia and the European Union' (European Council 1999a).

On the other hand, the EU's vision is also inclusive in that it envisions the two partners as part of one security complex built on a similar set of political values:[12]

> A stable, democratic and prosperous Russia, firmly anchored in a united Europe free of new dividing lines, is essential to lasting peace on the continent. ... The European Union welcomes Russia's return to its rightful place in the European family in a spirit of friendship, cooperation, fair accommodation of interests and on the foundations of shared values enshrined in the common heritage of European civilisation (European Council 1999a).

The second question raised by the EU's securitisation of its relations with Ukraine and with Russia pertains to the EU itself: What is the nature of its changing role as an international actor? The EU's attempts to foster the emergence of a regional security order cannot be dissociated from its own emergence as a security actor in the international arena. Obviously, the European integration project is intrinsically linked to security issues in that, in the EU's narrative, it was initiated to foster peace among former enemies. Even though it primarily developed through economic steps (even more so after the failure of the European Defence Community), the European project is thus primarily intended to reach security objectives. Security is also its core achievement: using Karl Deutsch's concept, the EU is a 'pluralistic security community' in that war is not conceivable among its members. Adler calls it a 'community-region', that is, a regional system of meanings 'made up of people whose common identities and interests are constituted by shared understandings and normative principles other than territorial sovereignty' (Adler 1997: 253). At the same time and paradoxically, the European Community remained during the Cold War period a minor element of the continent's security architecture. However, as far as it raised political challenges *par excellence*, the overthrow of communist regimes in Central and Eastern Europe made unavoidable an inflexion in the course of EU integration towards areas which, due to Member States' reluctance, were previously unexplored and highly sensitive. This resulted in the introduction

---

12   This discourse should be couched in the context of Russia's accession to the Council of Europe in 1996, which appeared as a major milestone for including Russia in a wider European area of shared values.

of the Common Foreign and Security Policy and Justice and Home Affairs as two intergovernmental pillars in the Treaty on the European Union.

Overall, with the common strategies the EU has undoubtedly stepped up its foreign policy and security profile in the former Soviet Union. From an institutional perspective, as explained by Haukkala (2000), the creation of common strategies finds its roots in the deep dissatisfaction with the CFSP's first years of implementation and with its cumbersome decision-making process. The EU's incapacity to take an active part either in preventing conflicts or in contributing to their settlement in the former Yugoslavia had been interpreted as a major failure for the new CFSP. In this context, one year after the peace agreement reached for Bosnia and Herzegovina near Dayton, the Intergovernmental Conference convened to revise those provisions of the Maastricht Treaty which gave rise to problems of implementation concentrated on foreign policy issues. While these were subject to deep divergences and bargaining among Member States (Haukkala 2000: 16–18), as a result of the Intergovernmental Conference the Amsterdam Treaty brought some improvements, *inter alia* the creation of the position of High Representative for the CFSP supported by a policy planning and early warning unit, the provision of a new foreign policy tool (common strategies) and the introduction of a qualified majority vote, with the dual safeguards of 'constructive abstention' and the possibility of referring a decision to the European Council if a member state resorts to a veto.[13]

Another important shift which is reflected in the common strategies on Russia and Ukraine pertains to developments in Justice and Home Affairs at the end of the 1990s, more specifically to their nascent external dimension, a development called upon by the Tampere European Council in 1999 and immediately reflected in EU–Russia and EU–Ukraine relations.[14] Against that background, the first common strategies appeared as a major test for the Union's ability to develop an EU approach in those areas where the Member States have important interests in common. Most importantly, both institutional developments and the EU's discourse reflect the EU's ascension as an appropriate level to deal with security threats in the international arena and principally in Europe. This is also tightly connected with the fact that security challenges are multidimensional and the majority of them are connected to non-military security, an evolution which suits the EU's distinctive security approach (Biscop 2004).

To sum up, the analysis of the policies pursued by the EU in the former Soviet Union at the end of the 1990s points to a twofold dynamics of politicisation and differentiation among post-Soviet countries. Politicisation is to be understood

---

13   The Amsterdam Treaty also incorporated the Petersberg tasks in Title V of the Treaty on the European Union and it opened the prospects for the integration of the Western European Union into the European Union. It also provided for expenditures on CFSP operations (except for military operations) to be funded from the European Community budget.

14   An EU–Russia Action Plan on Combating Organised Crime was signed in April 2000 and an Action Plan on Justice and Home Affairs was agreed upon with Ukraine in 2001. See also Antonenko 2005.

here in the institutional context of the European integration process, as the processes through which issues and instruments of the then second and third pillars of the EU have gained an increasing importance on the EU agenda in the post-Soviet area. Whereas the European Commission and the European Parliament still play a role in the making of EU foreign policy,[15] EU Member States become pivotal at the end of the decade. This offers a sharp contrast to the early 1990s, when first pillar activities managed primarily by the European Commission were central to the EU's action in the former USSR, due both to their greater flexibility and to the absence of political instruments at that time (Delcour 2002, 2005). As far as differentiation is concerned, it has been identified in Chapter 2 as a principle introduced by the EU in its policy framework *vis-à-vis* the New Independent States in the 1990s to take into account the specificities of each country; yet it gained substantial importance at the end of the decade, with Western NIS being subject to increased EU attention and benefiting from a broader array of policy instruments as compared to South Caucasus countries and to Central Asian republics.

A 'Projection-oriented Actor' (Charillon 2004: 252)? Building a Secure Neighbourhood as the Primary EU Policy Objective in the Former Soviet Union

This section will analyse the proposals which the EU put forward in 2002–3 to step up relations with its new neighbours. It will maintain that these proposals reflect a substantial shift in the EU's approach as compared to the end of the 1990s in that the EU's vicinity is identified as a new regional framework for EU policies.

The emergence of 'neighbourhood' as a concept in the EU's discourse results from a series of initiatives by EU actors and from compromises both within the EU and with external players. While the European Commission briefly referred to future neighbours of the EU in its enlargement progress reports at the end of the 1990s, the appearance of 'neighbourhood' as a referent object in the EU's discourse occurred only shortly before the accession of Eastern and Southern European countries to the EU. As mentioned by Cremona (2004), the concern grew among EU decision-makers that enlargement could act as a destabilising factor, which would further deteriorate security at the EU periphery. At the same time, the EU was confronted by a growing external demand for EU action, one of the major factors shaping EU foreign policy (Hill and Smith, 2005: 6). As the accession of Central European countries became imminent, the Union received increasing numbers of requests from its neighbours to review its policies, as shown by the growing importance of discussions related to enlargement in EU–Russia summits in 2001–2002. In the view of Northern countries, this called

---

15   The European Commission is 'fully associated' to the CFSP.

for considering a new global policy. Finland, Sweden,[16] Poland and, to a lesser extent, the UK were key actors in moving the issue onto the Council agenda. Northern Member States' call for a new proximity policy was meant to mitigate the negative effects of enlargement for Western NIS (Emerson 2004). The way they pushed their suggestion resonated with neighbouring countries' perceptions of their relationship *vis-à-vis* the EU and stressed the urgency to provide a signal answering their expectations.

At the same time, the concept of 'neighbourhood' was defined incrementally. EU Member States which had put proposals forward focused on Ukraine, Moldova, Belarus and Russia as the main targets of the future proximity policy. In April 2002, the Council asked the Commission to prepare contributions, together with the High Representative, for strengthening relations with future Eastern neighbours.[17] The document drafted jointly by Commissioner Patten and High Representative Solana (Patten and Solana 2002) questioned the geographical coverage of the future proximity policy, arguing that the EU's new neighbours would fall into three main regional groupings: 1) the Western Balkans, 2) Russia and the other Eastern neighbours and 3) the Mediterranean. The joint letter proposed to differentiate between these based upon the prospect of EU accession, which was explicitly foreseen for the Western Balkans, explicitly excluded for Southern Mediterranean partners and left open for Eastern neighbours. In the joint letter, the proximity policy was implicitly meant to target the latter group, which was deemed as being the most directly affected by the forthcoming enlargement. This policy would attempt to make Eastern neighbours' situation 'less ambivalent and more comfortable' (Patten and Solana 2002), that is, to take into account their expectations *vis-à-vis* the Union and to enhance political dialogue and trade links, while at the same time addressing potential security threats to the Union. Though it clearly advocated for a Neighbourhood Policy towards the Eastern periphery, the joint letter left open the issue of Russia's participation. The proposed geographical definition of the neighbourhood was further refined in 2003 (European Commission 2003) as a result of Southern Member States' pressures to include the Mediterranean partners, on the one hand, and of Russia's refusal to be part of the new policy, on the other hand (Delcour 2006). Moreover, as advocated both by the European Parliament (European Parliament 2003) and by the Council (Council of the European Union 2003), the three Caucasus countries were included in 2004 in the new neighbourhood policy, whereas they were not part of the Commission's proposal.

While also answering attending to local political developments (for example, the Rose Revolution in Georgia in 2003), the inclusion of the Mediterranean

---

16   Finland held the EU Presidency in the second half of 1999, Sweden in the first half of 2001.

17   General Affairs and External Relations Council, Minutes, 15 April 2002.

and, more specifically, of the Caucasus countries stemmed primarily from the EU's security concerns, as indicated in the EU's Security Strategy:

> Even in an era of globalisation, geography is still important. It is in the European interest that countries on our borders are well-governed. Neighbours who are engaged in violent conflict, weak states where organised crime flourishes, dysfunctional societies or exploding population growth on its borders all pose problems for Europe (Council of the European Union 2003).

Arguably, in launching the Neighbourhood Policy the European Union attempted to create a security complex, defined as 'durable patterns of amity ... taking the form of subglobal, geographically coherent patterns of security interdependence' (Buzan and Wæver 2003: 45). This construction of the neighbourhood had a considerable impact on EU policies *vis-à-vis* the post-Soviet area. The Neighbourhood Policy seeks to manage the growing interactions between the EU and its periphery by providing a framework for creating a stable and secure space surrounding the Union.[18] At the same time, such space is centred on the European Union, not only from a geographical perspective but also from a policy and governance angle. Harmonisation of neighbouring countries' legislation and the 'extension of EU policies' to its neighbourhood are foreseen as the major methods for fostering cooperation and regional stability. This entails new patterns of inclusion and exclusion in the EU's policies *vis-à-vis* the post-Soviet area between those countries targeted by this process and those left outside of the neighbourhood framework, either voluntarily (Russia) or not (Central Asia). More specifically, the 'nascent security community' (Adler and Barnett 1998) which may result from the new proximity policy raises the issue of the articulation of EU foreign policy between, on the one hand, this 'ring of friends' (European Commission 2003) of which the Union intends to be the core and, on the other hand, the adjacent countries facing, to some extent, similar security and political challenges. In this context, as envisioned by Chris Patten and Javier Solana (2002), the role played by Russia as a regional power is crucial for the EU, both in its neighbourhood and in the whole post-Soviet area: 'In the end, Russia is an indivisible part of the region – it is difficult to envisage strengthened regional cooperation without Russia.'

This chapter has highlighted a major shift in EU policies *vis-à-vis* the post-Soviet Union at the turn of the century, primarily resulting in ramping up EU involvement in the Western NIS and South Caucasus countries included in the EU's neighbourhood policy. The blurring of boundaries between internal and external security (Bigo 2001) was instrumental in the EU's securitisation of developments at its periphery and enhancement of its relations with its new neighbours, with a view to creating 'durable patterns of amity' (Buzan and Wæver 2003: 45) in its vicinity.

---

18   See Chapter 5 for a more detailed analysis.

The EU's stepping up its profile in its neighbourhood has been explained in the Union's narrative by the design of a 'vision', a term included in most policy documents related to the Neighbourhood Policy (for example, European Commission 2003). Yet, the term 'vision' should be discussed here in order to avoid overly simplistic interpretations. While it suggests a picture of the EU as a purely unitary, rational actor creating a strategic vision from whole cloth, this chapter has shown that such a picture is misleading. Rather, the design of a new EU policy framework results from an incremental process involving a number of actors, aggregating different interests and preferences and reacting to events in the areas concerned. In this process, some Member States and candidate countries emerged as pivotal actors; by pushing their foreign policy priorities forward they drew EU attention onto the former Soviet Union. However, this geographical emphasis found resonance in the EU arena in a specific context, characterised by the increasing importance of security issues on the EU agenda[19] and more specifically the growing entanglement between the internal and the external dimension of security.[20]

---

19 At Tampere in 1999, the European Council placed Justice and Home Affairs at the very top of EU political agenda.

20 The latter was given a decisive impetus at the Feira European Council in 2000.

Chapter 4

Russia: A Disruptive Other

While the EU initially – albeit hesitantly – included Russia in its initial design for a Wider Europe (Patten and Solana 2002), over the past five years the EU–Russia partnership and other EU policies in the former Soviet Union (principally, the European neighbourhood policy) have become increasingly distinct frameworks. The previous chapter has shown how the definition of its security interests led the EU to review its policies in the former USSR with a view to enhancing its relations with countries bordering the enlarged Union (first and foremost Ukraine, Moldova and Russia).

Against that background, how to explain the design of different policy frameworks between Western NIS and Russia, and the latter's increasing distinctiveness? According to a first set of explanations,[1] these dissociation dynamics coincide with a shift in Russian politics that can be roughly characterised as an evolution away from the democratic standards adopted in the 1990s[2] combined with both a growing assertiveness in the international arena[3] and strong economic growth in the early 2000s.[4] A second argument, mainly conveyed by Russian academics and policymakers, puts forward the notion of Russia's singular identity as a player on the international stage.[5] In both cases, it is thus taken for granted that the main reason for Russia's distinctiveness in the EU's post-Soviet policies is Russia itself. A third argument, however, points to the evolution of the EU's foreign policy toolbox and to the increasing use of strategic partnerships with regional or emerging powers to account for Russia's particularity in the EU's post-Soviet policies (Grevi and Vasconcelos 2008).

---

1   This view coincides with liberal views of international relations, according to which the internal political regimes influence the international behaviour of a given country (Battistella 2006: 178).

2   Sabine Fischer uses the term 'de-democratization' (Fischer 2006: 26). For a comprehensive analysis of Russia's political system, see Raviot 2008.

3   Whether such assertiveness has resulted in an increased international influence has been widely discussed by academics. Cf. the critical analyses by Anne de Tinguy (Tinguy 2007). Other analysts shed light both on the changes in Russia's foreign policy approach and on its weaknesses (Delcour 2007b, Monaghan 2008).

4   Russia's GDP growth has reached on average 6.4 per cent from 1999 to 2007. In 2007 real GDP grew by 8.6 per cent. See for example the International Monetary Fund's website (http://www.imf.org/external/pubs/ft/weo/2009/02/pdf/c2.pdf) and the European Bank for Reconstruction and Development's website (http://www.ebrd.com/pubs/factsh/country/russia.pdf).

5   See for example, Chizhov 2004.

Drawing upon the EU–Russia strategic partnership,[6] the present chapter will examine both external and internal factors that contribute to explaining Russia's increasing uniqueness regarding EU policies in the former Soviet Union.[7] Based upon the two main hypotheses presented in Chapter 1, this chapter will examine in further detail both exogenous arguments concerning Russia's evolution, expectations, preferences and uniqueness within the former Soviet Union as a global actor as well as endogenous explanations, including the effects of the fifth and sixth enlargements on the EU's approach *vis-à-vis* Russia, EU Member States' preferences and the emergence of strategic partnerships as a new and flourishing framework for EU relations with regional powers.

The following chapter will argue that both sets of arguments matter when accounting for Russia's distinctiveness in the EU's policy framework in the former Soviet Union, although not to the same degree. It will also analyse the multiple tensions that increasingly affect the EU–Russia partnership in connection to this distinctiveness. More specifically, the chapter will highlight a number of paradoxes that lie at the core of EU policies in the former Soviet Union:

First, Russia is undoubtedly the country with which the EU has developed the most varied array of policy tools and reached the most comprehensive institutionalised dialogue; at the same time, the EU–Russia partnership is repeatedly said (by either academics or policy-makers) to be stalling.

Second, the objectives promoted by the EU *vis-à-vis* Russia do not significantly differ from the ones asserted in the neighbourhood policy (Delcour 2007a), and yet, through its rejection of the EU's traditional methods and toolbox and through its insistence on developing an equal partnership, Russia questions the Union's soft power and disturbs the EU's vision of the continent's architecture.

The picture which emerges from this complex strategic partnership with Russia is one of a disruptive Other, a country with a different and sometimes contrary vision that poses a twofold challenge to the European Union: first, to its own integration process (especially to the structure of its foreign policy) and second, to its soft power in the former USSR.

---

6   The aim of this chapter is not to provide an in-depth analysis of the EU–Russia partnership, especially since that partnership has gradually expanded to cover a wide range of issues and to include a number of institutional mechanisms. EU–Russia relations will only be examined here, therefore, in the broader framework of the renovation of EU policies in the former Soviet Union.

7   This chapter will analyse the way in which Russia disturbs the EU's policy vision in the former USSR. Concrete examples of these disruptions will be given in Chapters 5 and 7, where EU–Russia interactions (or lack thereof) in the 'shared neighbourhood' and the compatibility of their policies in the post-Soviet area will be described at length.

Russia and the EU: Managing Interdependence with a Complex Partner, a Challenge for the European Union's Foreign Policy

Over the past decade, the EU–Russia relationship has been characterised by ambivalent processes which could be summarised as follows: owing to the growing interdependence linking both parties, the partnership is more and more indispensable; yet it is also more and more difficult to manage, as the partners are increasingly different from each other.

On the one hand, the EU and Russia have increasingly become interdependent within the context of EU enlargement, a shifting dynamic which called for the renovation of their relationship and the development of a strategic partnership following low-grade relations in the 1990s. A first indicator of the shift in EU–Russia relations at the turn of the century was the growing prominence of both partners in each other's foreign policy. Whereas the Union had consecrated in 1999 its first Common Strategy to Russia (Council of the European Union 1999), the EU also gained increased attention within Russia's foreign policy strategy. This coincided with President Putin's taking office. While being welcomed by a number of EU actors as being more predictable than his predecessor, the new Russian president was also initially considered as belonging to the Westerniser strand of Russian thinking on identity and foreign policy (Baranovsky 2000: 458). In the hierarchy of external priorities identified by President Putin upon his accession to the Presidency in 2000 (Conception of Foreign Policy 2000), the EU indeed ranked second after CIS countries (Ministry of Foreign Affairs of the Russian Federation 2000a); moreover, the Russian Ministry of Foreign Affairs responded to the EU Common Strategy by designing a medium-term strategy to develop relations with the EU (Ministry of Foreign Affairs of the Russian Federation, 2000b). In spite of their being quite general, both EU's and Russia's documents stressed the existence of common interests and hence acknowledged the strategic character of EU–Russia partnership and the need to develop it further to meet both parties' interests. In other words, the interdependence that would grow after EU enlargement was deemed desirable as far as it could pave the way for enhanced stability on the continent, in line with the vision expressed in the early 1990s by Jacques Delors.[8]

The new impetus given to EU–Russia relations found its first concrete expression in the energy sector with the launching of the EU–Russia energy dialogue at the Paris EU–Russia Summit (October 2000). The dialogue was based upon a strong complementarity: The EU was becoming increasingly dependent

---

8　See Chapter 2. Interestingly, despite the major changes that had affected Europe since the early 1990s, this vision of Russia and the EU being the two major poles on the continent was implicitly strengthened in the early 2000s when, while stressing its willingness to cooperate with the EU to foster pan-European stability, Russia clearly rejected the objective of EU accession in order to 'retain its freedom to determine and implement its domestic and foreign policies, its status and advantages of an Euro-Asian state and the largest country of the CIS.' Ministry of Foreign Affairs of the Russian Federation, 2000b.

on energy imports[9] and Russia was a geographically close supplier which also appeared to be reliable and stable, especially when compared to other countries or regions from which European oil and natural gas were then imported (for example, the Middle East).[10] The overarching objective of the dialogue was to facilitate trade and investment flows between the EU and Russia in the energy sector (Aalto 2008: 13); specifically, the EU sought to secure supplies from Russia and Russia sought to secure foreign investment and facilitate its own access to EU markets. Thus, the energy dialogue constituted a turning point in the EU–Russia relationship insofar as it was the first time both parties 'acknowledged the importance of [their] mutual dependency' (Grant and Barysch 2003). Furthermore, the dialogue itself aimed at increasing this dependency by 'binding Russia and the EU into a closer relationship in which all issues of mutual concern in the energy sector can be addressed.'[11] The EC discourse clearly reflected the functionalist approach which was at the root of the European integration process between its founding members, where energy was considered to be a basis for further cooperation by the European Commission (much the same as the early 1950s):

> Energy is an ideal sector in which relations can be progressed significantly – a kind of test case – for the further development of an EU–Russia strategic partnership. Success in the energy sector could then serve as a model for other areas of common interest.[12]

The review of the EU–Russia cooperation framework initiated in 2003 and pursued in 2005 resulted in a considerable expansion of the spheres of common interest, in new institutional mechanisms to sustain the partnership and in a new architecture based upon four common spaces.[13] True, the institutional network

---

9   See European Commission, DG Energy, *European Energy Outlook to 2020*, 1999 available at: http://ec.europa.eu/dgs/energy_transport/figures_archive/energy_outlook_2020. Retrieved in June 2008.

10   'The Russian Federation not only is our most important supplier of fossil fuels and uranium, it could also to a certain extent play a moderating role in international markets, being in some ways the most promising – and geographically the closest – alternative to the Middle East as energy supplier to Europe.' (European Commission 2004c: 2).

11   European Commission, DG Energy, presentation of bilateral cooperation with Russia, available at: http://ec.europa.eu/energy/international/bilateral_cooperation/russia/russia_en.htm. Retrieved on 20 October 2009.

12   Ibid.

13   The common spaces were launched at the EU–Russia summit held in St Petersburg in 2003. The four common spaces include a common economic space, with the objective of creating an open and integrated market between the EU and Russia; a common space of freedom, security and justice through which issues related to human rights and the rule of law, common threats such as terrorism and organised crime, and visa facilitation are addressed; a common space on external security providing for cooperation on international issues of common interests, *inter alia* crisis management, especially in the common neighbourhood;

set up under the PCA at the end of the 1990s was dense with regular meetings at various levels even before EU–Russia relations were reviewed, including PCA subcommittees in specific policy areas and meetings of the EU–Russia Parliamentary Cooperation Committee; moreover, Russia was already the unique PCA country with which summits of heads of state or government were held twice a year. Following the launch of the four common spaces and their corresponding road maps (Council of the European Union 2005),[14] new formats for cooperation proliferated. The Partnership Council, providing for meetings at the ministerial level, was transformed into a Permanent Partnership Council to allow for meetings as often as necessary in various policy areas. Cooperation between the European and Russian sides on a number of issues covered by the common spaces is now organised around approximately 30 dialogues, informal talks and working-group meetings for a specific technical area.[15] As a result, the EU–Russia partnership is the 'most intense dialogue the EU has ever had in the history of its external relations with any third actor', including the United States (Duleba 2009: 1).

Institutional mechanisms were created or strengthened to manage the increasing EU–Russia interdependence after EU enlargement to Central and Eastern Europe. Trade between the EU and Russia has more than doubled between 2004 and 2008.[16] Although, as a result of the economic crisis, it has slightly decreased in 2009 as compared to previous years, Russian trade with the enlarged Union (its biggest

---

and a common space on research, education and culture to capitalise on the strength of EU and Russian research communities and cultural and intellectual heritage.

14   The road maps providing for the implementation of the four common spaces were agreed upon at the EU–Russia summit in May 2005.

15   Dialogues in the first common space include an industry related dialogue, regulatory dialogue on industrial products, information society dialogue, trade related dialogue, public procurement dialogue, investment dialogue, competition dialogue, customs dialogue, financial services and macroeconomic policy dialogue, energy dialogue, environment dialogue, transport dialogue, phytosanitary measures dialogue, etc. In the second common space there is a Joint monitoring committee for the EC–Russia visa facilitation agreement, Joint monitoring committee for the EC–Russia readmission agreement, an EU–Russia visa dialogue, including expert dialogues on document security, including biometrics, on illegal migration, including readmission, on public order and security and on external relations, EU–Russia dialogue on counter-terrorism, informal dialogue on critical infrastructure protection, dialogues between Russia and Europol, Eurojust, Frontex, CEPOL and EMCDDA, EU–Russia Troika meetings on Drugs and expert dialogue on illegal content on the Internet, as well as informal talks on judicial cooperation in civil and commercial matters. See the website of the EC Delegation to the Russian Federation, http://trade. ec.europa.eu/doclib/docs/2006/september/tradoc_113440.pdf

16   EU–Russia trade totalled €129.697 million in 2004 and 278.770 million in 2008. European Commission, DG Trade, Russia Trade Statistics, September 2009, available at http://trade.ec.europa.eu/doclib/cfm/doclib_section.cfm?sec=138&langId=en

partner) is now 47.6 per cent of its total trade.[17] Russia is now the EU's third biggest partner after the United States and China, accounting for 7.9 per cent of the EU-27's total trade in 2009.[18] This increased trade is fuelled by Russia's share in the EU's energy imports, an increase which is due in part to the fact that Central and Eastern European countries which acceded to the EU in 2004 and 2007 are heavily dependent on Russian energy. Figures, however, show that the EU's dependence on Russian energy is weaker than is commonly stated and that both partners are indeed interdependent. The EU imports approximately 40 per cent of its natural gas from Russia and Russian gas accounts for around 25 per cent of European gas consumption, but only for 6.5 per cent of primary energy consumption (Noël 2008). The EU, in turn, accounts for two thirds of Russia's energy exports. As interdependence goes well beyond the economic sphere, the scope of EU–Russia interactions has expanded over the past five years to encompass a number of issues of mutual interest, for example, visa regime, stability in the common neighbourhood, and education. In other words, each partner has been faced with both opportunities (for example, trade, scientific exchanges) and challenges (traffics or illegal immigration) stemming from the existence, since the early 2000s, of a common border.

However, even as their interdependence was growing, the EU and Russia also were becoming more and more different from each other, an evolution which hinders progress in giving flesh to the strategic partnership. Over the past few years, especially since 2004,[19] Russia has increasingly been depicted as an exception in the post-1989 picture. It is analysed as a non-competitive democracy at best or, at worst, as an authoritarian regime driven by nostalgia for Soviet power and methods. Its economy now appears to be an 'administrated capitalism', with strategic sectors mostly controlled by the state via huge holdings. Finally, Russia is also increasingly seen as assertive or even aggressive in the international arena, especially in the former Soviet area where it seeks to preserve its influence or, according to some views, to restore its Empire. To sum up, almost 20 years after the collapse of the USSR, Russia has drifted away from what is often presented as a 'path'[20] – followed

---

17   Source: European Commission, DG Trade, EU bilateral trade with the world, Russia, 15 September 2010, available at: http://trade.ec.europa.eu/doclib/docs/2006/september/tradoc_113440.pdf

18   Ibid.

19   The Yukos case in 2003 was a first step in the 'de-democratization' (Fischer 2006: 26) of the Russian political regime. However, the major shift came as a result of two events which occurred in 2004 (hostage-taking in Beslan, South Ossetia, and particularly the Orange Revolution in Ukraine). Key political changes were decided in the wake of these events, for example, the appointment of governors by the President instead of their election, new electoral laws making it harder to register as a political party and to take part in elections and new laws on civil society organisations which strengthened the state's control over their funding and activities.

20   The concept of path has been widely used in the analysis of 'transition' processes, *inter alia* in Central and Eastern Europe; it has also been severely criticised, among others

by Central European countries and some former Soviet Republics – based upon democracy and a market economy as well as Europeanisation.

The purpose here, though, is not to analyse Russia's political evolution[21] but to highlight the growing discrepancy with the EU regarding the basis of their strategic partnership. Diverging values were often pointed out as the main illustration of this discrepancy: 'A stable, open and pluralistic democracy in Russia, governed by the rule of law' was presented as the first objective to be reached by the EU in the Common Strategy. The relationship was thus to be based on 'shared democratic values' (Council of the European Union 1999). A decade after the Common Strategy was designed, however, the values clearly appear to have been the EU's, whereas Russia seems to have developed its own conception of 'sovereign democracy.'[22] Clearly, as already emphasised by a number of scholars, 'values' have become obstacles to further progress in EU–Russia relations, and they can no longer form the main basis of the EU–Russia partnership.[23]

Another case in point is energy. Russia's energy market liberalisation was a cornerstone of the energy dialogue launched in 2000. In the EU's view, liberalisation could pave the way for the increased foreign investments needed to maintain production levels. However, as the EU was taking major steps to liberalise and harmonise its own energy market over the past few years,[24] Russia followed the opposite path. Soon after the EU–Russia dialogue was launched, the Russian authorities became aware of energy's strategic importance for both the country's growth and its international position. This realisation resulted in the state's asserting greater control over the energy sector.[25] Russia's refusal to ratify

---

for offering a predetermined explanation and applying a similar pattern to diverse situations (Dobry 2000, Kisilowski 2008).

21   It has been analysed in-depth in a number of publications, for example, Daucé 2008; Raviot 2008; Mendras 2008.

22   The expression was coined by Vladislav Surkov, Deputy Chief of Staff of the President of the Russian Federation. It emphasises both the Russian regime's democratic character and the country's sovereignty over its political model, excluding any foreign interference in the verification of compliance with international norms and standards.

23   Schematically, two views are opposed here. A first one argues that the EU should stick to its own political values in its relations with Russia and possibly use conditionality in case of breaches of democracy, human rights and the rule of law. According to a second view, the EU–Russia partnership should move forward on issues of common interest and set aside the issue of values to avoid any further standstills. For additional examples, see infra.

24   'The consolidation of the energy sector should be market driven if Europe is to respond successfully to the many challenges it faces and to invest properly for the future' (European Commission 2006). See the packages of measures on energy proposed by the European Commission in 2007.

25   Whereas Russia has engaged in the reform of 'natural monopoly', the Russian gas market is still state-controlled via Gazprom and oil is conveyed by a monopolistic company, Transneft. Other examples of the state's increasing control include the eviction of foreign

the European Energy Charter, which was considered a basis for the EU–Russia energy dialogue, clearly indicates the increasingly divergent nature of the two partners.

In other words, recent developments in EU–Russia relations highlight major paradoxes. Throughout the 2000s Russia and the EU have both come closer to each other in terms of political and economic interdependence as well as people-to-people contacts, and moved away from each other as far as values and interests are concerned. Whereas the common spaces identified areas for cooperation on the basis of shared interests, Russia and the EU now seem to have a different prioritisation of these issue areas and, as a result of the parties having different positions on issues of mutual interest, the very substance of their partnership seems to be in question: Its institutional architecture, presented as a basis for a new impetus, conceals disagreements and ambiguities and instead corresponds to 'the proliferation of the fuzzy' (Emerson 2005).

This convergence-divergence process presents a major challenge to the European Union in its partnership with Russia, particularly with respect to the coherence of the EU's foreign policy. Coherence in foreign policy is understood here as vertical coherence, that is, the consistency and existence of synergies between EU and Member States' foreign policies.[26] In this case, EU Member States' political and economic interests, historical experiences and links with Russia deeply differ, and the EU has been faced repeatedly with difficulties in building a common position. The last waves of enlargement have undoubtedly made the EU both more diverse and more fragmented when it comes to its relationship with Russia (Leonard and Popescu 2006). The harder stance advocated by most Eastern EU Members *vis-à-vis* Russia, a stance which can be understood principally through the memory of Soviet occupation, reflects divergent histories within the EU concretising into the advocacy of different policy options.

Over the past five years, these divergences have come to light on a number of occasions. It is therefore no coincidence that the principle of solidarity among Member States was first assessed *vis-à-vis* Russia at the EU–Russia summit of Samara (2007), in a context of crises with Poland and Estonia. Subsequent events have nevertheless shown that there is still much to be done in order to put flesh on this principle and have it incorporated into EU diplomacy on a consistent basis. It is true that, in reaction to Russia's decision to ban the British Council in a few Russian cities in 2007, the United Kingdom was supported by the EU and most

---

companies for non-compliance with Russian standards (for example, environmental) in exploiting oil and gas fields, or appointing persons closely connected to the Kremlin to leading positions within the major companies.

26   For an analysis of coherence in the EU's foreign policy, see in particular Gauttier 2004; Nuttall 2005; Hillion 2008; Portela and Raube 2009. Vertical coherence usually refers to the articulation between EU and Member States' policies, whereas horizontal coherence applies to the articulation between various EU policies or pillars. See Chapter 7 for a more detailed analysis.

Member States. However, ever since the Samara Summit – where the principle of solidarity was made clear to President Putin – the EU's vocal ensemble has been disrupted by a number of false notes. For instance, French President Sarkozy's warm congratulations to President Putin following United Russia's victory in the December 2007 elections offered a sharp contrast to other Member States and the European Commission's critical stance on the democratic character of these elections. Similarly, whatever their justifications may be, Poland's and Lithuania's vetoes on negotiations for a new agreement to replace the PCA have delayed the conclusion of a key foreign policy deal for the whole Union. In order to avoid further disharmony within the Union, it is therefore crucial to identify European interests *vis-à-vis* Russia which, more than any other country, requires from the Union a common approach based upon diverse experiences.

The 2008 conflict in Georgia offers an interesting illustration in this respect. The ceasefire agreement negotiated by France on behalf of the European Union gave rise to explicit disagreements between EU Member States: while it was welcomed by France and Italy as sealing the end of the fighting, Poland in particular denounced the lack of any reference to Georgia's territorial integrity. Moreover, President Sarkozy's decision to negotiate alone (albeit in the name of the EU) was perceived by some as an imposition of France's view of the conflict on the whole bloc. The initial stages of the war in particular saw the expression of different attitudes towards the conflict by Member States: The day the ceasefire was negotiated, the presidents of Poland and the Baltic states travelled to Tbilisi, together with Ukrainian President Viktor Yushchenko, to offer a public show of support to Georgian President Mikheil Saakashvili – and an equally public expression of suspicion towards Moscow. This disparity between Member States widened once it appeared that Russia would not respect its obligations under the ceasefire, with EU countries expressing widely divergent ideas as to how the bloc should respond. Roughly speaking, Member States were split into two main groupings.[27] On one side, the newer accession states (especially Poland and the three Baltic States, but also the UK and Sweden) advocated the taking of a harsh line towards Russia, including sanctions. For these countries, Russia's refusal to respect its obligations also seemed to confirm their criticisms of the ceasefire as being too vague and having left too much room for interpretation. On the other side, France, Germany and Italy favoured the preservation of a dialogue with Russia – with the proviso that Russia respect, at the least, the ceasefire agreement's provisions regarding the withdrawal of Russian troops from Georgian territory. This latter line prevailed at the Extraordinary European Council which reviewed EU relations with Russia on 1 September 2008: while the heads of state condemned Russia's recognition of the

---

27 Leonard and Popescu (2006) identify two main approaches *vis-à-vis* Russia within the EU: either 'soft containment', favoured by those Member States that sharply criticise Russia, or 'creeping integration', proposed by the proponents of an enhanced partnership with Moscow.

two breakaway regions and froze discussions for a new agreement with Moscow, they also renounced sanctions (European Council 2008).

Thus, Member States' histories, memories, perceptions of threat and economic links with Russia help account for the wide array of positions expressed *vis-à-vis* Russia.[28] As demonstrated here and noted by Leonard and Popescu, these positions are much more complex than a split between older and newer member states (Leonard and Popescu 2006: 2).[29] Differences among Member States have regularly proved to be an obstacle to the effectiveness of EU policy, a problem exacerbated by Russia's willingness to exploit those differences in order to fulfil its own interests. Several congruent factors explain Russia's bluntly realistic approach. First, even though Russian elites and policymakers have an overall positive image of the European Union (in sharp contrast to their negative perceptions of NATO, see Allison, Light and White 2006), they are not familiar with the European integration process (Trenin 2008: 134) and especially not with the institution which embodies the Union's general interest, the European Commission. Second, Russia has traditionally strong links with some of the largest countries and founding members of the EU, particularly with Germany, France and Italy; these countries are also seen as playing a pivotal role in the European integration process and are therefore the primary focus of the Russian Federation's attention in its European policy. Third, the accession to the EU of former Soviet satellites or republics (that is, the three Baltic States) has been negatively perceived by Russia concerning its partnership with the EU. According to Russia, these countries have adversely affected the EU's overall policy *vis-à-vis* Moscow.

Over the past few years indeed, owing to divergences being clearly expressed among Member States, the temptation for Russia has been to overlook Central and East European countries and to focus on those EU Member States with which it has preserved friendly relations. The latest foreign policy strategy document of the Russian Federation has conceptualised this approach by singling out a few Western countries in the paragraphs referring to the European Union, while it

---

28   Traditional foreign policy focuses, such as Sweden's advocacy of human rights, also play a role in formulating positions concerning Russia.

29   Leonard and Popescu identify five distinct policy approaches to Russia among EU Member States, that is, the pro-Russian 'Trojan horses' (Greece and Cyprus), the 'Strategic Partners' (for example, Germany, France, Italy), each of them having a special relationship with Russia; the 'Friendly Pragmatists' (for example, Austria, Belgium, Bulgaria, Finland, Slovakia) to which business interests prevail over political goals; the 'Frosty Pragmatists' (for example, Czech Republic, Denmark, Estonia, Latvia, Sweden, the UK) who focus more on political issues; and 'New Cold Warriors' (Lithuania and Poland) who have a tense relationship with Moscow. This typology could be discussed further, but it does have the merit of showing that differences go beyond the line between new and old member states. This was again demonstrated during the war in Georgia, with Slovakia criticising Georgia's attack on the breakaway region of South Ossetia, whereas Poland and the Baltic States asked for EU sanctions against Russia. See also the analysis by Kaczmarski and Smolar (2007), who study policy approaches by ten EU Member States.

clearly considers Russia–UK relations to be stalling and makes a brief and general statement on states of 'Central, Eastern and South-Eastern Europe'[30] (President of the Russian Federation 2008). To sum up, Russia's own evolution toward assertiveness and centralisation makes the EU's diversity more difficult for the EU. However, the recent shift in Polish–Russian relations may both tone down negative Russian perceptions *vis-à-vis* Central and East European countries and appeased divergences among EU Member States.[31]

Overall, the EU–Russia relationship is a challenge to the EU as far as it mirrors European integration's weaknesses. In other words, Russia confronts the EU with the limits of its own integration process. Again, this is a unique position in EU foreign policy. Areas which lie at the core of the strategic partnership are precisely those which are underdeveloped in the EU integration process, that is, where there is not yet a common policy or where the EC has few competencies. The obvious example here is energy.[32] The EU and its Member States have pointed out both insufficient transparency regarding Russia's energy market and aggressive measures in Moscow's external energy policy. Nevertheless, the EU's vulnerability is first and foremost linked to the lack of a common energy policy. Over the past few months, a number of Member States have thus conducted bilateral energy

---

30   'The Russian Federation will develop its relations with the European Union, which is a major trade, economic and foreign-policy partner, will promote strengthening in every possible way the interaction mechanisms, including through establishment of common spaces in economy, external and internal security, education, science and culture ... The Russian Federation is interested in the strengthening of the European Union, development of its capacity to present agreed positions in trade, economic, humanitarian, foreign policy and security areas.

The development of mutually advantageous *bilateral relationships* [italics by the author] with Germany, France, Italy, Spain, Finland, Greece, the Netherlands, Norway and some other West European States is an important resource for promoting Russia's national interests in the European and world affairs, as well as contributing to putting the Russian economy on an innovative track of development. Russia would like the potential for interaction with Great Britain to be used along the same lines ... .

Russia is open for further expansion of pragmatic and mutually respecting cooperation with the States of Central, Eastern and South-Eastern Europe taking into account genuine readiness to do so on the part of each of them'.

31   It is still too early to provide a fully-fledged assessment of the consequences of the Russian–Polish *rapprochement* following Russian authorities' shift on the Katyn tragedy and Polish officials' plane crash near Smolensk in April 2010. The Polish Presidency of the Council of the EU, during the second semester of 2011, will be a test in this respect, even more so as relations with the Russian Federation and Eastern neighbours are identified as key priorities under the Polish Presidency. An evolution of Poland's attitude towards Russia (subject, *inter alia*, to Russian authorities keeping in line with their recognition of the USSR's role on the Katyn tragedy) would undoubtedly have important consequences on EU policy *vis-à-vis* Moscow.

32   It is, however, not the only one. For instance, much remains to be done to forge a common EU policy on issues pertaining to justice, security and freedom.

talks with Russia, sometimes at the expense of other Member States. Whereas the Russian–German Nord Stream project bypasses Poland and the Baltic States, the involvement of Bulgaria, Italy, Greece and more recently France in the South Stream project unavoidably weakens the planned Nabucco pipeline, which is strongly supported by the EU.[33]

Russia is thus a difficult partner as far as it points to the EU's weaknesses, whether those linked to the Union's foreign policy or to its own integration process. In the 2000s, the emergence of the Russian Federation as 'the most divisive issue in the European Union' (Leonard and Popescu 2006: 1) had wide-ranging consequences going beyond the bilateral strategic partnership and affecting the EU's policy vision in the former USSR.

Russia in EU Policy: From Object to Subject?[34] Challenging the EU's Vision of a Wider Europe

As shown in the previous chapter, security issues have played a major role in shaping a EU strategic vision for its neighbourhood in the context of 2004 enlargement. Nevertheless, starting from the very moment it was conceived, the EU's vision has been challenged by Russia. It is argued here that Russia's rejection of the EU's 'Wider Europe' proposal (European Commission 2003) primarily finds its roots in the country's perception of an unbalanced relationship. It has been further nourished by the fear of an increasing EU influence in Moscow's backyard. As a consequence, Russia's blunt behaviour in the shared neighbourhood and its insistence on developing a partnership of equal footing with the EU have resulted in the EU's questioning its conception of the eastern neighbourhood.

Russia's contest over its relationship with the EU should be placed in the wider context of its evolving foreign policy. The country went through a deep disenchantment after developing a pro-western stance[35] in the early 1990s that brought little benefit (Baranovsky 1992: 111). From the mid-1990s onwards the

---

33   See Chapter 7 for a more detailed analysis.

34   Sergey Prorozov has remarkably analysed Russian perceptions of a 'subject-to-object' relation with the EU and Russia's willingness to move to a 'subject-to-subject' partnership (Prorozov 2005).

35   By that time, Russian elites underlined the need for returning to the 'civilised world' and Russian media frequently used the word *normal'nyi* when referring to the Western world. Cf. the communications presented at the seminar 'Russia-Europe', Ecole des Hautes Etudes en Sciences Sociales, Paris, 1997, especially A. Shubin, 'Europe's influence on Russia's transformations in the 1980s–1990s' and A. Berelowitch, 'Europe as Utopia of Normality.' Cf. also Raviot 2008. These references to 'normality' or to the 'civilised world' were based upon two assumptions. First, they implied that Russia's past was abnormal, if not monstrous. Thus, it seemed as if seven decades of communist rule were to be considered as an abnormal period in Russian history (just like Tatar invasions in the 13th century) and as if this moment was to be followed by a rapprochement with Europe considered as the normal course of

Russian Federation increasingly sought to assert and to defend its own interests (Delcour 2007b).[36] This entailed the re-examination of those agreements and policy frameworks that had been developed at a time, following the USSR's collapse, when Russia was weak. NATO represented a target for Russia's newly rediscovered assertiveness and was the first Western organisation Russia explicitly opposed at the end of the 1990s.[37] The EU was not targeted as such, but the way it had managed its relationship with Russia was critically appraised. The overall policy framework was deemed inadequate and therefore ineffective. Researchers pointed to the lack of European strategic vision *vis-à-vis* Russia (Maresceau 1998: 261, Delcour 2002) and stressed that the full potential of the EU–Russia relationship was not being tapped.[38] EU policy was thus assessed as a 'patchwork' of activities, programmes and agreements (Maresceau 1998: 262).

Specific EU policy tools and initiatives were also criticised by Russia. Technical assistance provided under TACIS was subject to a broadside of diatribes. For a state that succeeded one of the largest assistance providers, becoming a beneficiary country was generally perceived as humiliating.[39] More specifically, the EU's assistance procedures and modalities were assessed as unsuitable to Russia's needs. The TACIS programme's approach had indeed been replicated from other EC schemes elsewhere[40] and consultants hired to implement assistance projects had generally little experience with Russia in the 1990s.[41]

The Northern Dimension also struck Russian critics[42] as being 'an EU policy on Russia rather than a framework of EU–Russian relations' (Prozozov 2005: 20).

Russian policy. Second, 'normality' was considered to be a quality inherent to the Western world rather than the result of decades or centuries of efforts.

36   Even though the 'romantism' (Baranovsky 1992: 111) of the early 1990s had already been abandoned before, the appointment of Evgeny Primakov as Minister of Foreign Affairs in January 1996 can be considered a major turning point in the evolution of Russian foreign policy.

37   Stressing that the Atlantic Alliance did not act upon a UN mandate, Russia fiercely opposed NATO's intervention in Yugoslavia and condemned the strikes against Serbia. This war witnessed the first head-on confrontation between Russia and the West since the end of the Cold War.

38   At the end of the 1990s, one of the most prominent Russian specialists on EU–Russia relations, Yuri Borko, considered the partnership to be still 'virtual' (Borko 1998).

39   This opinion was widely expressed in the interviews held in the Russian Federation for the author's PhD research in 1995–2000 (Delcour 2002).

40   More specifically, TACIS was initially modelled in large part after PHARE, the EC programme launched in July 1989 to support central European countries and which drew upon previous EC assistance experience. The two programmes took different paths, however, once PHARE became a cornerstone of Central and Eastern European countries' accession process.

41   Many of them had experience with the EU programme in Africa, a record that was considered particularly humiliating for Russia (Delcour 2002).

42   See Joenniemi and Sergounin 2003.

This last comment reflected a general desire on the part of Russia to develop a more balanced relationship with the EU.[43] On the whole, owing to the ineffectiveness of the EU–Russia policy framework and to developments on the continent, Russia felt relegated to Europe's periphery (Baranovsky 2000: 448). Even though Russia did not put forward any wide-ranging initiatives to enhance its partnership with the EU, the country repeatedly expressed both dissatisfaction with the current status of EU–Russia relations and fear over the forthcoming eastern enlargement. Most of all, it asked for a partnership on an equal footing.

While there was agreement among Russian policy and academic circles upon the need to enhance Russia's partnership with the EU, the policy documents related to the Wider Europe initiative and the subsequent EU strategy for the ENP (European Commission 2004) triggered scepticism (Sergounin 2004: 123). The EU's hesitant proposal to include Russia in the new policy (Patten and Solana 2002) was harshly criticised in Moscow and finally rejected for two main reasons. One reason for this rejection was Russia's claim of uniqueness among European nations and in the international arena. As far as it gathered countries with different levels of development and objectives,[44] the EU proposal was interpreted as neglecting or even denying Russia's distinctiveness as a global actor (Delcour 2006). As noted by Hiski Haukkala, 'in essence, Russia felt insulted that it was grouped together with Moldova, Morocco and other countries in the southern Mediterranean together in the same "neighbourhood" basket' (Haukkala 2008a: 38). In other words, Russia could not possibly be included in a single policy framework together with other Western NIS, even less so with Mediterranean partners which were included in the ENP strategy in 2004 (Sergounin 2004: 123). The principle of differentiation underlying the ENP, which could have been seen as a means to take Russia's unique status into account, was analysed as a lack of clear EU priorities among neighbours (Arbatova 2004).

Another reason for Russia's rejecting the ENP is the neighbourhood policy's methods (that is, the export of EU norms and the partial adoption of *acquis communautaire* by neighbours, the use of conditionality), which were not acceptable to Moscow (Haukkala 2008a: 37). They were considered to be both incompatible with the country's preferences for an equal partnership and an expression of the EU's interference in Russia's internal affairs. This rejection coincided with the shift discussed above in both Russian political evolution and

---

43   In sharp contrast to the years following the collapse of the Soviet Union, this reflects a new assertiveness on the part of Russia. Referring to EU–Russian relations in the 1990s, a former Soviet ambassador to the EU, Vladimir Shemiatenkov indicates: 'It was golden time for the EU policy-makers. Whatever they proposed was sooner or later accepted by the Russian side' (Shemiatenkov 2002).

44   According to the Russian Federation's Ambassador to the EU, 'this is an attempt to reduce to the least common denominator groups of countries and individual states that are entirely different in their level of development and that, in addition, have different objectives with respect to the EU itself.' See Chizhov 2004: 85.

its foreign policy. As far as the latter is concerned, the defence of national interests was consecrated as the primary policy objective.[45] In placing the emphasis on the defence of its national interests, Russia also made it clear that it can accept neither a systematic alignment based on norms and standards forged by a foreign organisation nor any conditionality imposed by such an organisation.

Such an interpretation of the ENP led Russian authorities to urge the EU to develop a tailor-made relationship in which Russia could equally participate in shaping the agenda and the rules. This gave rise to the Common Spaces, launched in St Petersburg in 2003. The principle of equality between partners framed policy formulation and was embedded in all policy documents. For instance, the Roadmap for the Common Space for Freedom, Security and Justice mentions as its first overarching principle for EU–Russia cooperation the recognition of 'equality between partners and mutual respect of interests' (EU–Russian Roadmaps 2005). Cremona and Hillion (2006) note an additional example:

> The conceptualisation of the Common Economic Space was the task of an EU–Russia High Level Group consisting of an equal number of Russian and EU representatives, rather than the exclusive job of the Commission and the Council services.

This is a major difference with the ENP, where the EU has – via the use of conditionality – considerable leverage at its disposal. The tough negotiations for the content of EU–Russia roadmaps, especially those for the Common Economic Space as well as Justice and Home Affairs, highlight Russia's attempts to shape the content and tools of cooperation according to its areas of interest.

In particular, Russia pushed hard to include visa-related issues on the bilateral agenda and to progress towards liberalisation of the visa regime, which was first identified as a major issue in the context of EU enlargement, especially in light of Kaliningrad's specific situation. The visa facilitation and readmission agreement signed in 2006 was therefore the result of a bargaining process in which Russia used the EU's concerns over immigration as a trade-off to put forward its own policy interests. On the one hand, the EU was increasingly concerned by the role of transit countries played by NIS for illegal immigrants on their way to Europe (Potemkina 2002). On the other hand, Russia had repeatedly expressed its dissatisfaction with the costly and cumbersome procedures imposed on its citizens by many EU Member States. At the same time, the EU was concerned with damaging its image as well as its economic and scientific cooperation with Russia. Moscow therefore accepted the readmission agreement as a trade-off against a

---

45 The defence of national interests had already been asserted as a major foreign policy objective by Yevgeny Primakov (Minister of Foreign Affairs and then Prime Minister) at the end of the 1990s. The shift noted in the early 2000s is therefore not so much conceptual. Rather, in a new economic context, it refers to Russia's increased capacities to effectively promote and defend its national interests. See Delcour 2007b.

simplified visa regime. This entailed simplified procedures, shorter delays for obtaining EU visas, reduced visa fees for short-stay visas (35 Euros instead of 60) and simplified criteria for multiple-entry visas pertaining to certain categories of persons. As far as EU concerns and interests were quite similar, the visa facilitation and readmission agreement signed with Russia was soon replicated with other NIS included in the neighbourhood policy, for example, Ukraine and Moldova.[46] In other words, the documents signed with ENP countries were modelled after an agreement largely shaped by Russian preferences.[47]

Whereas priorities, agreements, steps and rules governing the strategic partnership are in fact defined through a joint process, Russia has not totally rejected rapprochement with EU laws and standards. However, such a rapprochement follows a similarly utilitarian logic. Indeed, the Russian Federation considers legal approximation to EU laws to be a selective process[48] used for fulfilling its own policy interests. Approximation is limited either in depth (that is, the degree of approximation, Meloni 2007) or in width (that is, to selected policy areas). It is primarily targeted at the adoption of rules and standards for facilitating trade relations and improving Russia's integration into the world economy, thus answering Russia's economic and, especially, political interests. As mentioned by Shemiatenkov (2002: 9), approximation is to be seen as 'a vital factor of [Russia's] radical societal transformation.' The adaptation of EU laws in the field of competition, for instance, is expected to improve the domestic situation, even as the adaptation process is facilitated by the historical lack of Russian regulations in that field. The Partnership for Modernisation which was first discussed during the EU–Russia summit in Stockholm (November 2009) and then formally launched at the EU–Russia summit held in Rostov-on-Don (31 May–1 June 2010) offers a good illustration of this selective approach. It is conceived as a 'flexible framework for promoting reform, enhancing growth and raising competitiveness', *inter alia* through promoting alignment of standards and fostering investment in major economic sectors (Council of the European Union 2010). The workplan for activities under the Partnership for Modernisation published in December 2010 highlights a disjunction between technical and depoliticised issue areas, in which EU–Russia cooperation is developing, and areas which are considered more sensitive by Russia (for example, justice and civil society), in which the EU alone puts proposals forward. In other words, Russia is reluctant to follow any EU-based convergence path (Barbé, Costa, Herranz and Natorski 2009: 846); rather than

---

46 Visa facilitation and readmission agreements were signed at the EU–Ukraine Summit on 27 October 2006 in Helsinki; the EU–Moldova summit on 10 October 2007 in Brussels. Following the 2008 conflict in Georgia, the Extraordinary European Council held on 1 September mentioned the objective of concluding a similar agreement with Georgia and negotiations were opened in 2009. See Chapter 7 for a detailed analysis.

47 See also Barbé et al. 2009.

48 Cf. Gabriella Meloni's PhD, defended at the European University Institute, Florence, 2007.

Europeanising, the country has chosen to socialise with the EU, a process which can only be voluntary (Kratchovíl 2006: 13).

This voluntary process of selective rapprochement, however, raises an additional challenge to the EU. As indicated by Hiski Haukkala (Haukkala 2008a: 39), Russia's opting out of political conditionality (a cornerstone of EU foreign policy) creates a precedent that can undermine the EU's external legitimacy. Russia indeed appears as a free-rider exploiting the EU's model for the purpose of its own modernisation process. This appears to be especially the case under the Partnership for Modernisation which apparently brings together Russia and the EU around the common objective of modernisation. This new initiative, which makes the EU a privileged (yet non exclusive) partner in Russia's modernisation process, may indeed bring to light different visions between the two partners. On the one hand, the EU's vision connects modernisation to a broader political, economic and social environment; in the EU's approach, good governance, the rule of law and democratisation are considered as prerequisites to effective modernisation. On the other hand, modernisation is deemed crucial by the Russian Federation[49] to cope with the negative consequences of globalisation[50] and to enhance its competitiveness on the world economic stage; in this context, modernisation is primarily understood as innovation and it is principally (although not only)[51] considered through an economic angle.

In other words, the EU's room to manoeuvre is much more constrained with Russia than in the case of countries included in the ENP. This appears as a major challenge to the EU, even more so since its objectives with Russia do not significantly differ from those it pursues with ENP countries, that is, rapprochement in the economic, security and foreign policy spheres to foster stability, prosperity and security on the continent;[52] the focus on modernisation is also a common feature

---

49   Modernisation has emerged as the core priority of the current Medvedev Presidency, as shown both by the President's discourse and the launch of an 'innovation city' 'Innograd') to develop new technologies in Skolkovo near Moscow. See in particular President Medvedev's article 'Rossia vpered! ('Forward Russia!'), http://archive.kremlin.ru/eng/text/speeches/2009/09/10/1534_type104017_221527.shtml

50   In the latest National Security Strategy of the Russian Federation, globalisation is analysed as both the main trend in international relations and a source of threats, as far as it triggers increased competition for resources and strengthens inequalities among countries (National Security Council of the Russian Federation 2009).

51   President Medvedev's 2009 State of the Nation speech also points to the fight against corruption and to the 'consolidation of democracy' as necessary steps towards modernisation. Cf. D. Medvedev, 'Presidential Address to the Federal Assembly of the Russian Federation', 12 November 2009. Available at: http://archive.kremlin.ru/eng/speeches/2009/11/12/1321_type70029type82912_222702.shtml

52   The similarity of the objectives pursued by the EU *vis-à-vis* Russia and Western NIS included in the neighbourhood policy was underlined by an EC official from DG Relex (interview in September 2007). This entails *inter alia* the conclusion of visa facilitation, readmission agreements and further visa liberalisation; trade liberalisation with the objective

in the EU's relations with Russia and with Eastern neighbours. Yet, by rejecting conditionality by contributing to shaping the agenda regarding its relationship with the EU and by developing competing policies in the shared neighbourhood, Russia questions the foundations of the EU's influence, described as 'normative' or 'soft power.'[53]

Moreover, while Russia clearly positions itself outside the EU and out of its traditional modes of influence, its claims to be a part of Europe (as put by its Foreign Affairs minister) are another obstacle for the EU's vision of its role on the continent:

> The rigid Anglo-Saxon model of socio-economic development has again started to fail, as it did in the 1920s … On the other hand, there is the socially-oriented Western European model, which was a product of European society's development throughout the 20th century, including the tragedies of the Second World War, the Cold War and the Soviet Union's experience … Therefore, by proclaiming the goal of creating a socially-oriented economy, the new Russia appeals to our common heritage. This is yet more evidence of Russia's compatibility with the rest of Europe (Lavrov 2008).

As clearly shown in the above quotation, Russia, considering itself part of Europe, draws upon a common heritage and picks up elements of what is called the 'socially-oriented Western European model.' It is therefore clear that Russia has no intention of challenging this model through the proposal of an alternative. Nevertheless, Russia challenges the prevailing EU interpretation and instead sees itself contributing to shaping the European model. In other words, it denies the EU's exclusive prerogative to develop the European model according to its own norms and standards.

Conclusion

Over the past decade, the EU's policy toward Russia has undoubtedly been deeply altered by the Union's own transformations, first of all by its Eastern enlargement. It is also forged and constrained by the degree of European integration in those areas which are crucial in the EU–Russia partnership, for example, energy or the visa regime. Moreover, the EU's policy toward Russia (more than any other third country) mirrors the evolving balance between EU actors and institutions. Clearly, whereas the European Commission played an important role in designing and managing this policy in the first half of the 1990s, EU Member States are more and more pivotal in the strategic partnership. This evolution is connected to the

---

of creating a free trade area; and enhanced dialogue on foreign policy issues. See also Delcour 2007a.

53   See Chapter 1.

prevalence of 'high politics' stakes (that is, issues pertaining to Member States' competences) in the EU–Russia partnership. At the same time, the Council's increasing importance is combined with a greater diversity stemming from the two last waves of EU enlargement. EU integration dynamics have therefore made both the design and the implementation of EU policy *vis-à-vis* Russia more complex. Since an agreement upon the relationship the EU wants to develop with Russia is more and more difficult to reach among Member States, the EU has not been proactive over the past few years. Since the Wider Europe proposal was rejected by Moscow in 2002–2003, the Union has not put forward any new strategic vision. In other words, in the EU–Russia partnership the EU does not appear as a unitary actor following a well-conceived strategy.

The EU's reactive rather than proactive stance is not only the result of these internal dynamics. Russia's increasing distinctiveness in the EU's policy framework stems first and for most from the country's own specificities. It corresponds to Moscow's 'renewed self-perception as a global player' (Fischer 2008: 117) and it is therefore a recognition of its role as a pole contributing to shaping the world system, a position that no other country in the former Soviet Union can claim to have. The development of a strategic partnership therefore reflects the EU's acknowledgement 'that the international distribution of power is fluid enough to warrant establishing "special" relationships with aspiring world players while, at the same time, focusing on its primary goal of promoting global and regional governance and effective multilateralism' (Vasconcelos 2008: 26). At the same time, the strategic partnership in its current form derives from Russia's use of both realistic and pragmatic lenses. This entails relying upon bilateral relations with specific Member States in those areas where the EU is deemed to be weak. This also means that cooperation is limited to those areas in which both partners have convergent interests (Fischer 2008: 118). Russia's growing assertiveness has thus narrowed down the content of the strategic partnership, excluding *de facto* from the dialogue issues which are central to the EU, such as values; opened in 2008, negotiations for a new agreement to replace the PCA are unlikely to change the situation.[54] Combined with its considerable weight in the former USSR, Russia's questioning of EU soft power has far-reaching implications for the Union's overall influence in the post-Soviet area.

---

54   The final text of the forthcoming agreement between Russia and the EU will be a major indicator of both partners' vision of their partnership. The EU indeed supports a detailed contractual framework while Russia favours a basic framework agreement.

Chapter 5

The Eastern Neighbourhood: A New Region for a Flagship Policy

The European Neighbourhood Policy (ENP) was created in 2003–2004 to 'reinforce stability and security' (European Commission 2004a: 4) in adjacent areas, either with Southern or Eastern neighbours. It was conceived as a 'response to the new situation' stemming from EU enlargement to Central European and Mediterranean countries.[1] Accordingly, the overall self-portrait reflected by the EU in both its Security Strategy (2003) and ENP founding documents (European Commission 2004) is that of an 'interventionist actor in its near abroad' (Charillon 2004) and a 'motor for ensuring regional security' (Bengtsson 2008). As such, the policy undoubtedly marks a shift in the nature of EU engagement in the post-Soviet area. It is an unprecedented EU proposal for specific guidance as well as external monitoring and benchmarking to carry out comprehensive domestic reforms in the post-Soviet states, with a view to aligning Eastern neighbourhood countries with EU norms and standards in a number of areas.

The ENP has emerged as a cornerstone of the EU's foreign policy. Its central importance is evidenced by steps[2] such as the inclusion of provisions dedicated to the neighbourhood in the Treaty of Lisbon.[3] The prominence given to the ENP in EU foreign policy also speaks volumes about the self-perceptions of the EU[4] and reflects the EU's willingness to take up responsibilities commensurate with its status as the major power and pole of attraction on the European continent. Given its ambitions, the ENP is undoubtedly a major capability test for European foreign policy (Delcour and Tulmets 2007: 3), more specifically for the EU's capacity to

---

1   The European Neighbourhood Policy applies to the EU's immediate neighbours by land or sea: Algeria, Armenia, Azerbaijan, Belarus, Egypt, Georgia, Israel, Jordan, Lebanon, Libya, Moldova, Morocco, Palestinian Territories, Syria, Tunisia and Ukraine.

2   Symbolic steps also include the change in the title of the Commissioner on external relations in the 2004–2009 Commission. In the European Commission appointed in 2004, Benita Ferrero-Waldner was commissioner for external relations and the neighbourhood policy. The ENP is currently included in the portfolio of the Commissioner for Enlargement, Stefan Füle.

3   The Lisbon Treaty commits the EU to the 'development of a special relationship with neighbouring countries aiming to establish an area of prosperity and good neighbourliness, founded on the values of the Union and characterised by close and peaceful relations based on cooperation.' For that purpose 'the EU may conclude specific agreements with the countries concerned' (art. 8 TEU).

4   On this topic, see Kratochvíl 2008.

deal with security challenges in its vicinity (as explained in Chapter 3) and for the EU's soft power[5] in its neighbourhood. Aside from the notable exception of Russia, which rejected the ENP despite its geographical contiguity with the EU, six New Independent States are part of the policy: Ukraine, Moldova, Belarus,[6] Armenia, Azerbaijan and Georgia.[7] The incentives provided by ENP and its expected results have been studied at length, quite often in connection with the enlargement policy[8] and with the EU's modes of governance.[9] Yet the regional dimension, which is both a constitutive feature of the EU's integration process and a cornerstone of its external policies, is neglected in the current ENP research. Even the recent Eastern Partnership is most often analysed either from the angle of EU capacities or from the perspective of norms convergence,[10] and much less so through the prism of region-building.[11] Chapter 2 stressed the low profile of the EU when it comes to regional cooperation in the 1990s and the weak regional dimension of its policies in the post-Soviet area. The ENP reflects an enhanced EU engagement in the region, but does it also constitute a watershed in the EU's approach to region-building? To what extent has the EU committed to regional cooperation for fostering stability, security and prosperity in its neighbourhood, and has the EU policy mix between bilateral and regional approaches produced results sufficient to pass the above-mentioned capability tests in its Eastern neighbourhood?

---

5   Understood here, based upon Nye's definition (Nye 1990 and 2004), as the ability to get what you want through attraction rather than coercion.

6   Belarus's participation in the policy is theoretical, taking into account the low grade of EU–Belarus relations due to the country's political regime. Belarus and the EU have not signed a partnership and cooperation agreement, and the contractual framework for their relationship is still provided by the 1989 trade and cooperation agreement signed with the USSR. Relations slightly improved in 2009, as suggested by both the visit of the High Representative for the Common Foreign and Security Policy to Minsk in February 2009 and the suspension of travel bans for high-level Belarus officials in March 2009. However, EU–Belarus relations deteriorated again in the wake of the 2010 presidential elections and subsequent repression of protests, with the European Parliament adopting a tough resolution on Belarus and the EU Council deciding on a visa ban for 158 Belarusian officials. On the evolution of Belarus's political regime, see Goujon 2009, more specifically Chapter 5; see also Silitski 2009. On EU–Belarus relations, see Fischer 2009, more specifically the contribution by Gromadzki.

7   The three Caucasus countries were not targeted by the European Commission's initial proposal (European Commission 2003). They were included in the ENP in 2004.

8   For an overview of this literature see Delcour 2007a. For a theoretical analytical framework on the ENP see Kratochvíl and Tulmets 2010.

9   The external governance approach analyses the connection between EU internal and external modes of governance and the extension of EU rules beyond its borders. See in particular Lavenex 2004, Lavenex and Wichmann 2009, Lavenex and Schimmelfennig 2009, Barbé, Costa, Herranz and Natorski 2009.

10   See for instance Mikhelidze 2009, Shapovalova 2009, Tardieu 2009.

11   See the presentation of the Eastern Partnership's regional dimension by Hillion and Mayhew 2009: 11–16.

To answer these questions, this chapter will assess the respective weight of the three independent variables selected in the analytical framework presented in Chapter 1. The regional dimension in the EU approach to its neighbourhood is first affected by partner countries' policy interests and preferences, that is, by the existence of cooperation schemes among the six countries concerned or, conversely, by their preference for bilateral ties with the EU. The second factor relates to the relative influence of the policies developed by a major actor in the area, namely Russia, and to the general orientation reflected in their approach to the ENP, that is, competitive or cooperative. The third factor analysed in this chapter pertains to the structure of European foreign policy, that is, the interplay between not only different actors and levels of action but internal integration and external policy as well. While this factor is a constant component of EU foreign policy, it is argued here that it plays a particularly prominent role in the case of the ENP.

All three factors are closely intertwined and react with one another in the implementation of the neighbourhood policy. This chapter will argue that these factors adversely affect one another and that their interplay results in tensions which influence both the EU's vision of its Eastern neighbourhood and the emphasis (or lack thereof) given to the regional dimension in its policy mix.

Differentiation as the Preferred Tool for Converging with the EU

The ENP did not constitute *per se* a rupture with previous EU policies in the post-Soviet area regarding approaches to region-building. In spite of initial attempts by the European Commission to include regional cooperation in the ENP, bilateralism remained a cornerstone of the approach promoted by the Union as a result of partner countries' preferences for a policy tailor-made to their specific needs, expectations and situation.

The European Commission had originally foreseen giving an impetus to regional cooperation in the EU's vicinity. The initial Commission communication (European Commission 2003) on the future neighbourhood policy clearly followed the traditional EU foreign policy approach and identified regional cooperation as a key to stability and prosperity (two of the new policy's major objectives). This cooperation had to be stimulated by the Union, which perceived itself as having a duty to act as region-promoter at its periphery, including – implicitly – areas where no regional integration existed: 'The EU must act to promote the regional and subregional cooperation and integration that are preconditions for political stability, economic development and the reduction of poverty and social divisions in our shared environment' (European Commission 2003).

However, while regional cooperation was envisioned in initial ENP documents, it has since remained an essentially empty shell in the policy's Eastern component. This mostly unrealised vision for the East stands as a sharp contrast to the Southern component of the ENP. Interestingly, in the EU discourse developed in the years

2003–2006, the need for regional cooperation was exclusively illustrated through references to Southern Mediterranean countries. Expressions describing the 'EU Mediterranean policy' or integration 'between Mediterranean partners' (European Commission 2003) implied both the existence of a regional EU policy *vis-à-vis* its Southern partners and an agreement among these partners to reach a degree of integration in specific areas. The discrepancy between the ENP's two components from the angle of region-building was further confirmed by references to Southern partners as the 'Mediterranean region' and to Eastern partners as 'Western NIS' or 'Eastern Europe.' Conversely, the principle of differentiation underlying the neighbourhood policy was quite often exemplified in policy discourse by Eastern partners, in particular Ukraine. Clearly, Western NIS (to which the South Caucasus countries were added in 2004) were not perceived by the EU as constituting a region. The introduction of regional initiatives in the Eastern neighbourhood was impeded by two obstacles. Unlike in the Mediterranean area, the ENP could not build in the East upon a previous record of EU support for regional cooperation.[12] When launching the neighbourhood policy, the EU was able to build in the South upon toolbox of the Barcelona process and record in region-building, that is, upon a policy in which regional cooperation was a major pillar, whatever its actual achievements may be.[13] Furthermore, introducing a regional dimension did not match Eastern neighbours' expectations.[14]

Eastern partners' reticence towards regional cooperation can be explained by the combination of two factors. First, the reform process undertaken by the former Soviet republics in the wake of the USSR collapse has so far resulted in different paces and paths of reform, thus ushering in divergence rather than convergence. At the time of the 'Wider Europe Initiative' in 2002–2003, political and economic options taken by Western NIS and Caucasus countries were quite different. They became even more disparate, if not divergent, in the following years. The Rose Revolution in Georgia at the end of 2003 and the Orange Revolution in Ukraine resulted in a shift towards democratisation and pro-Western foreign policy orientation in these countries, albeit with many nuances and differences in processes as well as in outcomes.[15] Political transformations and shifts are still ongoing in these countries: to take one example,

---

12   See Chapter 2.

13   Fostering regional cooperation is foreseen in all three components of the Euro-Med partnership, that is, political, economic, social, and cultural; regional programmes also constituted a large part of the funds disbursed under the MEDA assistance programme. The regional dimension is considered by the EC as 'one of the most innovative aspects of the Partnership.' See http://ec.europa.eu/europeaid/where/neighbourhood/documents/ barcelona_qa_en.pdf. However, achievements are limited as suggested, among other data, by the low figures of trade between Southern Mediterranean partners.

14   To some extent, this is also the case with the Southern Mediterranean countries among which political and economic cooperation is poorly developed.

15   Silvia Serrano (Serrano 2008) argues that Georgia's evolution reflects the assertion of its identity and of its sovereignty *vis-à-vis* Russia; the country follows a way out of Empire. On Ukraine's path see Fischer 2008.

developments in Ukraine since presidential elections suggest that the country has reoriented the course of its foreign policy towards Russia as compared to the previous five years; political life has also changed over the past few months. Though it was ruled by a communist President until 2009, Moldova maintained to some extent a balanced foreign policy in spite of period of tensions with Russia;[16] the country, now being rule by a pro-European coalition, is confronted to political instability. As a third example, Belarus' evolution towards authoritarianism and 'sultanic presidentialism' (Goujon 2009: 169) is an exception within the Western NIS. Yet, it shares some features (for example, the extension of presidential powers through plebiscite referendums and subsequent amendments to the Constitution) with developments in Azerbaijan in the past few years.[17] As far as Armenia is concerned, it can be named a 'non competitive democracy',[18] that is, a regime in which it is difficult to mark out the boundary between democracy and authoritarianism. To sum up, while post-Soviet countries still share common legacies from the USSR and are at the same time undergoing a long-term wide-ranging transformation process, they are increasingly different from one another when it comes to political systems as well as economic or foreign policy preferences.

The second factor in addition to divergence in policy choices is the disintegration dynamics that have affected the post-Soviet area since the early 1990s, which have either distended or strained the links between former republics, thus adding to regional fragmentation. This is especially true for the area encompassed by the neighbourhood policy, owing in particular to the so-called 'frozen conflicts.' In the case of South Caucasus countries, most regional cooperation programmes have been hampered by the Armenian–Azerbaijan dispute over the unresolved conflict of Nagorno-Karabakh. The lack of relations between the two countries complicates the development of either endogenous or exogenous regional initiatives. To a lesser extent, the same goes for Transnistria: When the neighbourhood policy was launched, the breakaway region appeared as a black hole between Moldova and Ukraine from which various traffics reached Western Europe. As a consequence of such disintegration dynamics, regional and subregional cooperation initiatives and organisations in the countries included in the neighbourhood policy have yielded little, whether initiated by local or by external players. Neither GUAM (Georgia Ukraine Azerbaijan Moldova), due to different political options taken by

---

16   According to Emerson (Emerson 2004: 8), the country's primary foreign policy objective 'seems to be to gain recognition as a full partner in the regional mechanisms of South East Europe.'

17   In March 2009, a referendum was organised in Azerbaijan to decide on the abolition of presidential terms limitations. The proposed measure was approved by more than 87 per cent of voters; in June 2010, a law was passed to coordinate the legislature's annual agenda with the presidential administration (June 2010).

18   The expression was coined by Jean-Robert Raviot in his analysis of Russia's political system. See Raviot 2008.

its members, nor the Community of Democratic Choice,[19] though driven by a pro-Western orientation shared by all members, have reached tangible results.

Under these circumstances, it is particularly difficult for the EU to promote its traditional approach favouring regional cooperation under the ENP, and the difficulties are exacerbated by Eastern neighbours who are also diverse in their expectations *vis-à-vis* the EU (yet another factor affecting their policy preferences on regional cooperation). Ukraine offers a good illustration in this respect. As early as the end of the 1990s, the country had declared its intention to join the EU and designed a strategy to that purpose (President of Ukraine 1998). It then set up various mechanisms to further its strategy, with special emphasis on approximation with EU legislation. Thus, Ukraine clearly positioned itself as a would-be candidate for EU accession (Delcour 2007a). In light of this engagement, the ENP was perceived as highly disappointing in Kyiv, even more so after the Orange Revolution which confirmed the country's European choice. Being included in a single policy framework together with countries that had no accession perspective was considered by Ukraine as a way to discard its European aspirations. As Ukraine considered its position within the ENP to be quite specific, it met any EU attempt to develop multilateral instruments with reluctance (Lytvynyuk 2007).

Moreover, whereas the Ukrainian authorities have repeatedly and strongly criticised the ENP for reflecting the EU's lack of commitment to future accessions, they have at the same time sought further differentiation inside the ENP policy framework. Kyiv has thus managed to gain the recognition of an 'advanced status' (European Commission 2006) within the ENP by taking advantage of the differentiation principle enshrined in policy documents. In the years 2007–2009 in particular, Ukrainian authorities have tried to get the utmost out of the ENP's bilateral instruments and benchmarks. By striving to ensure effective implementation of PCA and ENP Action Plan,[20] they positioned the country as the good pupil among neighbours (Delcour 2008). This resulted in obvious policy gains: Ukraine was the first country, in March 2007, to open negotiations with the EU for an enhanced agreement, (subsequently renamed 'association agreement'); it was also one of the main beneficiaries of EU funding allocated under the current ENPI (European Neighbourhood Partnership Instrument) programming, as well as under the Governance Facility set up in 2007. In this context, other Eastern neighbours are perceived as laggards in their relationship to the EU; as such, inclusion with them in a regional framework would be a step backward for Ukraine.

The Eastern context, characterised by the 1990s disintegration process and by the reluctance of several former Soviet republics to develop new forms of regional cooperation, explains the shift in EU policy discourse on the regional dimension of the ENP in 2004. Both regional cooperation in the ENP framework and the role of

---

19   Initiated by the Borjomi Declaration and signed jointly by Viktor Yushchenko, President of Ukraine and Mikheil Saakashvili, President of Georgia, in 2005.

20   Interviews with civil servants of the Ministry of Justice, Kyiv, March 2006; interviews with experts on PCA implementation, Kyiv, October 2008 and January 2009.

the EU in fostering links at a regional level were then attenuated. The Commission's strategy paper formalising and launching the policy stated that the ENP 'will reinforce *existing* [emphasis mine] forms of regional and subregional cooperation' (European Commission 2004a). Accordingly, the EU no longer perceived itself as a region-builder through the ENP, but merely as a region-supporter; *de facto*, this could not apply to Western NIS which lacked effective mechanisms for regional cooperation. From the outset of the process for policy implementation, the ENP thus clearly focuses on bilateral instruments. Country Reports are prepared by the European Commission with a view to assessing the situation and prospects in a specific neighbouring country, while Action Plans defining a medium-term agenda for reforms are then negotiated bilaterally with each country. Monitoring is also carried out by the Commission on a country-by-country basis, even though the EC also issues overall reports on the ENP implementation. Finally, under the ENPI, the new assistance instrument created to replace TACIS and MEDA, the share of regional programmes is limited to 14.7 per cent of the indicative funding for 2007–2010.[21] To sum up, partner countries' preferences for bilateral ties with the EU and reluctance toward regional cooperation have been instrumental in the EU's promotion of differentiation as a stepping stone for the neighbourhood policy. The proximity policy is therefore conceived as a flexible framework offering a variety of tools to meet the specific needs of each partner country, as clearly indicated by the Commission:

> The point of departure for the Action Plans is a common set of issues, which correspond with the ENP's objectives ... However the drawing up of an Action Plan and the priorities agreed with each partner will depend on its particular circumstances. These differ with respect to geographic location, the political and economic situation, relations with the European Union and with neighbouring countries, reform programmes, where applicable, needs and capacities, as well as perceived interests in the context of the ENP (European Commission 2004a: 8).

ENP Implementation Gaps in Western Nis and South Caucasus Countries: The Need for a Region-wide Approach

Whereas the ENP is still a recent initiative, tensions arising from policy implementation have been instrumental in gradually refining the policy, especially with a view to defining region-wide strategies in major sectors. As a result of gaps noted in the implementation process, cooperation among Eastern neighbours has incrementally emerged as a necessary component in the ENP.

---

21   The Eastern component of regional programmes totals €223.5, that is, less than four per cent of total commitments under the ENPI. See European Commission, European Neighbourhood Partnership Instrument funding 2007–2013, available at: http://ec.europa. eu/world/enp/pdf/country/0703_enpi_figures_en.pdf

To analyse the ENP, scholars have most often used the external governance approach which was initially applied to the EU's accession process. They have moved this analytical framework beyond the enlargement policy reference while also initially stressing the importance of conditionality in the EU's attempts to project internal solutions in the ENP (Lavenex 2004). This approach mostly draws upon institutionalist explanations, according to which 'EU external governance is generally shaped by existing EU institutions. They provide the template for the externalisation of EU policies, rules, and modes of governance and condition their effectiveness' (Lavenex and Schimmelfennig 2009: 802). From this perspective, factors such as the degree of EU competences within a specific field or the internal structure of policy-making are salient for explaining EU policies in its neighbourhood. The external governance approach seeks to grasp the way in which the EU expands its rules abroad. According to this approach, the EU uses its bargaining power to export its own rules and to ensure compliance with its standards (Schimmelfennig and Sedelmeier 2004). Such bargaining power derives from the asymmetrical relationship between the EU and its neighbours: as noted by Karen Smith, 'the EU is clearly the dominant actor in the relationship' (Karen Smith 2005: 772). However, even though there is indeed an asymmetry between the EU and its neighbours, what the EU does in its neighbourhood is not limited either to rule expansion or to its bargaining power. Insofar as the ENP is not about enlargement, 'joint ownership' is a core principle in the ENP (European Commission 2003 and 2004a). Therefore, policy reception and implementation by partner countries matter (Delcour 2007a, Parmentier 2008).[22]

A brief analysis of policy implementation[23] highlights a first series of tensions originating in the discrepancy between the ENP's objectives and toolbox, on the one hand, and partner countries' policy preferences and domestic structures on the other hand. This obviously relates to the well-known mismatch between the lack of membership perspective in the ENP and individual partner countries' aspirations to join the EU (for example, Ukraine's, Moldova's and, to a lesser extent, Georgia's).[24] Since the ENP is clearly distinct from any accession prospect (see for example,

---

22   This is explicitly acknowledged by the European Commission: 'The responsibility for this [progressing towards prosperity and stability] lies primarily with the countries themselves' (European Commission 2006: 2).

23   ENP implementation is unexplored in academic research. Systematic field research is necessary in order to assess the degree of convergence with EU norms and standards and to gather comparative data on the effectiveness of policy implementation. This is even more important as there is no fully-fledged institutionalised monitoring system for ENP implementation in partner countries, although such a system is currently being set up in Ukraine. As a result, ENP monitoring is often performed by think-tanks (for example,. the Razumkov centre in Ukraine) or civil society organisations.

24   See for example, Petrov 2007, Smith and Webber 2008: 79. Gabriella Meloni deepens the argument by concluding that the ENP's instruments, borrowed from the enlargement process, do not match its objectives, which still need to be further clarified as there is no convergent vision, either within the EU or with neighbouring countries (Meloni 2007).

European Commission 2006: 2), methods borrowed from the 1990s enlargement process (that is, mainly conditionality) are less likely to generate results than in the case of candidate countries. In other words, the EU lacks strong leverage in its neighbourhood. ENP Action Plans are 'political documents'[25] relying upon partner countries' commitments; they do not constitute a legal framework. The situation is similar for the Association Agenda which has been adopted with Ukraine once the ENP Action Plan came to an end.[26] Implementation of the objectives identified under the Action Plans is therefore a major issue for the effectiveness of the ENP in all partner countries. However, the incentives offered are not sufficient to induce Eastern neighbours to effectively converge with EU norms and standards, especially in comparison to the costs incurred by neighbours. For instance, while Ukraine has concluded negotiations with the EU on 31 policy areas where it is expected to harmonise its legislation with EU acquis, the Association Agreement with the EU, a major incentive for Kyiv, cannot enter into force before talks on a deep and comprehensive free trade area are completed.[27] Georgia offers another illustration. The launch of negotiations for an association agreement (July 2010) provided the country with a strong political signal and additional incentives to converge with EU norms. However, the fact that the opening of negotiations for a DCFTA is subject to strict EU preconditions is perceived negatively in Tbilisi.[28] The cost (both financial and administrative) of approximation with the EU acquis is therefore considerable for countries lacking accession perspective.

Another issue is the mismatch between the domestic policy agenda and ENP priorities; Georgia offers a good illustration in this respect. While over the past six years territorial integrity and state-building have ranked at the top of Georgia's policy agenda, the EU's approach in this country focused on the rule of law as a prerequisite for stability (Di Puppo 2009). As a result of this mismatch, ENP objectives play no major explicit role in the Georgian government's programmes drafted in the years 2006–2008.[29] Overall, the purpose of legal approximation is not clearly understood in the absence of any EU membership perspective. In all Eastern neighbours, an additional gap lies at the institutional level, between the reforms requested under the ENP and partner country administrative resources.

---

25   Cf. for instance the text of the Plan signed with Armenia: 'The EU Armenia Action Plan is a political document laying out the strategic objectives of the cooperation between Armenia and the EU.' Available at: http://ec.europa.eu/world/enp/pdf/action_plans/armenia_enp_ap_final_en.pdf

26   The Association Agenda was adopted by the EU–Ukraine Cooperation Council on 23 November 2009.

27   This point was raised by Alexander Duleba during the Slovak Foreign Policy's Association Conference 'Strategic Framework for the EU's Eastern Policy', Bratislava, October 2010.

28   Interviews with the Chief Advisor to the Prime Minister and with Chief Negotiator for the EU–Georgia Association Agreement, Tbilisi, November 2010.

29   This statement is based upon observations made during the mission conducted in Georgia in 2008 to evaluate European Commission's assistance.

The implementation of the ENP is hindered by unstable political environments (for example, in Ukraine, see Wolczuk 2004, 2007 and 2008; Delcour 2008), policy shifts, insufficient resources and frequent staff turnovers. Secondary legislation and the administrative capacity to implement the reforms are identified by the European Commission as the main challenge (European Commission 2008a: 6). As a result of the discrepancy between ENP incentives and priorities and partner countries' expectations and preferences, convergence with the EU *acquis* is uneven across sectors and countries.[30] Furthermore, owing to weak capacities, approximated legislation is far from being thoroughly applied.

The second series of tensions affecting the implementation of the neighbourhood policy stems from the influence of another major player in the former Soviet countries covered by the ENP: Russia. As shown in the previous chapter, Russia's refusal to participate in the ENP prompted the tailor-made design of a strategic partnership with the EU; however, the impact of Russia's decision has been at least as important on the European Neighbourhood Policy (Delcour 2006). Given Russia's influence in the region, security challenges in the Western NIS and the South Caucasus prompted an enhanced cooperation between the EU and Russia to enhance stability and security in their common neighbourhood (Lynch 2003a: 19). Regional security – more specifically the management of unresolved conflicts – was thus meant to become a cornerstone of the EU–Russia Common Space on External Security. Yet EU–Russia cooperation in the Western NIS and the South Caucasus countries has remained an empty shell as a result of 'competing rationalities' (Averre 2009). Over the past six years, Russia has been reluctant to accept growing EU involvement in its 'near abroad.' The EU's increasing power to attract Western NIS was indeed perceived in Moscow as a loss of influence for Russia in its traditional backyard and as a source of 'rivalry in the post-Soviet space' (Arbatova 2006: 16). With a view to accounting for such rivalry, analysts have often pointed out differences in the way in which Russia and the EU exert their influence. Russia is often presented as pursuing a realist approach and usually resorting to coercive instruments in its backyard, whereas the EU is described as a post-modern and benevolent construction relying primarily upon its soft power in the Western NIS and South Caucasus.

Yet, as convincingly put by Haukkala (2008a) and Averre (2009), the picture is much more complex. On the one hand, whereas Russia indeed resorts to coercion in its near abroad, as shown by the 2008 conflict in Georgia, it has also developed over the past few years a 'normative agenda' (Haukkala 2008a: 37) and pays increasing attention to non-military instruments likely to enhance its attraction power, such as the Russian language (Delcour 2007b). On the other hand, the notion of the EU as a benevolent actor in its neighbourhood, particularly in the Eastern periphery, needs to be reviewed (Kratochvíl 2008, Averre 2009). As Zielonka puts it, 'the EU's efforts to spread its norms [are] truly imperial in the sense that the EU tries to

---

30   Pressure to align with EU norms is of course much weaker for those partner countries who have less expectations *vis-à-vis* the EU and therefore more bargaining power, such as Azerbaijan.

impose domestic constraints on other actors through various forms of economic and political domination' (Zielonka 2008: 471). Hettne and Söderbaum (2005) refer to 'soft imperialism,' which they define as 'an asymmetric form of dialogue or even the imposition or strategic use of norms and conditionalities enforced for reasons of self-interest rather than for the creation of a genuine (interregional) dialogue' (Hettne and Söderbaum 2005: 539). In other words, to some extent the EU uses its civilian instruments in a coercive manner.[31] The issue is therefore not so much about contrasted international actors. It is rather about the way in which Russia's rejection of the ENP erodes the EU's normative power *vis-à-vis* the Western NIS and South Caucasus countries included in the ENP (Haukkala 2008a), *inter alia* by creating a discrepancy between EU policies at its periphery. Russia also develops economic and normative politics competing with EU policies as a means to retain influence. This is particularly the case for the Customs Union which is not compatible with talks for a deep and comprehensive free trade area launched by the EU with Ukraine and foreseen with other partner countries. This requires from the EU additional efforts both to take into account the role of a competitive region-builder at its Eastern periphery and to articulate the ENP and its strategic partnership with Russia (Delcour 2006); in other words, it requires 'a foreign policy adjustment to the realities of the post-Soviet space' (Smith and Webber 2008: 83).

The unresolved conflicts are the best illustration of the way in which a regional hegemon which chooses to opt out can undermine the ENP. While the South Caucasus was identified in the Security Strategy as an area where the Union should take a 'stronger and more active interest' (Council of the European Union 2003), both the EU's engagement and its achievements have been limited. This is primarily connected to Russia's high involvement in the conflicts which has also resulted, at the EU level, in divergences among Member States. The European Commission has explicitly acknowledged the ENP's shortcomings when it comes to conflict resolution and the need for better cooperation with Russia:

> The ENP has achieved little in supporting the resolution of frozen or open conflicts in the region ... If the ENP cannot contribute to addressing conflicts in the region, it will have failed in one of its key purposes ... There is also a need, in the interest of all concerned, to engage Russia in closer cooperation in preventing conflicts and enhancing stability across Eastern Europe and the Southern Caucasus (European Commission 2006b: 4 and 9).

In the case of Nagorno–Karabakh, the EU has kept a low profile. The Union as such is not involved in the Minsk Group providing an international framework for conflict resolution and its role has been limited to supporting the OSCE-led negotiation process, while meetings and negotiations between Armenia

---

31 Examples include the EU Border Assistance Management Mission (EUBAM) in Moldova and Ukraine (Parmentier 2008) and the visa facilitation and readmission agreements signed with Russia, Ukraine and Moldova. See also Chapter 7.

and Azerbaijan have mainly been undertaken under the auspices of the Russian Federation. The EU's influence over conflict settlement is further undermined by its lack of discursive coherence in ENP policy documents: whereas the Action Plan concluded with Azerbaijan mentions territorial integrity, the ENP AP negotiated with Armenia refers to the principle of self-determination (see also Alieva 2006 and Mikhelidze 2009). The fact that the EU is not even 'a demandeur for a greater role' in the conflict settlement (Popescu 2007) contrasts both with the South Caucasus countries' expectations in this respect (Alieva 2006: 13) and with its own security interests.

In Georgia, the EU has been among the biggest contributors to efforts toward the peaceful resolution of internal conflicts by supporting confidence-building measures and economic rehabilitation projects in both the Abkhazia and South Ossetia conflict zones, as well as through projects to improve the living conditions of internally displaced persons (European Commission 2009: 22). As noted by Popescu (2007), the EU also chose to focus on Georgia's reform process as a precondition to conflict resolution; it regarded further reforms and progress in the democratisation process as prerequisites to the country's efforts for reintegrating the two breakaway regions (Nilsson 2008: 103). This approach explained the focus on rule of law, including under the European Security and Defence Policy through the EUJUST–THEMIS mission assisting the Georgian government in drafting a new strategy for the criminal justice system. In other words, the EU did not engage directly in conflict resolution whereas Russia had been playing a major role since the collapse of the Soviet Union, either through its role in the 1990s ceasefire agreements and subsequent peacekeeping missions (Gordadze 2008: 34– 5), through its scheme delivering passports to the citizens of the breakaway regions (the so-called *pasportizatsiya* policy) or through its willingness to provide these regions with military equipment (Illarionov 2008).

The EU's approach to conflict resolution can therefore be characterised as a 'policy limbo between action and non-action' (Lynch 2005: 35). The EU's maintenance of such a low profile can also be explained by divergences among Member States, with France, Germany, Italy and Belgium opposing the dispatch to Georgia of a border monitoring mission in 2005 that was backed by the UK and the Baltic States (Smith and Webber 2008: 93). The EU's mediation in the 2008 conflict with Russia[32] was its first direct engagement in conflict settlement. Even though the EU's involvement can be considered a success to the extent that they put an end to the armed conflict, EU efforts were strongly constrained by Russia's behaviour, as evidenced by Moscow's non-compliance with provisions of the ceasefire agreement and by the access denied to the EUMM (European Union Monitoring Mission) observers in the breakaway regions.

To sum up, while 'in principle the EU and Russia share similar interests regarding the stabilisation of their neighbourhood' (Fischer 2008: 122), they pursue

---

32   As noted in Chapter 4, this mediation also gave rise to deep divergences among EU Member States.

different approaches to regional security (Averre 2009: 1707) and this discrepancy is also a major stumbling block for the effectiveness of the EU's neighbourhood policy. As a result, EU commitments and intentions, when it comes to conflict prevention, have often fallen short at the time of implementation. While the EU has to some extent enhanced its profile in conflict resolution in the wake of the 2008 Georgia conflict, it still does not appear as a major regional player. The Turkish–Russian rapprochement and the Turkish proposal of a stability platform for the South Caucasus, involving Ankara and Moscow while excluding the EU and the US, are only the most recent examples of such exogenous constraint – even though the stability platform has not materialised.

As a consequence of both the role played by Russia and the different degrees of commitment and timelines for policy implementation among ENP partner countries, fragmentation appears as a major risk for the ENP's Eastern component. Interestingly, the main amendment proposed by the EC to tackle the weaknesses noted in ENP implementation is the introduction of a multilateral dimension:

> Thus far, the ENP has largely been bilateral … Nevertheless, there are a number of cross-cutting themes where the EU and its ENP partners … share common interests and concerns and which could usefully be addressed in a multilateral context' (European Commission 2006b: 8).

The Eastern Partnership: Building a Regional Dimension for Europeanisation in the Eastern Neighbourhood?

The Eastern Partnership proposed in 2008 and launched in 2009 thus marks a shift in prior EU approaches to region-building in that it introduces a multilateral dimension to the ENP, more specifically with a view to fostering the convergence with EU norms and standards.

The Eastern Partnership results from a joint Polish–Swedish initiative (Polish–Swedish Proposal 2008) presented both at the General Affairs and External Relations Council (GAERC) in May 2008[33] and at the European Council in June 2008.[34] Poland played a major role in designing the Partnership and pushing it forward onto the EU agenda. In the early 2000s, the country had already advocated for a specific Eastern dimension of the EU's foreign policy[35] that would step up

---

33   2870th General Affairs and External Relations Council 26–27 May 2008, Press release. Slovenian Presidency's website, available at: http://www.eu2008.si/en/News_and_Documents/Council_Conclusions/May/0526_GAERC-prE.pdf

34   Conclusions of the European Council, 19–20 June 2008. Slovenian Presidency's website, available at: http://www.eu2008.si/en/News_and_Documents/Council_Conclusions/June/0619_EC-CON.pdf

35   An initial Polish position was presented to the EU Presidency in June 2001. It was then detailed and specified in the Non-Paper presented by the Polish Ministry of

relations with Ukraine, Moldova and Belarus after the 2004 enlargement. At the Copenhagen European Council in December 2002, Polish representatives called for 'a coherent, comprehensive framework that will enable individual development of relations with each of the countries concerned'[36] and supported by regional action plans combined with country action plans (Ministry of Foreign Affairs of the Republic of Poland 2003: 86). However, while important elements of the Polish non-paper[37] were retained in the final formulation of the ENP (European Commission 2004), the idea of a specific Eastern dimension was discarded owing to Southern EU Member States' pressure for also including the Mediterranean partners.

A few years later, the proposal by the French President of a Union for the Mediterranean, initially put forward in 2007 and endorsed at the EU level in 2008,[38] opened a window of opportunity for Poland to ask for a balance between Eastern and Southern neighbours and to move its foreign policy priorities to the top of the EU foreign policy agenda. Two concerns are salient in Poland's efforts to promote a new Eastern dimension. First, among EU Member States Poland is one of the strongest advocates of Western NIS/South Caucasus European aspirations. This support is closely interwoven with its own democratisation experience, in parallel to the EU's accession process, since 1989; like other Central and Eastern European countries, more specifically like the Baltic States, Poland has experienced a path similar to the one Ukraine has engaged on, transforming itself from a communist regime to a genuine democracy. When compared to the Western EU Member States, Poland (as well as other new Member States) therefore has a comparative advantage in its relations with former Soviet republics, based upon a specific know-how of the reform process.

Moreover, Polish support for having Western CIS join the EU can be better explained by understanding the country's geopolitical security interests. After its accession to the EU, Poland was concerned about its marginal location at the outskirts of the Union (Natorski 2008: 74). This concern was even more worrying as the East was perceived as a potential source of threats. Since Ukraine's Orange Revolution, in which Poland played a key role, and more specifically over the years 2005–2008, Polish–Russian relations have drastically deteriorated (Natorski 2008: 69). The

---

Foreign Affairs in January 2003. For an analysis of Poland's initiatives and policies in its neighbourhood, see Natorski 2008.

36   Ministry of Foreign Affairs of the Republic of Poland, 'Non-Paper with Polish proposals concerning policy towards new Eastern neighbours after EU enlargement', January 2003, in: Stefan Batory Foundation, EU Enlargement and Neighbourhood Policy, February 2003, 86.

37   For example, methods underpinning the ENP: the use of conditionality, the principle of differentiation and related individual Action Plans (Ministry of Foreign Affairs of the Republic of Poland 2003).

38   Nicolas Sarkozy proposed a new EU project for the Southern Mediterranean countries during his campaign for the French 2007 presidential elections. This proposal originated in a poor assessment of the Euro-Med Partnership launched in 1995. See Liberti 2008.

newly-elected Polish President Lech Kaczyński and the governments supported by his Law and Justice party (2005–2007) advocated for an adamant position *vis-à-vis* Moscow. As convincingly put by Natorski, in order to put forward its foreign policy priorities onto the EU agenda, Poland attempted to give a European dimension to its security concerns, *inter alia* through raising arguments on the need for avoiding new dividing lines on the European continent (Natorski 2008: 70).[39]

Despite the clever framing of Polish concerns within a European context, support for the Polish initiative from another EU Member State – Sweden – was crucial[40] in bringing the Eastern neighbourhood onto the EU agenda. The Swedish Prime Minister, Carl Bildt, indeed shared Poland's hard line on Russia (Meister and May 2009). The joint Polish–Swedish proposal was welcomed by other EU Member States who asked the Commission to prepare a proposal (European Council 2008, European Commission 2008d). The Eastern Partnership was then launched under the Czech Presidency in May 2009 (Council of the European Union 2009).

A few months after the creation of the Union for the Mediterranean, the new initiative was designed to step up EU's relations with its Eastern neighbours 'without prejudice to [their] aspirations for their future relationship with the EU' (European Commission 2008d: 2). In other words, the Eastern Partnership is about 'accelerating political association and further economic integration' between the EU and its neighbours (Council of the European Union 2009: 6) while the issue of accession is left aside. To that end, the bilateral track remains predominant. In particular it entails increased convergence with EU norms, standards and *acquis communautaire* for upgrading contractual relations towards association agreements,[41] for setting up deep and comprehensive free trade areas and for progressing towards visa liberalisation. The whole process of convergence is thus still managed individually, including cases related to administrative capacities.[42] The bilateral track therefore

---

39 Concerns about new dividing lines in Europe were raised at the end of 2007 when the new Central and Eastern EU member states acceded to the Schengen area. This accession implied a full adherence to Schengen rules and thus put an end to the cheaper visa fees and simpler procedures applied by Central European States *vis-à-vis* their neighbours since they had joined the EU, with a negative impact on borderlands with strong historical ties such as the Polish–Ukrainian border. See Boratynski, Gromadzki, Sushko and Szymborska 2006; Truner and Kruse 2008; Delcour 2010.

40 Germany had previously declined the Polish Minister of Foreign Affairs' proposal for a Polish–German initiative as far as Russia was not taken into consideration (Meister and May 2009). The need for another Member State's support confirms Copsey's and Pomorska's thesis of an overall limited Polish influence on the EU's Eastern policy (Copsey and Pomorska 2010).

41 After Ukraine in 2007 and Moldova in 2009, negotiations for association agreements have been launched with the three Caucasus countries in July 2010.

42 Under the Eastern Partnership, Comprehensive Institution-Building (CIB) Programmes will be developed with each partner country in order to strengthen their administrative capacities and to enable a more effective enforcement of the legislation approximated with EU *acquis*. The idea underlying CIB programmes clearly originates in

includes the most important objectives in EU-partner countries' cooperation. It can therefore be argued that the Eastern Partnership will, at least initially, strengthen differentation between partner countries, especially between South Caucasus countries which were traditionally considered as a subregional group by the EU. At the same time, the multilateral track foreseen under the Eastern Partnership 'will provide a new framework where common challenges can be addressed' (European Commission 2008: 3). It envisages regular high-level meetings gathering officials from the countries involved[43] and four thematic platforms corresponding to the major ENP areas of cooperation.[44] In addition, the Eastern Partnership envisages the establishment of an interparliamentary assembly between the European Parliament and Eastern neighbours' parliaments, as well as the creation of an Eastern Partnership Assembly of Regional and Local Authorities.

To the extent that 'differentiation needs to remain at the heart of the policy' (European Commission 2006b: 8), the multilateral track is envisioned as a complement to bilateral activities under the ENP. The words 'multilateral' and 'thematic' are widely used in the EU's policy discourse, at the expenses of the word 'regional', which is barely used in the Polish–Swedish joint proposal and carefully avoided both in the Commission proposal and in the Declaration launching the Partnership. This contrasts with the 2008 European Council conclusions which underlined 'the need to further promote regional cooperation among the Eastern neighbours and between the EU and the region', in parallel to bilateral cooperation (European Council 2009: 20). It is argued that the elements concerning multilateral cooperation included in the Polish–Swedish proposal (that is, a project-based, practical and concrete cooperation) were then refined by the European Commission based upon its own thinking and observations drawn from the ENP implementation. As early as 2006, the Commission had pointed to the need for multilateral activities as a complement to the bilateral part of the policy (European Commission 2006b). In a dedicated non-paper (European Commission 2007a), it then gave flesh to the concept of thematic cooperation that underpins the Eastern Partnership multilateral track. This new concept illustrates a shift in the Commission's thinking on region-building. Cooperation is to be organised among Eastern partners and between these partners and the EU around cross-cutting themes, subject to two conditions being fulfilled: common interests for these topics shared by the EU and its partners and the existence of an added value for addressing them in a multilateral context (European Commission 2007a: 1). This shift toward a multilateral thematic approach to the Eastern Partnership states indicates that the EU does not intend to tackle regional

---

the 1990s enlargement process, which highlighted the need for institutional strengthening in order to have the approximated legislation effectively implemented.

43   Meetings of the Ministers of Foreign Affairs are foreseen every year and meetings of Head of State or Government are planned to be held every two years (Council of the European Union 2009: 8).

44   That is, democracy, good governance and stability; economic integration and convergence with EU policies; energy security; and contacts between people.

issues as such; this coincides with partner countries' reticence toward regional cooperation. Rather, the Eastern Partnership addresses specific issues on a multilateral basis, where the word 'multilateral' (as used by the European Commission in its 2007 non-paper) is conceived as cooperation that is, not necessarily connected to geographical regions but in fact can go beyond them.[45] In the framework of the Eastern Partnership, the multilateral track envisages the participation of the EU and possibly Member States together with partner countries.

It is argued however that both the bilateral and the multilateral tracks of the Eastern partnership may, over time, have region-building effects in the Eastern neighbourhood. The deepening of EU-partner countries' relations foreseen under the bilateral track implies further approximation with the EU *acquis*, especially with trade-related *acquis* for the negotiation of Deep and Comprehensive Free Trade Agreements and with Justice and Home Affairs-related *acquis* for the conclusion of Mobility and Security Pacts. As a consequence of this wide-ranging Europeanisation, the convergence between partner countries' norms and standards may well increase over time, with EU norms becoming the common reference.

As far as the multilateral track is concerned, the thematic platforms are unlikely to foster regional links *per se*; as stressed above, partner countries have embarked on different political paths and the thematic platform on democratisation, good governance and stability will probably not bring them closer to one another. Also, it is highly unlikely that the multilateral track will contribute to overcoming the existing conflict between Armenia and Azerbaijan. Yet, like the interparliamentary assembly and the assembly of local authorities, in principle it provides a forum which, combined with greater incentives and stronger EU leverage under the bilateral track and subject to the frequency of meetings and the participation of partner countries, may nurture dialogue on concrete issues among Eastern neighbours. In other words, the underlying logic is to foster socialisation and 'links among the partners themselves and [to] be a natural forum for discussion' (European Commission 2008: 10). Such logic also explains the emphasis put on civil society exchanges in the Eastern Partnership, *inter alia* through the Civil Society Forum. The Eastern Partnership may thus result in the emergence of Western NIS and the South Caucasus as a distinct regional area over time by bringing them closer to the EU and differentiating them further from other ENP/NIS countries.

On the one hand, even though it was presented as a trade-off for Poland's acceptance of the Union for the Mediterranean and thus as a counterbalance between the two ENP components, the Eastern Partnership is likely to further differentiate Eastern partners from South Mediterranean countries. Indeed it entails an implicit distinction between Eastern and Southern neighbours, based upon the existence of an accession perspective grounded in article 49 of the Treaty on the European Union. In other words, the Eastern Partnership confirms the distinction between

---

45   For instance, the Non-Paper issued by the Commission mentions the possibility of having both Eastern and Southern countries cooperating on specific issues together with the EU. See European Commission 2008e.

European neighbours and Europe's neighbours,[46] initially formulated in 2007 by Germany in its proposals for strengthening the Eastern policy of the EU (Copsey 2007: 11). The Partnership is clearly conceived by its main initiator, Poland, as a facilitator or as an antechamber for integration of Western NIS into the EU which, according to the Polish Minister of Foreign Affairs, would only seem 'natural'[47] at a later stage. Poland has always been one of the strongest proponents of Western NIS's (especially Ukraine's) accession into the EU. The project was inspired by Poland's own experience of regional cooperation within the Visegrád Group, which served as preparation for EU integration (Cianciara 2008). Nevertheless, owing to the reluctance of the bulk of EU Member States to enlarge the Union further, the Partnership does not mention EU accession as an objective. As a consequence, the project may suffer from the same mismatch with Eastern neighbours' expectations as the whole ENP. In its current formulation, the proposal has elicited sharp criticism from the Ukrainian authorities, for whom it does not significantly differ from the ENP on the issue of EU accession. The Ukrainian Ministry of Foreign Affairs has called for a clear step forward to give Eastern neighbours a real EU perspective:

> We believe that the initiative of the 'Eastern Partnership' should envisage a clear EU membership perspective to those European neighbours of the EU who can demonstrate seriousness of their European ambitions through concrete actions and tangible achievements.[48]

On the other hand, the Polish–Swedish initiative was also implicitly meant to further differentiate Western NIS from the other post-Soviet Republics, above all from Russia. Such an objective is tightly linked to Poland's tense relations with Russia. Currently, however, the objectives of the EU's relations with Russia do not significantly differ from those of the ENP with Western NIS, even though Moscow opted out (Delcour 2007a). For instance, Russia was the first former Soviet Republic to conclude a visa facilitation and readmission agreement with the EU;[49] the negotiations for a new EU–Russia agreement, opened in June 2008 at Khanty-Mansiysk to replace

---

46   That is between 'European countries that are neighbours of the EU' and 'non-European neighbours' (Copsey 2007: 11).

47   Cf. the conference of the Polish Minister of Foreign Affairs, Radoslaw Sikorski, in Brussels, 26 May 2008: 'In Poland we distinguish between the EU's Southern and Eastern neighbours: in the south we have neighbours of Europe, in the east we have European neighbours of the EU that – if they fulfil the criteria – will one day be able to apply for membership.' Cf. also his comments in *Europe's World*, No. 12, Summer 2009: 'Although EU membership for EaP states is not yet on the agenda, we in Poland feel that the prospect of accession should be kept open.'

48   Ministry of Foreign Affairs of Ukraine, 'Statement regarding the development of the eastern dimension of European Foreign Policy,' 26 May 2008. Available at: http://www.mfa.gov.ua/eu/en/news/detail/13105.htm.

49   The agreements were signed at the EU–Russia Summit on 25 May 2006 in Sochi and at the EU–Ukraine Summit on 27 October 2006 in Helsinki.

the PCA, also include the perspective of a free trade area. However, should it be implemented as such, the Polish–Swedish proposal could push partner countries further away from Russia. Even though the initiative intends to associate Russia under specific, local initiatives (for example, around Kaliningrad), it has been (at least initially) perceived as a threat by Moscow.[50] The Eastern Partnership is clearly meant to foster links among Western NIS based upon EU values and with the EU as a reference point. Russia itself is unlikely to become fully engaged in the process, since this would constitute its tacit acceptance of EU norms as a reference, which it is ready to do only on a selective basis and if this coincides with its own interests. Furthermore, while Russia is for the time being a key economic and political partner to all Western NIS, its influence may decrease together with the conclusion of thematic agreements using the EU as a reference. However, the costs incurred by neighbours for converging with EU norms may also bring them closer to Russia, whose market is more accessible than the EU's.

Conclusion

This insight into the ENP's approaches to region-building confirms the picture of an EU foreign policy which has been shaped gradually, as EU institutions and policymakers adjust policy tools and content according to experience.

If considered from the perspective of support for regional cooperation, the European Neighbourhood Policy as designed by the EU in 2003–2004 does not mark a shift from previous EU approaches to region-building in the former USSR in that it provides very limited support to cooperation between partner countries. The policy framework reflects a 'hub-and-spoke' model in which the centre – the EU – works out its relations with its neighbours bilaterally (Emerson 2004: 10). While remaining in line with the EU's previous policies *vis-à-vis* CIS countries, the emphasis on differentiation in the ENP is also similar to the approach adopted during the 1990s enlargement process (Karen Smith 2005: 355). The ENP thus confirms the post-Soviet exception in EU approaches to region-building.[51] The decision to

---

50 Cf. the reaction of Alexander Babakov, vice-chairman of the Duma, to the Polish–Swedish proposal: 'To maintain the partner-like attitude begun during the Polish prime minister's visit to our country earlier this year, it would be better for such new initiatives to emerge, if not in partnership with Russia, then at least after prior consultation with Moscow. In the Eastern European region and – of course – on the territory of the Commonwealth of Independent States, it is not worth ignoring the warranted, fully justified and by now traditional interests of Russia', www.warsawvoice.pl

51 Michael Emerson notes that the EU tends to promote with its other neighbours (for example, countries belonging to the European Economic Area, or even Southern Mediterranean partners) a 'cobweb approach', in which 'the centre seeks to simplify and order the system with the neighbours grouped according to their shorter or longer geographic/political distance from the centre, with elements of multilateralism or standardisation for each group' (Emerson 2004: 10).

emphasise differentiation can principally be explained by exogenous factors. Deep differences and conflicts between Eastern partner countries have prevented the Union from relying on its traditional support for regional cooperation.

However, as noted by Smith and Webber (2008: 73), 'dealing with regional stabilisation has been a central rationale of the ENP.' This objective has not been reached through the prevailing bilateral approach in the ENP, owing to implementation gaps and discrepancies with partner countries' expectations. Moreover, the effectiveness of the ENP approach has been strongly constrained at a regional level by the intervention of other regional powers, primarily Russia. The weight of exogenous factors is even more important as it combines with endogenous weaknesses, for example, lack of substantial incentives offered to partner countries, the EU's relative inexperience in some parts of the neighbourhood (for example, South Caucasus) as well as dissension among EU Member States who are divided on major issues such as the prospect of accession for Eastern neighbours.

While granting that it is still early to provide any well-grounded assessment, the Eastern Partnership may be a watershed in EU policies *vis-à-vis* its Eastern neighbours. From the perspective of association agreements, deep and comprehensive free trade areas and visa liberalisation, it provides greater incentives to partner countries on a bilateral basis, in particular to those which so far had not been offered such perspectives (for example, the three South Caucasus countries). Subject to the effectiveness of implementation, it may thus favour convergence among partner countries through increased Europeanisation, just as 'regionalism in Europe is encouraged through enlargement of the EU itself' (Karen Smith 2005c: 347). Subject to their effective functioning, the additional socialisation mechanisms provided by the multilateral track may contribute to the progressive emergence of the 'Eastern neighbourhood'[52] as a region. This also may be facilitated by local developments, for example, the current decrease in tensions between, on the one hand, Poland and Russia,[53] and on the other hand Russia and Ukraine.[54] Nevertheless, the major question mark relates to Eastern neighbours' actual degree of convergence with EU norms in light of the administrative, political and financial costs incurred and in the absence of accession perspective.

---

52   The expression is broadly used by the EU, more specifically by the European Commission in its policy documents.

53   As indicated in Chapter 4, Russian authorities' shift regarding the Katyn massacres (for example, joint declaration by Prime Ministers Donald Tusk and Vladimir Putin on 7 April 2010) and Russia's cooperation and compassion following the crash of the Polish presidential plane over Smolensk on 10 April 2010 offer an opportunity for a new start in Polish–Russian relations.

54   The rapprochement between Russia and Ukraine is a consequence of Viktor Yanukovich's election in January 2010. The meeting of the newly elected President with his Russian counterpart on 21 April 2010 resulted in signing agreements on Russia's Black Sea Fleet and gas deliveries, two issues that had been at the core of the tensions between the two countries.

Chapter 6

The EU: A Latecomer in Central Asia's Great Game

In many respects, the countries of Central Asia present a unique set of circumstances regarding region-building within the former Soviet Union. When compared to other post-Soviet republics, Central Asian republics have two major distinctive features.

First, owing to similar cultural, political and/or economic features and to the transnational character of the major challenges with which the area is confronted, there is *a priori* a strong case for developing regional cooperation among the five countries concerned (Kazakhstan, Uzbekistan, Kyrgyzstan, Tajikistan and Turkmenistan). Among these similar features is the fact that Central Asian countries had not existed as states prior to the collapse of the Soviet Union. As explained in Chapter 2, they were strongly dependent upon the centre and lagged behind in the USSR's dissolution process. Another similar feature is the use of Russian, which has remained widespread in the region, with bilingualism prevailing in the majority of countries (Atnachev 2001).[1] To sum up, Central Asian countries share, to a certain extent, a 'unity of language, culture and history' (Peyrouse 2006: 65) as well as a strong Soviet legacy. At the same time, they are also confronted with analogous challenges, e.g. drug trafficking and environmental (particularly water) issues. Such similarities in turn provide strong incentives among Central Asian countries to develop 'inside-out' (Neumann 1994) regional dynamics.

Second, Central Asia's strategic position makes it the core of several regional projects and organisations which have emerged since the 1990s and in which external actors play key roles. The rivalries among great powers in the region have increased since the turn of the century, owing mainly to energy issues and to the war on Afghanistan launched after the September 11 attacks. For over a decade, Russia, China, and the United States, along with less influential powers, have started to play a new 'great game' around Centrasiatic countries. As a consequence, there is also a strong case for fostering 'outside-in' (Neumann 1994) regional dynamics in Central Asia.

Central Asia thus combines both internal and external factors that propel cooperation or integration projects. As a result, the region is an interesting case study for analysing EU policies from the angle of region-building. The hypothesis

---

1   This is especially the case in Kazakhstan and Kyrgyzstan. To some extent, Uzbekistan constitutes an exception in this picture, with Uzbek language being largely predominant and the Cyrillic alphabet being replaced by Latin letters.

here is that, owing to the two distinctive features mentioned above, Central Asia offers fertile ground for the EU to implement its traditional regional approach. To what extent, then, has the EU been able to build upon the existence of regional challenges to design a political vision for the area and to encourage cooperation between Centrasiatic republics? How far has it developed inter-regional links with other regional organisations? How does it interact with other region-builders in Central Asia?

This chapter will argue that after a decade of weak EU involvement in Central Asia (though the EU's presence there has been strengthened since the mid-2000s), both the EU's influence and its contribution to region-building have been limited in the region, owing both to local and international factors.

Central Asian Republics in the 1990s: The Forgotten Partners

Throughout the 1990s, the EU has kept a low profile in Central Asia. The EU's limited commitment mostly reflects the low ranking on its external agenda of what was then considered from Brussels a remote and relatively stable region.[2] The area remained a *terra incognita* to many EU stakeholders. Among EU member states, only Germany opened an embassy in all five countries and France and the UK in most of them,[3] whereas some other EU countries reportedly covered the region from Moscow or Ankara (Melvin 2008: 2). The same pattern holds true for EU institutions. While European Commission delegations in the 1990s became major diplomatic tools for the EU worldwide (Bruter 1999), the EC opened, in 1994, only one delegation (in Kazakhstan) responsible for all five republics, the activities of which mainly focused on aid cooperation management throughout the decade (Delcour 2005).

True, Central Asian republics were included in the EU policy toolbox designed in the early 1990s after the collapse of the Soviet Union through PCAs, as well as the TACIS programme. However, a closer look into EU instruments highlights the scant attention paid by the EU to the region and reveals a discrepancy when compared to Western CIS, with EU commitments being much weaker in Central Asia.

First, as far as the contractual framework is concerned, PCAs came into force later in Central Asia (as well as in the three Caucasus countries) than in Russia or in Ukraine.[4] Moreover, despite the design of a specific type of agreement common to all former Soviet Republics, the EU introduced in the PCAs a degree

---

2   Especially keeping in mind the wars on the European continent (in the Balkans) in the early 1990s.

3   France and the UK have embassies in all countries except Kyrgyzstan.

4   PCAs entered into force on the 1 July 1999 for Kazakhstan, Uzbekistan and Kyrgyzstan, as compared to December 1997 for Russia. The PCA between the EU and Tajikistan was concluded in October 2004 and came into force only in January 2010. Whereas it was signed in 1998, the PCA with Turkmenistan is still under ratification.

of differentiation clearly reflecting its priorities in the former USSR. An analysis of the various agreements concluded with NIS shows that the scope and depth of these documents is more limited in the case of Central Asian (and the Caucasus) countries than for Russia, Ukraine or even Moldova. All agreements pursue the same broad objectives:

- provide an appropriate framework for developing a political dialogue
- support partner countries' efforts to consolidate their democracy, develop their economy and complete the transition into a market economy
- promote trade and investment
- provide a basis for legislative, economic, social, financial, civil, scientific, technological and cultural cooperation.[5]

But the PCAs signed with Russia, Ukraine and Moldova set an important additional objective which is not included in the PCAs signed with the Caucasus or Central Asian countries, that is, 'to create the necessary conditions for the future establishment of a free trade area covering substantially all trade in goods between them, as well as conditions for bringing about freedom of establishment of companies, of cross-border trade in services and of capital movements.'[6] Moreover, the political dialogue developed with Central Asian countries (or the Caucasus, for that matter) in the 1990s within the framework of the PCA has not reached a level similar to the one that the EU had with Russia or Ukraine at the same time. True, the institutional framework is the same for all PCA countries: a Cooperation Council at the ministerial level, regular meetings at the senior official level, and a Parliamentary Cooperation Committee at the parliamentary level. But on top of this framework, the agreements concluded by the EU with Russia and with Ukraine envisage annual or bi-annual meetings between these countries' Presidents on the one hand, and the President of the Council of the European Union and the President of the Commission of the European Communities on the other. Such meetings were not foreseen in the agreements signed with Central Asian republics. Overall, the PCAs concluded in the 1990s with Central Asian and Caucasus countries reflect low-grade relations with the EU as compared to Russia, Ukraine and Moldova. While, as shown in Chapter 5, relations with South Caucasus countries have been significantly enhanced since the mid-2000s, especially so with the opening of negotiations for Association Agreements,

---

5   See for example, Article 1 of the PCA signed with Kazakhstan in July 1995, available at: http://ec.europa.eu/external_relations/central_asia/pca/index_en.htm.

6   Article 3 of the PCA signed with Russia, available at: http://eur-lex.europa.eu/ LexUriServ/LexUriServ.do?uri=CELEX:21997A1128(01):EN:HTML. Article 4 of the PCAs signed with Ukraine and with Moldova also envisage the creation of a free-trade area. See: http://trade.ec.europa.eu/doclib/docs/2003/october/tradoc_111612.pdf (EU–Ukraine PCA); http://www.delmda.ec.europa.eu/eu_and_moldova/pdf/pca_moldova_en.pdf (EU– Moldova PCA).

Central Asian countries' relations with the EU are still based upon a contractual framework designed in the 1990s, which is not yet fully in force in all countries and which at the same time appears outdated in other republics.[7]

Second, financial assistance provided by the EC under the TACIS programme to Central Asian republics in the 1990s amounted to significantly less than the funds received by some other NIS. Over the decade, the bilateral amount committed by the EC for all five countries totals €311.8 million,[8] as compared to €1.274 million for Russia and €460.8 million for Ukraine. True, the set of demographic, political and economic criteria used by the EC to dispatch TACIS funds among the NIS can, to some extent, explain such a discrepancy: Central Asian countries are far less populated than Russia or Ukraine, for instance.[9] Moreover, political factors have played a role in the dispatch of EC assistance. The authoritarian character of Central Asian regimes and the lack of progress towards democracy (Laruelle and Peyrouse 2006) can also help explain the limited amount of EC funds disbursed to the region; in the case of Tajikistan, civil war (1992–1997) and security conditions impacted negatively on EC commitments for technical assistance, even though other types of assistance were provided. Finally, as far as the economy is concerned, in the first part of the 1990s, Central Asian republics particularly suffered from the dissolution of Soviet economic mechanisms, combined with 'a complete absence of previous experience with market institutions, coordination and practice, attitudes of the population as well as the challenge of building new national economies' (Kalyuzhnova and Lynch 2000: 166). As a result, the economic reform process in Central Asia kept lagging behind other former Soviet republics. These economic conditions explain the use of specific EC aid mechanisms outside the TACIS framework, such as the Food Security Programme (in favour of Kyrgyzstan or Tajikistan)[10] or humanitarian aid managed by the European Commission Humanitarian Office (ECHO), especially in the case of Tajikistan.

Overall, the EU's policy *vis-à-vis* the five Centrasiatic republics in the 1990s and in the early 2000s highlights a weak commitment on the part of the Union. Central Asia had generally remained off of the EU 'radar screen' (Matveeva 2006: 1) for the decade following the collapse of the Soviet Union. Clearly, EU activities have mainly concentrated on technical and humanitarian assistance as well as

---

7   The EU is about to consider the next generation of agreements with Kazakhstan. (Council of the European Union 2010: 4).

8   The breakdown is as follows: €111.9 million for Kazakhstan, €102.5 million for Uzbekistan, €49.8 million for Kyrgyzstan, €39.9 million for Turkmenistan and €8 million for Tajikistan. Central Asian countries also benefited from TACIS regional programmes. European Commission 2000.

9   For instance, Kazakhstan's population amounts to approximately 15,400,000 and Uzbekistan's, Central Asia's most populated country, to 27,600,000 as compared to approximately 142,000,000 in Russia and 46,000,000 in Ukraine.

10   The Food Security Programme was also widely used in the South Caucasus.

development cooperation for the only post-Soviet countries which were then classified as developing countries by the Organisation for Economic Co-operation and Development's Development Assistance Committee (OECD DAC). At the same time, EU activities reflect a vision of Central Asia as forming a coherent region. This is evidenced by the establishment of a single EC Delegation, by the low degree of differentiation among the PCAs concluded and by the regional dimension of assistance projects such as INOGATE and TRACECA, the two programmes (analysed in Chapter 2) meant to open up Central Asia and strengthen its links with the EU via the Caucasus. Though negatively defined when contrasted with the relatively stronger relations established with Russia or Ukraine, a subregional dimension for Central Asia was nonetheless apparent in the embryonic EU policy *vis-à-vis* the post-Soviet area.

Interwoven Factors, Actors and Instruments: The Complex Building of a 'New Partnership' with Central Asia

While regional powers such as Russia and China increased their presence in Central Asia as early as the mid-1990s, the region was thrust to the forefront of broader international relations following the September 11th attacks. These events – instrumental in engaging the US in a region considered as strategic in the context of the war on Afghanistan – led to a new Great Game in Central Asia. They also (directly or not) triggered an increased presence on the part of both Russia and China, as well as a strengthening of regional organisations under their aegis (Laruelle and Peyrouse 2008). By comparison with the aforementioned, the EU's involvement has been much more incremental. A brief policy review reveals the combination of several factors at work in the agenda-setting phase and the interplay of various EU actors in the formulation of a new policy *vis-à-vis* Central Asia. The EU's enhanced involvement in the region features a two-stage process characterised both by the use of EC instruments as a first response to the situation in Central Asia and by the Council's subsequent takeover of the design of a political strategy in the region. This two-stage process also reflects the emergence of two sets of issues on EU agenda with Central Asia: security issues after 2001 and energy security in the wake of the Russian–Ukrainian gas crisis in 2006.

The initial EU response in Central Asia following the September 11 attacks consisted of increased assistance to tackle security challenges. The main instrument used by the EU was the BOMCA/CADAP programme, which merged two initially different initiatives. Whereas the Central Asia Drug Assistance Programme (CADAP) was proposed as early as 1996, the Border Management Programme in Central Asia (BOMCA) clearly emerged as an answer to the September 11th attacks. By introducing into Central Asia European-style integrated border management methodologies, BOMCA pursues two interconnected objectives: the enhancement of border security and the facilitation of legal transit and trade in the region. Interestingly, even though they are now managed by the EC, EU

Member States played a key role in pushing these initiatives onto the European agenda. CADAP was initially proposed by France, while BOMCA grew out of an Austrian initiative in the Ferghana Valley – known as the Central Asia Border Initiative (CABSI) – which was supported by several other EU member states.[11] However, the European Commission's legal competencies to execute EC policies, as well as the experience previously accumulated in providing technical assistance to the former USSR, enabled it to become the major player in the programmes' implementation. Funded under the TACIS programme, BOMCA and CADAP were managed by the EC, which also decided to link the two initiatives. In addition, the EC's subcontracting BOMCA to the United Nations Development Programme (UNDP) did not favour Member States' ownership of the programme (as noted by Anna Matveeva).

EU Member States nevertheless continue to play a role in the implementation process both through the reporting mechanism to the CABSI established by the Austrian Ministry of Interior and through the contribution of suggestions for refinement of the programme. In particular, the UK's financial and staff contribution to BOMCA in Tajikistan and Germany's focus on Afghanistan led to a greater emphasis on the Tajik/Afghan border after the programme's revision in 2005. Thus, the initial EU response to the political and security upheavals around Central Asia is mainly, yet not exclusively, based upon first pillar policies. The TACIS programme provided an appropriate framework for funding new initiatives. As in other areas previously,[12] EC instruments (especially assistance) collectively constituted a suitable basis for the EU to quickly react to a changing environment and to gradually enhance its presence in Central Asia. As a result, the EU opened, in 2004, a new 'Europa House' (an implementation and management support office) in Uzbekistan as well as new EC Delegations in both Kyrgyzstan and Tajikistan.

Yet, these efforts remained marginal as compared to the leap forward in EU relations with Russia, Western NIS and, from 2004 onwards, South Caucasus. With the ENP being launched and new perspectives being offered to neighbouring countries (for example, visa facilitation, free-trade area), Central Asia clearly appeared as a laggard in the EU's policy framework in the former Soviet Union until the mid-2000s. The growing importance of security issues on the EU agenda and the increasing strategic importance of Central Asia following EU enlargements then prompted the strengthening the Union's involvement in the region. The Council played a major role in this process. Even though Central Asia is not mentioned in the 2003 Security Strategy, it is implicitly referenced in discussions about most of the threats detected in the Strategy, for example, terrorism or organised crime. The Council's emphasis on the need to address 'distant threats'[13] thus prompted the Union

---

11   See Matveeva 2006: 96 and also BOMCA's Webpage: http://bomca.eu-bomca.kg/en/about/history

12   For example, in Central and Eastern Europe with PHARE.

13   'In an era of globalisation, distant threats may be as much a concern as those that are near at hand' (Council of the European Union, 2003).

to increase its political presence in Central Asia, *inter alia* through the nomination in July 2005 of a Special Representative under the CFSP.[14] The Special Representative's mandate reflects the EU's willingness to be more engaged in the region through increasingly close monitoring of political developments in the region; it also paves the way for 'developing a comprehensive strategy towards Central Asia.'[15]

Three factors are salient in explaining the EU's enhanced political involvement and the design of a comprehensive strategy for Central Asia. First, political developments in the region over the last decade have shown that the apparent immobility of Central Asian regimes conceals various economic, social or religious trends which may in the end destabilise those countries (Peyrouse 2006, Poujol 2006). Uzbekistan and Kyrgyzstan are probably the best examples. The repression of Andijan's insurrection in 2005, while triggering EU sanctions,[16] also moved the Union's attention toward the rule of law and democratisation as core issues for the region's future and for the EU's intervention. Kyrgyzstan's chronic political instability after the Tulip Revolution in 2005, the deep political crisis and the violent riots which took place in the first half of 2010 further invalidate this picture of stability. Second, political and security issues became even more important in the mid-2000s in light of EU enlargement and of the design of a neighbourhood policy. On the one hand, the creation of the ENP disconnected Central Asian republics from Western NIS and from Russia, as reflected in the institutional changes within EuropeAid[17] and in the evolution of EC assistance programmes.[18] On the other hand, the inclusion of the three South Caucasus countries in the ENP in 2004 clearly called for increased EU attention towards Central Asia, owing to the tight economic links between these countries, especially around the Caspian Sea. Of particular concern were economic links related to energy flows,[19] which can be considered as the third explanatory factor in the

---

14   The Council first nominated Jan Kubis, a former OSCE Chair. He was replaced in October 2006 by Pierre Morel, a former French ambassador (*inter alia* to the Russian Federation, to Kyrgyzstan and to Georgia).

15   Council Joint Action L199/100, 2005/544/CFSP, *Official Journal of the European Union*, 29 July 2005.

16   The EU decided to suspend the Cooperation Committee and subcommittees' meetings under the PCA. General Affairs and External Relations Council, Conclusions, 3 October 2005.

17   In 2005 Central Asia was moved to Directorate D of EuropeAid together with Asia, whereas it was previously part of the same directorate as other NIS. However, relations with Central Asia are still managed within Directorate E of DG Relex, which also includes (albeit under different units) Russia and ENP partner countries.

18   From 2007 onwards, the TACIS programme no longer exists. ENP partner countries (and Russia) benefit from ENPI; whereas Central Asian republics are included in the Development and Cooperation Instrument. See also Chapter 7.

19   'The Southern Caucasus countries are also important in this respect in terms of new energy supplies to the EU from the Caspian region and Central Asia.' European Commission 2004 a: 17.

design of a EU comprehensive strategy *vis-à-vis* Central Asia. As shown by the INOGATE programme and the Baku initiative, the EU had been concerned for years about connections between Central Asia, Caucasus countries and Europe. Such concerns clearly became a priority after the Ukrainian-Russian 2006 energy crisis, which led the EU to seek diversification of its energy suppliers.[20]

As important as these factors may be, the rise of Central Asia onto the EU's external agenda and the design of an EU strategy also result from member states' preferences. In this case, Germany – among the most active EU member states in Central Asia and in Afghanistan – pushed Central Asia to the top of external priorities during its presidency in the first semester of 2007 and played a major role, together with the Council, in formulating the strategy. The unprecedented importance granted to Central Asia was part of a broader German vision for a 'new Eastern policy' (*eine neue Ostpolitik*). In the case of Central Asia, the Presidency and the Council appeared to be the political entrepreneurs, while the Commission remained (to some extent) behind the scenes and the European Parliament played a marginal role.[21] Initially, both the Council and the Commission had different approaches regarding the strategy to be formulated for Central Asia, with the Council being more ambitious.[22] The German presidency played an active role by presenting a first draft during the first meeting of the EU troika with Central Asian Foreign Ministers in Astana on 27–28 March 2007, by issuing several non-papers and by asking for the Commission and the Council to work together on the final version.[23] Owing to the Commission's delay and work overload, however, the final document mostly reflects the views of the Presidency working closely with the EU's Special Representative; interestingly, the latter's mandate was amended twice[24] in order to incorporate competencies for providing input concerning the formulation of energy security and anti-narcotics aspects of the CFSP with respect to Central Asia.

The Strategy adopted by the European Council in June 2007 serves as an overall framework for the EU policies in the region. However, its added value stems mainly from its existence, that is, from the EU's enhanced political profile and the impetus given to deepened relations with Central Asian republics. Considering

---

20   See Chapter 7 on this issue.

21   The European Parliament adopted several resolutions on Central Asia, in particular those of 26 October 2006 on Uzbekistan, of 16 March 2006 on Kazakhstan and of 12 May 2005 on the situation in Kyrgyzstan and Central Asia. These mainly concentrate on human rights-related issues. The Parliament also welcomed the increased EU focus on Central Asia in a resolution on the Strategy for a New Partnership adopted on 20 February 2008.

22   Interview with a European Commission official, DG Relex, Brussels, October 2007.

23   Ibid. See also the German Presidency's website, http://www.eu2007.de/en/News/Press_Releases/March/0328AATroikaAstana.html?

24   Council Joint Action 2007/113/CFSP of 15 February 2007, Official Journal of the European Union L 46, p. 83 and Council Joint Action 2007/634/CFSP of 1 October 2007, *Official Journal of the European Union* L 256, p. 28.

policy objectives and instruments, the Strategy (Council of the European Union 2007) does not constitute a breakthrough *per se*. In order to reach security and stability (identified as the EU's interests in the region), it aims at:

- enhancing respect for the rule of law, human rights and good governance;
- developing transparent democratic political structures;
- promoting economic development, trade and investment;
- strengthening energy and transport links;
- improving environmental and water sustainability;
- combating common threats and challenges (for example, trafficking, illegal migration).

To achieve these goals, the Strategy will exploit the potential of Partnership and Cooperation Agreements, the EC Regional Assistance Strategy 2007–2013, Member States programmes, cooperation frameworks (such as the Baku Initiative and political dialogue), Twinning and secondment of staff.[25]

To sum up, the Strategy for a New Partnership fills a gap in the EU's foreign policy, a policy that, until the mid-2000s, had been particularly timid in Central Asia. Though it takes stock of the experience accumulated by the EU in Central Asia and neighbouring regions, it is mainly to be seen as a starting point for an enhanced EU visibility and presence in the region. Its first three years of implementation are interesting in this respect. They indeed confirm the increasing importance of Member States in EU policy in the region, through an active participation in the implementation of the Strategy.[26]

The EU's Strategy in Central Asia: A Delicate Balance between Bilateral and Regional Approaches

According to the Strategy for a New Partnership, the EU promotes in Central Asia a 'balanced bilateral and regional approach' (Council of the European Union

---

25   Twinning and TAIEX are new instruments in the toolbox of EU policies in Central Asia, but after their creation in the 1990s within the framework of the enlargement policy, they had already been used as a foreign policy tool in the context of the neighbourhood policy (Delcour and Tulmets 2008).

26   See Council of the European Union 2010: 5: 'France and Germany, with the support of the Commission, act as "lead coordinator" for the Rule of Law Initiative, while Italy has taken on the same role for environment and water, supported by the Commission and Romania as Presidency of the Working Group on Eastern Europe, Caucasus and Central Asia for the EU Initiative for Water. In the area of education, where the Commission is the 'lead coordinator', Latvia has taken on the role of local coordinator in Tashkent, while Poland does the same in Ashgabat.'

2007: 11). What are the factors explaining this combination and how is it reflected in the toolbox used by the Union in Central Asia?

The arguments in favour of a regional dimension for EU policies are connected both to local conditions and to EU preferences. The main challenges identified by the EU in its strategy are clearly regional or transnational and need to be tackled at a regional level, involving all five countries. Most of these challenges have become more acute since the early 2000s. This applies in particular to security-related issues such as border management in connection with the situation in Pakistan and Afghanistan, migration, the fights against organised crime and international terrorism, as well as human, drugs and arms trafficking. For instance, Central Asia had already been identified in the 1990s as one of the main transit routes for drugs originating from South-East Asia, Afghanistan or Pakistan and crossing all five Republics (mainly Tajikistan) on their way to Russia and Europe. Since then, while trafficking has developed even further following the increase in the cultivation of drug crops after the international intervention in Afghanistan (Matveeva 2006: 42), Central Asia itself has also become a place for drug production and transformation, with all countries being concerned about and confronted with related public health or corruption challenges (Hohmann 2006).

Although not identified by the EU as a challenge as such, Islamic fundamentalism provides yet another example of a transnational issue. While Centrasiatic republics – as former Soviet republics – share a common secularist legacy, various Islamic groupings emerged in the 1990s, mainly in Tajikistan and Uzbekistan. Even though some of those (for example, the Islamic Movement of Uzbekistan) are rooted in specific countries, others (for example, Hizb-ut-Tahrir al Islami) have a transnational dimension (Khalib 2006: 106) and potentially can constitute a threat to the entire region. Beyond security issues, other challenges such as hydro-energetic resources and environmental questions also require regional cooperation to be solved. Tackling security and other major challenges on a regional basis (including engagement, when necessary, of neighbouring countries such as Afghanistan) would thus reflect a rationalist view on the part of the EU.

The second set of factors explaining the regional approach in the EU's strategy relates to the Union itself. As stated in the Strategy for a New Partnership, 'the EU can offer experience in regional integration leading to political stability and prosperity' (Council of the European Union 2007: 6). This statement clearly goes beyond the necessary cooperation to solve common challenges and suggests a potential integration among Central Asian countries modelled, to some extent, after the EU's pattern. This form of integration coincides with the preferences expressed by some Central Asian republics. Since the USSR collapsed, Central Asian countries have indeed engaged in various attempts at integration, most of which were put forward by Kazakhstan. The first of those, the Eurasian Union created in 1994, clearly followed the pattern of the European Economic Community; it envisaged the creation of a common economic space based upon the four freedoms. Over the two past decades, Kazakhstani President Nazarbaev has always been at the forefront of regional integration initiatives; as indicated in 2006, he wants Kazakhstan to play the role of a 'regional locomotive' (Kushkumbayev 2008: 12). Moreover, in the framework of the country's multi-vector foreign policy, the European Union is seen as an important actor with whom relations should be further developed. The EU's experience is therefore of great interest to Central Asia's most important country, as far as it coincides with its own foreign policy and regional interests. Conversely, beyond its huge energy resources (which are of great importance to the Union from the perspective of its suppliers' diversification), Kazakhstan is considered by the EU to be a stable country that has achieved substantial progress on the path of economic reforms, though much remains to be done regarding democratisation. Astana is thus seen (although not explicitly) both as an anchor in the region and as a key partner in the Union's efforts to support regional integration. Hence, the EU's support for cooperation among Central Asian countries coincides with the regional power's own interests and preferences, while at the same time it confirms that regional integration is a core norm promoted by the EU in its external action' (Lavenex 2004: 695).

The regional dimension of the EU's policy can thus be explained through a combination of rationalist and institutionalist interpretations. On the one hand, owing to the transnational character of threats identified in Central Asia, the EU's Central Asian policy best serves its own interests (that is, stability and security). On the other hand, following the path dependency argument, it constitutes an exportation of the EU's patterned practices and the EU's tendency to 'reproduce itself' (Bretherton and Vogler 1999: 249) in its relations with third countries. This 'copy-paste'[27] habit, however, seems to be responsive to some partner countries' preferences (as in the case of Central Asia and Kazakhstan), and therefore does not entirely correspond to the routine-based behaviour described by path dependency theory.

Within the framework of its Strategy for a New Partnership, the European Union channels a number of its own instruments at a regional level. The EC assistance strategy 2007–2013, including priority sectors, was designed at a regional level. Its first priority area, amounting to approximately one third of EC financial commitments, relates directly to regional cooperation and good neighbourly relations, with four focal priorities (networks, environment, border/migration management and education).[28] Beyond EC assistance, the Strategy for a New Partnership also envisages the establishment of a regular regional political dialogue at the Foreign Minister level. In this context, meetings and conferences are held at a ministerial level on an annual basis.[29] Other regional initiatives correspond to the main priorities identified in the

---

27   Interview with a European Commission official, DG Relex, Brussels, October 2007.

28   European Community 2007: 23.

29   The first meeting was held in April 2008 in Ashgabat, followed by a Ministerial Security Forum in Paris in September 2008. See http://europa.eu/rapid/pressReleasesAction.

Strategy for a New Partnership; they include a regular energy dialogue in the wake of the Baku initiative, a 'European Education Initiative' and an 'EU Rule of Law Initiative.'[30] However, the balance sought with the bilateral approach developed *vis-à-vis* the five republics is delicate. Since the USSR collapsed, the major trend in Central Asia has undoubtedly been towards differentiation and dislocation. The process of state- and nation-building has facilitated a retreat into national symbols and history, both of which in turn were quite often constructed in the aftermath of the Soviet Union's collapse, since the current Central Asian republics had not previously existed as such before (Poujol 2006: 71). That process has also resulted in differentiated policy choices: Whereas Kazakhstan and Kyrgyzstan pursue economically liberal policies, Uzbekistan pursues an economic path in which the state still plays a predominant role. Central Asia's fragmentation is especially visible when one examines the low level of intraregional trade figures, reflecting trade barriers among the republics; for instance, the other four countries together only represent 3.1 per cent of Kazakhstan's foreign trade (Koblandin 2008: 27). Overall, as underlined by Richard Pomfret (Pomfret 2006), nowhere else has the dissolution of the Soviet Union led to greater economic disintegration than in Central Asia, where old coordination mechanisms disappeared and new national borders appeared.

Moreover, the trend towards compartmentalisation is mirrored in the way Central Asian countries have dealt with regional challenges. For instance, as indicated by Anna Matveeva, drug trafficking has not yet been dealt with at a regional level; the way it has been tackled by Central Asian governments – through the introduction of harsh border regimes – has only aggravated the situation (Matveeva 2006: 42). The situation regarding hydro resources has highlighted sharp divergences between upstream (Kyrgyzstan, Tajikistan) and downstream countries (Kazakhstan, Uzbekistan) that have impeded any progress towards a sustainable solution. Owing to the different interests and perceptions of the five countries concerned, all attempts at regional integration have so far failed. The rivalry between Kazakhstan and Uzbekistan for regional leadership is a major factor in these failures. Uzbekistan has rejected the regional cooperation proposals put forward by Kazakhstan, while these proposals were systematically approved by Astana's closest ally in the region, Kyrgyzstan. Whereas Uzbekistan had taken part in an informal summit held in Astana in October 2006 with a view to enhancing regional cooperation and discussing the creation of an interstate Union, its President, Islam Karimov, rejected in April 2008 Kazakhstan's initiative for a regional Union (Kushkumbayev 2008: 13). Still other mutual suspicions have hindered regional projects, for example, between Tajikistan and Uzbekistan (Allison 2004: 474) or between Turkmenistan and other countries, as evidence

---

do?reference=IP/08/541&format=HTML&aged=0&language=EN&guiLanguage=en, retrieved on 6 May 2009.

30   The Rule of Law initiative is a joint undertaking of the Commission and Member States with the five Central Asian countries. It was launched at a ministerial meeting in Brussels on 27 November 2008.

by Ashgabat's staying apart from regional institutions. Overall, 'regionalization – understood as an active process of change towards increased cooperation, integration, convergence, coherence and identity – has not been an obvious feature of security (or other policy interactions) in Central Asia' (Allison 2004: 465).

Compartmentalisation and differentiation are therefore major features of Central Asia's situation which make striking a balance with the regional dimension of EU policies difficult to achieve. Before its Strategy for a New Partnership was designed, the EU's regional approach and instruments in Central Asia had been criticised for being ineffective.[31] The International Crisis Group thus recommended in 2006 that 'Europe ... moves away from largely unsuccessful policies, particularly the promotion of region-wide projects, and take on a more focused and active role geared to the distinct characteristics of each of the region's five states' (International Crisis Group 2006: i); similar recommendations were put forward by other experts and think-tanks (Kimmage 2008: 18). Discussions held with Central Asian republics to prepare the Strategy for a New Partnership confirmed their reluctance *vis-à-vis* a systematic regional approach.[32]

Consequently, even though it seeks to promote a balanced approach between the regional and bilateral dimension in its strategy, the EU insists on the 'special importance' of the latter (Council of the European Union 2007: 11). In other words, a regional approach is only needed when and where the bilateral dimension is not effective enough to solve challenges. Bilateral instruments still play a major role in the implementation of EU policy. The Partnership and Cooperation Agreements offer a natural framework to develop bilateral links with Kazakhstan, Uzbekistan and Kyrgyzstan, the three countries in which PCAs are in force.[33] In parallel to a regional strategy, EC assistance also includes bilateral programmes tailor-made to the needs of each country. In addition, political dialogue as well as thematic dialogues are conducted bilaterally as much as at a regional level.[34] Bilateral links have enabled the EU to develop further its

---

31　This is not specific to the EU: Richard Pomfret assesses regional assistance provided by multilateral organisations as ineffective in the 1990s–early 2000s (Pomfret 2006).

32　Interview with a European Commission official, DG Relex, Brussels, October 2007. See also Laruelle and Vinatier 2007.

33　Bilateral links have also developed with Tajikistan and Turkmenistan. Joint Commitee meetings have taken place since 2004 with Turkmenistan and since 2001 with Tajikistan; over the past years a Human Rights Dialogue has also been established between the EU and each of the these countries. The President of the European Commission José Manuel Barroso's first official visit to Ashgabat, in January 2011, is another illustration of the new impetus the EU wants to give to its relations with Turkmenistan. Finally, a Europa House was opened in Achgabad in 2008, modelled after the one already opened in Tashkent.

34　During the Portuguese Presidency of the Union (second semester of 2007), the EU Troika visited four out of five Central Asian countries with a view to discussing implementation of the Strategy with the local authorities and devising priority projects for individual countries. Council of the European Union, General Secretariat, 2007 Annual Report from the Council to the Parliament on the main aspects and basic choices of the

relations with several Central Asian countries and to tailor them to its partners' expectations. For instance, bilateral visits by the EU's Special Representative Pierre Morel were considered fundamental for the gradual EU reengagement with Uzbekistan and the fostering of closer contacts with Turkmenistan following the change of leadership in that country. When it comes to Kazakhstan, the EU's main interlocutor in the region,[35] the authorities there are committed to a closer strategic cooperation with the Union as part of their multi-vector foreign policy. This is achieved *inter alia*, through a policy dialogue and advice facility providing EU expertise and assistance in the implementation of the government's reform programme. Kazakhstan's chairmanship of the OSCE in 2010, as well as the modernisation programme 'Path to Europe' initiated by President Nazarbaev in 2008, undoubtedly create a window of opportunity for enhancing bilateral ties (Emerson, Boonstra, Hasanova, Laruelle and Peyrouse 2010); considerations on the next generation of agreement to replace the PCA should give further impetus to the EU-Kazakh relationship. The growing stress on bilateral relations in EU policy *vis-à-vis* Central Asia is also a key factor explaining the expansion of the EU's diplomatic presence, either through EC Delegations and offices or through the CFSP High Representative and the Special Representative's increasing number of trips in the field.

The Strategy for a New Partnership represents a shift in the EU's approach to Central Asia from the angle of region-building. To some extent, the EU has moved away from its traditional regional vision. The growing importance of bilateral links reflects the different situation of each partner country, and their various expectations *vis-à-vis* the EU, as much as the Union's own interests. At the same time, the regional level selected for political or thematic dialogues shows that the EU still pursues region-building objectives over the long term; the prevalence of a regional dimension in areas such as education and science is indeed meant to foster confidence and to develop contacts between all five countries.

The EU and Regional Organisations: Competing Region-Building Efforts and the Absence of Inter-regionalism

Whereas the main trend in Central Asia has been towards disintegration since the collapse of the Soviet Union, the area also has become the core of a network of regional forums and organisations since the mid-1990s. This offers both a sharp contrast to other parts of the former USSR and, *a priori*, a potential basis for the EU to develop inter-regional links. However, this hypothesis has not materialised

---

CFSP, Available at http://www.consilium.europa.eu/uedocs/cmsUpload/EN_PESC.pdf on 8 May 2009.

35   Interview with a European Commission official, DG Relex, Brussels, October 2007.

yet. The EU's interactions with other regional organisations remain at a weak level, owing to the configuration of the regional landscape.

Regional organisations playing a major role in Central Asia include the Shanghai Co-operation Organisation (SCO), the Eurasian Economic Community (EurAsEc) and the Collective Security Treaty Organisation (CSTO). Founded in 1996 as a forum with a view toward fostering good neighbourly relations, SCO[36] became an organisation in 2001 and its activities gradually expanded, especially in the security sphere. Established in 2000, EurAsEC[37] originated from the custom unions project between Russia, Belarus and Kazakhstan; it aims at creating a free trade regime and a customs union among its members. The CSTO[38] grew out of the CIS Security Treaty signed in 1992 with a view to preserving political/military links among members and fostering peace and stability in the former USSR.

These organisations share two important features (Delcour and Ternova 2007). First, even though all regional organisations include members originating either from other former Soviet areas or from Asia, Central Asia is undoubtedly a major strategic area for all main issues on their agendas. It is highly concerned about the fights against terrorism and organised crime, and these are among the key objectives currently pursued both by SCO and CSTO. Central Asia is also crucial when it comes to energy issues that matter both to SCO[39] and to EurAsEc.[40] Second, even though Central Asia is at the core of regional organisations' concerns, Russia and/ or China have been the main actors in the processes leading to the creation of these organisations, to their institutionalisation and to the expansion of their activities. As shown by Roy Allison, Central Asian republics have 'bandwagoned' with Russia and/ or China (or, sometimes, with the United States) in response to security concerns, that is, 'security challenges have not been addressed on an exclusively regional basis' (Allison 2004: 467). Regional security organisations' objectives clearly reflect, above all, Russia's or China's interests and their vision of the international arena condemning US unilateralism (Laruelle and Peyrouse 2008); for instance, the SCO can be seen primarily as 'a balancing mechanism developed by Russia and China to counteract American hegemony' (Allison 2004: 478).

The fight against terrorism in the region must also be understood as a fight against separatism, in a context characterised not only by the September 11 attacks but by growing perceptions in China and Russia of separatist threats, *inter alia* emanating from Uighur populations spanning across Western China, Kazakhstan and other Central Asian countries. China and Russia also share the same concern for stability

---

36   Its members currently include China, Russia, Kazakhstan, Uzbekistan, Tajikistan and Kyrgyzstan; India, Pakistan, Mongolia and Iran are observers.

37   Its members currently include Russia, Belarus, Kazakhstan, Uzbekistan, Tajikistan and Kyrgyzstan.

38   Its members currently include Armenia, Belarus, Kazakhstan, Kyrgyzstan, Russia, Tajikistan, and Uzbekistan.

39   A dialogue on energy issues was established by the Bishkek Declaration in 2007.

40   EurAsEc's objectives include the creation of a common energy market.

in the region and therefore support the current authoritarian regimes through regional organisations. At the same time, Russia and China, and more generally major powers, are also competitors in Central Asia (Allison 2004: 464; Laruelle and Peyrouse 2008). Russia has tried to contain China's growing economic power in the area by pushing forward EurAsEc. Moscow also uses CSTO as the main channel to serve its security objectives, rather than the Shanghai Cooperation Organisation, where it has to cope with China. Thus, Central Asia appears to be a scene dominated by great powers which use regional forums as a means to preserve or to increase their influence in the area. In this case, regionalism is not supported by inside dynamics but is 'hegemon-sponsored' (Allison 2004: 468).

Against that background, developing inter-regional links is particularly difficult for the European Union, which is perceived as both a latecomer and a weak player when compared to Russia and to China. The Strategy for a New Partnership clearly states the EU's desire for a dialogue with other organisations.[41] The EU's Report on the Strategy's first year of implementation stresses the need for strengthened dialogue and concrete cooperation with other regional organisations, for example, in such fields as border and water management, as well as the fight against drug trafficking and trans-border crime (European Commission and Council of the European Union 2008). One potential option in this regard, argued for by Oksana Antonenko, is the case for strengthened cooperation with the SCO wherein the SCO/EU dialogue should cover a broad range of areas, including issues of common interest such as energy or Afghanistan (Antonenko 2007). However, in spite of the case for cooperation, there is currently little room for an institutionalised dialogue with the SCO or EurAsEC. While some EU member states either consider the SCO to be an anti-Western organisation or condemn human rights violations perpetrated by some of its members (Antonenko 2007), it seems that Brussels is keen on obtaining observer status within the SCO.[42] However, the EU may be seen as a competitor by Russia (International Crisis Group 2006: 25) and, to a lesser extent, by China, whether in the SCO or in other regional organisations. Thus, the EU's support for thematic regional platforms among Central Asian countries can also be explained through both the limited current possibilities of inter-regionalism and the desire to foster new region-building attempts which could eventually form the basis for a strengthened inter-regional dialogue.

Conclusion

For more than a decade after the USSR's collapse, Central Asia has remained a *terra incognita* on the map of the EU's foreign policy. The EU's presence was

---

41   'The EU is prepared to enter into an open and constructive dialogue with regional organisations in Central Asia and to establish regular ad hoc contacts, that is, with EURASEC, the Shanghai Cooperation Organisation (SCO), CICA, CSTO, CAREC and CARICC.' Council of the European Union 2007: 1.

42   Interview with Kazakh officials, Astana, July 2007.

circumscribed to EC assistance under TACIS and to the cooperation programmes and policies implemented by a few member states, mainly Germany and the UK. However, the attacks of September 11 – and, subsequently, the neighbourhood policy resulting from EU enlargements – moved Central Asia onto the list of EU priorities. Such a process is tightly linked to the growing importance of security challenges, including hard and soft security threats (e.g. drug trafficking, energy security). Owing to the crucial character of security issues, the Council was the main actor in engaging the EU in Central Asia, either through its Special Representative or, mainly, through the Presidency, with the more active EU member state in the region, Germany, playing a major role in the design of a Strategy for a New Partnership.

Even though it is not an influential actor in a region where other major powers play a crucial role, the EU's enhanced political profile in Central Asia corresponds to Central Asian republics' expectations.[43] States such as Kazakhstan indeed perceive themselves as a crossroads between Asia and Europe and therefore welcome the EU's involvement as a means to modernise their countries and to balance their foreign policies.[44] However, the EU is not able to fully utilise its traditional regional approach in Central Asia. This is primarily due to centrifugal trends that have prevailed since the early 1990s. As a result of this fragmentation process, the extent to which Central Asia exists as a region can currently be questioned (Kimmage 2008: 13). The focus on country-specific issues and bilateral relationships in the Strategy for a New Partnership hence reflects a pragmatic EU approach, inclusive of partner countries' preferences. Nevertheless, the shift from the traditional 'support to regional cooperation' approach is relative. Whereas the EU's action in Central Asia is also strongly constrained by other region-builders that are reluctant to forge inter-regional links, the regional dialogues initiated by the Strategy for a New Partnership allow the EU to assert its specificity as a soft power. Indeed, thematic issues chosen for regional dialogues, such as the rule of law or education, are meant to build confidence between Central Asian countries over the long term, but they also reflect the EU's different approach *vis-à-vis* other region-builders dealing with economic or military issues in the framework of regional organisations. As such, the regional dialogues initiated in 2007 may serve as a test for the EU's influence in Central Asia and its ability to assert a distinctive profile. Moreover, the EU may benefit from Central Asian republics' attempts to balance Chinese and Russian influences that are, for different reasons, feared by political and economic elites in the region, thus limiting the bandwagoning processes observed in the SCO, CSTO and EurAsEc. Yet, as mentioned by

---

43 See Council of the European Union 2010: 2: 'The adoption of the Strategy was a reflection of the realisation by the EU of the growing importance of Central Asian countries for the EU, notably in terms of security, governance and energy, and in response to a growing interest on the part of Central Asian countries to strengthen relations with the EU'.

44 See for instance Kazakhstan's modernisation programme 'Path to Europe', announced by President Nazarbayev in his annual address to the nation, 6 February 2008.

Emerson, Boonstra, Hasanova, Laruelle and Peyrouse (2010), the EU's support to regional cooperation in Central Asia further needs to be articulated with an enhanced commitment towards a wider regional cooperation, that is, an EurAsian dimension (Emerson, Boonstra, Hasanova, Laruelle and Peyrouse 2010: 3) going beyond the existing EU policy framework[45] and contributing to '[disenclaving] land-locked Central Asia' (ibid.).

---

45   See Chapter 7 for a more detailed analysis.

Chapter 7

Consistency as a Major Challenge for EU Policies in the Post-Soviet Space

As shown in previous chapters, EU policies in the former Soviet area have been extensively overhauled during the last decade. Security issues were instrumental in the EU's development of new subregional policies across the post-Soviet area. Although the initial EU reflection (Patten and Solana 2002) primarily imagined an enhanced relationship with all NIS bordering the enlarged Union (thus implicitly dividing the post-Soviet area among EU neighbours and non-neighbours) an EU 3-area policy framework has been progressively shaped. Russia's opting out of the new proximity policy resulted in the formulation of a specific strategic partnership singling out the country. Consequently, it is clearly differentiated in the EU policy framework from Western CIS and South Caucasus countries included in the ENP and increasingly referred to as forming an 'Eastern neighbourhood.' Central Asia has emerged as the third subregion in the EU policy framework in the post-Soviet area as a result of the EU's increased role in the region (roughly, from the launch of the 'New Partnership' onwards).

Whereas the differentiation between these three subregions arose naturally from differences in both EU interests and partner countries' preferences, one may argue that it also has important consequences. Indeed, the subregionalisation of EU policies entails the EU's utilisation of distinct policy toolboxes and modes of governance, in contrast to the 1990s, during which a similar contractual framework was designed for all NIS with only marginal differences in the EU instruments. From the institutional and contractual perspectives, and owing to their proximity with the EU, Russia and neighbouring countries benefit from a much more advanced status in the EU's policy framework (for example, forthcoming association agreements for ENP countries, perspectives of free-trade areas and visa liberalisation) and thicker and more complex networks with the EU than does Central Asia. At the same time, neighbouring countries and Russia deeply differ in their policy methods; for instance, in the case of ENP countries, the EU resorts to conditionality for leverage, which it does not use with Russia. In other words, the differentiation applied by the EU among subregions is not only formal. As a consequence, as indicated in Chapter 5 and based upon the example of the Eastern Partnership, differentiation is also likely to have region-building effects over time in the post-Soviet area.

Yet, while it has increasingly developed three distinct policy frameworks, the European Union also pursues transversal policy interests across the former Soviet Union. It is argued that these are connected to the broader EU foreign policy objectives as defined in the consolidated version of the Treaties as signed on 13 December 2007 in Lisbon:

> The Union shall define and pursue common policies and actions, and shall work for a high degree of cooperation in all fields of international relations, in order to:
>
> (a) safeguard its values, fundamental interests, security, independence and integrity;
> (b) consolidate and support democracy, the rule of law, human rights and the principles of international law;
> (c) preserve peace, prevent conflicts and strengthen international security, in accordance with the purposes and principles of the United Nations Charter, with the principles of the Helsinki Final Act and with the aims of the Charter of Paris, including those relating to external borders;
> (d) foster the sustainable economic, social and environmental development of developing countries, with the primary aim of eradicating poverty;
> (e) encourage the integration of all countries into the world economy, including through the progressive abolition of restrictions on international trade;
> (f) help develop international measures to preserve and improve the quality of the environment and the sustainable management of global natural resources, in order to ensure sustainable development;
> (g) assist populations, countries and regions confronting natural or man-made disasters; and
> (h) promote an international system based on stronger multilateral cooperation and good global governance (Council of the European Union 2008a, Title V, Chapter 1, article 21.2).

In other words, support for democratisation processes, integration in the world economy and assistance in conflict prevention can be defined as transversal priorities for the EU in an area undergoing a complex transformation process. Addressing key threats and building stability are further singled out as the overarching goals pursued by the EU on the international stage in the EU Security Strategy (Council of the European Union 2003) and the *Report on the implementation of the European Security Strategy* (Council of the European Union 2008c). More specifically, terrorism, proliferation of weapons of mass destruction, organised crime and energy security are identified in these documents as major challenges to the EU and all of them concern a number of former Soviet republics.

Against that background, how does the EU reconcile the promotion of these large-scale, transversal and cross-country interests with the increasing geographical differentiation of its policy frameworks across the post-Soviet space? To what extent is it able to build bridges between its various policies in order to promote transversal objectives and to tackle pervasive threats either at its borders or farther east?

The present chapter analyses the degree of consistency in, and between, current EU policies in the post-Soviet area. It first discusses the notion of coherence and proposes an analytical framework upon which the empirical analysis of the implementation of EU policies in the post-Soviet area can be built. Based upon examples drawn from major transversal issues on the EU agenda in the region, it then points to existing gaps between EU policies stemming from their increasing compartmentalisation. It shows how these gaps are explored and exploited by other region-builders: Russia, to take one example, still perceives the former USSR as its own sphere of influence and acts to influence the region accordingly. More specifically, the chapter argues that Russia has so far thwarted all EU attempts to link its various geographical policies and to promote a trans-regional approach, especially with respect to energy.

Analysing Consistency in the EU's External Action: The Need to Take into Account Geographical Coherence

The issue of coherence is central to a complex foreign policy-making system such as the EU's. It has been extensively studied in the literature (Gauttier 2004, Nuttall 2005, Portela and Raube 2008), including the latest developments introduced by the Lisbon Treaty (Cremona 2008, Gaspers 2008). Two major dimensions of coherence,[1] each of them giving rise to related sub-categories, have been identified as crucial for the EU's foreign policy effectiveness. Vertical consistency refers to the coherence between EU external policies and Member States external policies (Nuttall 2005: 96–8). A related notion is interstate consistency, which centres on the coherence between policies designed and implemented by EU Member States (Gaspers 2008: 21). Horizontal consistency pertains to the coherence between 'intergovernmental and *communautaire* aspects of EU foreign policy and the consistency of individual policies formulated within these two dimensions' (Gaspers 2008: 21).[2] A sub-category is institutional consistency, that is, the coherence of approaches between the institutions and their bodies involved in foreign policy-making (mainly the European Commission and its Directorate Generals and the Council of the European Union). All four notions thus relate primarily to the internal or input side of the EU external action. Yet, they miss important questions of coherence

---

1   For reasons pertaining to the analytical framework explained in the paragraph to follow, the words 'coherence' and 'consistency' are used indifferently in this chapter. Nuttall also notes that 'attempts to distinguish between [coherence and consistency] risk ending up in linguistic pedantry' (Nuttall 2005: 93).

2   Horizontal coherence has often been referred to as the coherence between the three EU pillars defined by the Maastricht Treaty; the entry into force of the Lisbon Treaty on 1 December 2009 made this division into pillars obsolete.

which mainly relate to the external or output side:[3] to what extent are EU approaches and policies coherent across a geographical area?

In order to fill this gap and to take into account the geographical dimension in the analysis, Tulmets (2008a) proposes a distinction be made between internal and external coherence based upon a criterion privileging stages in the public policy process. She contrasts stages pertaining to policy conception and formulation from the implementation process and assimilates internal coherence to the former, whereas external coherence is categorised as related to the latter. In her proposal of an analytical framework to investigate coherence in the EU neighbourhood policy, Tulmets further differentiates consistency from coherence as follows: 'while consistency is checked against criteria defined in advance, coherence reflects the overall result of the policy' (Tulmets 2008a: 111). She also justifies the demarcation between policy conception and policy implementation in light of the changes brought to the European foreign policy system by the entry into force of the Lisbon Treaty.[4] By suppressing the three pillars and by increasingly merging intergovernmental and *communautaire* aspects of foreign policy (Gaspers 2008: 26), these are indeed expected to have important effects on the coherence of EU external action, which call for a review of the analysis grids used so far.

Yet, whereas the output side of the EU external action needs to be further investigated (as rightly pointed out by Elsa Tulmets), external coherence cannot be gauged strictly against stages of the policy process. From a legal perspective, the differentiation between policy conception and implementation does not exist as such in EU treaties, even though the role of each institution varies from one stage of the policy process to the other.[5] From an institutional perspective, the appointment of a 'Union Minister for Foreign Affairs' (Gaspers 2008) may result in her having a major role in formulating the EU strategy while leaving the operational side to the European External Action Service. However, it is argued that, owing to the specificities of the European foreign policy system, the demarcation between policy

---

3   Christophe Hillion also emphasises the need for a positive definition of coherence going 'beyond the assurance that the different policies do not legally contradict each other' and consisting in a 'quest for synergy and added value in the different components of EU policies' (Hillion 2008: 17).

4   Together with the above-mentioned suppression of the categorisation of EU activities into pillars, these include: the creation of the post of 'Union Minister for Foreign Affairs', the High Representative of the Union for Foreign Affairs and Security Policy, also acting as Vice-President of the Commission and as Commissioner for External Relations; the establishment of a joint European diplomatic service, the European External Action Service. See Gaspers 2008.

5   'The common foreign and security policy is subject to specific rules and procedures. It shall be defined and implemented by the European Council and the Council acting unanimously, except where the Treaties provide otherwise. The adoption of legislative acts shall be excluded. The common foreign and security policy shall be put into effect by the High Representative of the Union for Foreign Affairs and Security Policy and by Member States.' Council of the European Union 2008a, Title V, Chapter 2, Article 24.

conception and policy implementation is not sufficiently clear to provide a well-grounded analysis of the geographical dimension of coherence. As put by Smith and Webber (2008: 95), 'as always in the case of EU foreign policy, incremental steps are very important, as are learning-by-doing and the symbols and rhetoric involved in creating the EU's global identity.' In other words, distinguishing policy conception from policy implementation is tricky in the case of a policy 'in the making' and therefore constantly evolving, in which lessons from the implementation process involving external actors feed back into strategy design. As a result, it is also difficult to contrast consistency and coherence on the basis of the criteria proposed by Tulmets.

For the purpose of the present analysis, it is therefore proposed to take into account the geographical dimension by examining the extent to which various EU policies (either at a conceptual or at an operational level) within a given geographical framework are compatible with one another. It is proposed to refer to this dimension as geographical coherence. Why does geographical coherence matter in the case of the former Soviet Union? Why should the EU pursue compatible policies across CIS countries which, arguably, have followed different paths over the past two decades? Such a question is far from merely rhetorical. On the contrary, it is indeed central from an analytical perspective.

If one considers that the EU 3-area policy framework in the former USSR reflects existing disintegration dynamics in the field, one implicitly starts from the assumption that, owing to the collapse of the USSR and the subsequent transformation process, the post-Soviet area is no longer a region. In this case all three EU policies do not necessarily have to be coordinated or compatible with each other, since each subregion is clearly distinct from the other and has different expectations *vis-à-vis* the EU. Such logic is often reflected in academic analyses of EU policies in the former USSR, which quite often are not grounded on systematic and comparative field research. Interestingly, while over the last decade EU policies in the former Soviet Union have been increasingly investigated, the bulk of research has been conducted by European studies scholars[6] and therefore from the predominant angle of EU policies.[7] As a result, the majority of analyses presupposes the division of the post-Soviet space into three distinct areas.

---

6   This holds especially true in the case of the European neighbourhood policy. Many scholars conducting research on this policy previously investigated the EU enlargement process or other internal EU policies. While such background allows one to highlight the blurring of boundaries between internal and external EU policies, so far important aspects such as EU policies' reception and implementation have been underestimated owing in particular to the paucity of field research.

7   EU–Russia relations are an exception in this picture. Major publications and research on this topic were often produced as a result of field research and by scholars having a background in East European/Russian studies and an in-depth knowledge of the Russian context. Such an approach was crucial in accounting for the stumbling blocks of the strategic partnership.

The opposite assumption, which will be the basis of the empirical analysis developed in this chapter, argues that the EU 3-area policy framework as reviewed since the early 2000s is a social construction and therefore does not necessarily correspond to regional realities. True, the post-Soviet Union does not constitute a region, as implicitly suggested by references to a country that no longer exists to point to the group of states that gained independence in the aftermath of its collapse. Arguably, there is neither a common political culture/shared identity between NIS (at least within the geographical framework of the former Soviet Union), nor common institutional development through regional integration schemes. In other words, the New Independent States do not define themselves together as a 'we' (Adler and Crawford 2002: 5).[8] However, there are still a number of political, economic, cultural and security interactions among former Soviet republics. For instance, Russia is still the major economic partner of a number of them. Whatever transformational path each state may chose, economic interdependence persists even outside of the 'former centre-former periphery' scheme. Interactions now follow a different rationality; for example, an economic logic based upon a cost-benefit analysis, as shown by Kazakhstan's important investments in Georgia after the Rose Revolution. Another example, this time from the cultural angle, is the fact that the Russian language is still broadly used as a vector of communication among NIS (Atnachev 2001), whereas the use of English remains limited even in those countries which have adopted a pro-Western stance. The point is therefore to examine how these interactions between post-Soviet republics are taken into account by the EU in the formulation and implementation of its policies and how the Union strives to reach some degree of consistency in the geographical area that once constituted a State. The definition of geographical coherence given here therefore pertains to what Christiansen calls coherence 'in terms of systemic outputs.'[9] Other dimensions of coherence will be considered as well in this chapter, as far as they contribute to the overall consistency of EU foreign policy. Indeed, in spite of the modifications and simplifications brought by the Lisbon Treaty, challenges related to vertical, horizontal, institutional and interstate consistency will persist (Gaspers 2008: 47) as much as the structural complexity of European foreign policy will survive (Cremona 2008).

To examine the consistency of EU policies across the post-Soviet area, the empirical part of this chapter will focus on two cross-cutting issues, energy and visa regimes. These have been chosen due to their importance within the EU's agenda

---

8   Yet, as shown in Chapters 5 and 6, such features currently do not exist within the 'Eastern neighbourhood' (that is, Western NIS and South Caucasus) and, to a lesser extent, in Central Asia. In other words, while the post-Soviet area cannot be considered a region geographically, politically or economically, the geographical areas retained by the EU for two of its policies cannot either. This confirms the argument of regions being, including in the case of EU policies, social constructions.

9   Defined as 'the way in which the substance of different policies generated by the EU forms part of a coherent whole' (Christiansen 2001: 747).

either in the partnership with Russia, in the Eastern neighbourhood or in Central Asia. Moreover, these two topics are also central in post-Soviet countries' interests *vis-à-vis* the European Union. Finally, it is argued that both energy and the visa regime are crucial in interactions between the former Soviet republics. As far as energy is concerned, CIS countries possess the biggest gas reserves in the world and significant reserves of oil (Centre for Social and Economic Research 2008: 178). Since most of these countries are also transit routes to convey oil and gas westwards to Europe, interactions in this field are important and complex. They are further complicated by common Soviet legacies, either when it comes to the energy sector structure, aging transit infrastructures or energy prices. The visa regime is a major factor for explaining the persistence of a high level of interaction among the former Soviet Republics. Since the USSR collapsed in 1991, the post-Soviet area has widely remained a visa-free area. Exceptions are linked to the assertion of national sovereignty combined with political tensions with other former Soviet Republics, quite often with Russia; for instance, the Baltic States set up a visa system nearly immediately after their independence, in the wake of their strict citizenship and language policies; Georgia also introduced a visa for Russian citizens, which can easily be explained by a long record of disputes since 1991. Nevertheless, visa-free movement remained largely a reality in a post-Soviet space where borders are recent and not always tangible or fixed. Against that background, the conclusion of visa facilitation and readmission agreements with several NIS, which reflects the extension of EU Justice and Home Affairs policies, is undoubtedly a watershed. This chapter will therefore examine the way in which the EU takes into account the interdependence between CIS countries on these topics and the degree to which the EU policies implemented within subregional frameworks are compatible with each other as far as energy and visas are concerned.

Energy Security at the Nexus of Vertical, Interstate and Geographical Coherence

Over the past decade, energy security has moved to the top of the EU's security agenda. In 2003, the EU Security Strategy noted that 'energy dependence is a special concern for Europe' (Council of the European Union 2003: 4), yet it was not included in the list of threats elaborated by the Council. Five years later, the Report on the implementation of the EU Security Strategy identified energy security as an increasing challenge to the EU's interests (Council of the European Union 2008: 5). Whereas the EU's dependence on oil and gas imports has steadily increased, developments in the post-Soviet area are a major factor for explaining the growing perception of energy insecurity as being a threat to the Union's interests.

In a context of weak economic growth and increasing energy demand, the decline of EU production and the prospect of a growing dependence on imports had already triggered a reflection among EU institutions (first of all within the European Commission) at the turn of the century (European Commission

1999b). The EU response consisted of both internal and external elements. On the demand side, reducing energy consumption in Europe emerged as the major objective. On the supply side, as explained in Chapter 4, the EU–Russia Energy Dialogue was also originally envisioned as a tool for mitigating the effects of increasing energy dependence by ensuring a reliable supply of imports. At the time the Dialogue was launched, the EU did not have such a developed energy strategy *vis-à-vis* the other former Soviet Republics. Russia's share in EU energy imports further increased as a consequence of 2004 and 2007 EU enlargements; many among the new Member States were indeed largely dependent on Russian gas for their imports, some of them (Bulgaria, Estonia, Latvia, Lithuania, Romania and Slovakia) at 100 per cent.[10] In this context, repeated disruptions in supplies of Russian gas to Ukraine and to Belarus in 2006–2007 were perceived by the EU as a major shift, further deteriorating its energy security[11] and elevating the issue to the top of EU agenda. The crisis between Ukraine and Russia was instrumental in shaping the debate for a EU energy policy that, quite oddly, was still lacking five decades after the European integration process started precisely with the coal and steel sectors (Delcour 2008a: 37; Natorski and Herranz Surrallés 2008: 73). In other words, the agenda-setting process for enhanced integration in the energy sector was largely grounded in external stimuli. As further stressed by the major EU policy documents issued on this topic, external and internal aspects of energy security cannot be disentangled and therefore a comprehensive approach requiring a combination of internal and external policies is needed (European Commission 2006b: 1).

What, then, are the interactions of the EU energy security debate with its external policies (specifically, those in the former Soviet Union)? The Russian–Ukrainian dispute in 2006 did not only pave the way for further progress towards an Internal Energy Market and it did not serve as a mere wake-up call for the EU's vulnerability to imports. It also deeply affected EU stakeholders' perceptions of potential suppliers. Specifically, as noted by Westphal (2006: 45), temporary cuts considerably damaged the image of Russia as a reliable supplier. Russia presented its arguments over its dispute with Ukraine as being predominantly of an economic nature.[12] Since the collapse of the USSR, all former Soviet republics had benefited from subsidised energy prices. As part of the process to raise gas tariffs to world market prices,

---

10   See the figures of EU Member States' natural gas imports quoted by Feklyunina (2008: 132). Finland is also totally dependent on Russian natural gas imports.

11   Such disputes, however, were not new. As noted by Stern (2006: 2), they regularly occurred in the 1990s for similar reasons: high levels of Ukrainian debt and suspicions of diversions by Ukraine of Russian natural gas transiting to Europe, which prompted temporary natural gas cuts by Moscow.

12   Ukrainian arguments were guided by a similar logic. In early 2005, the Yushchenko administration suggested raising natural gas transit prices to European levels which, as noted by Stern (2006: 5), triggered Gazprom's counter proposal to raise natural gas tariffs to European levels.

Gazprom required a 4.5 times increase in 2006 gas prices for Ukraine as compared to 2005 (Westphal 2006: 45). While Ukraine responded that such an increase should be phased in over a period of time (Stern 2006: 6), Moscow also accused Kyiv of overdue payments.[13] However, the withdrawal of Russian price subsidies was largely interpreted within the EU as a political weapon levelled against a country that had chosen a pro-Western path with the Orange revolution the year before. The Russian energy dispute with Belarus over gas prices and oil siphoning in 2007 and the increase in gas tariffs for Armenia were further indications of Moscow's use of a similar leverage with other former Soviet republics, regardless of whether they were considered its close allies. Conversely, Russian authorities pointed to transit countries (that is, Ukraine and Belarus) as sources of potential threats in the delivery of Russian oil and gas to the EU (Feklyunina 2008: 138).

Nevertheless, a number of EU actors expressed growing concerns over Russia's status as the primary energy supplier of the Union. A brief overview of their positions highlights different concerns, though they resulted in the advocacy of similar solutions.[14] Among EU Member States, Poland and the Baltic States clearly perceived the use of energy in Russian foreign policy as a threat and strongly advocated for reduction of Russia's share of EU supplies. During early 2006, those Member States and candidates countries which were the most dependent on Russian gas worked out a joint action plan calling for the diversification of supplies.[15] Such reduction of dependence on Russia has also been repeatedly called upon both by the European Commission and by the European Parliament. Beyond the use of energy as a political tool, the former pointed to the increasing state control over the energy sector in Russia and the country's refusal to ratify the Energy Charter as major sources of concern:[16] 'Some major producers and consumers have been using energy as a political lever. Other risks include the effects on the EU internal energy market of external actors not playing by the same market rules nor being subject to the same competitive pressures domestically' (European Commission 2006b: 1).

The evolution of the energy sector management was especially alarming for the European Commission at a time when it was preparing the completion of the Internal Energy Market as the basis for EU energy policy.[17] The European

---

13   The reasons behind the dispute are simplified here for the sake of the argument. For a detailed analysis, see Stern 2006.

14   For an in-depth analysis of EU actors' policy discourse on energy security, see Natorski and Herranz Surrallés (2008).

15   That is, Poland, Czech Republic, Slovakia, Austria, Hungary, Slovenia, Croatia and Romania. Poland also put forward a proposal for a legally binding instrument, a 'European energy security treaty' aimed at fostering mutual assistance in case of energy cuts. See Natorski and Herranz Surrallés (2008): 81.

16   Such concerns had been raised a few years before the Russian–Ukrainian dispute in 2003 with the Yukos case that reflected the strategic character of the energy sector for Russian authorities.

17   See the speech by Energy Commissioner Piebalgs (2007): 'At the core of our energy policy is a well-functioning internal energy market.'

Parliament further emphasised major shortcomings in the management of the energy sector in Russia, for example, aging infrastructure, lack of investment and waste in the domestic market, as additional risks for the EU, that is, stagnation in Russian oil and gas production (European Parliament 2006b, point 66). For the European Parliament, such risks called for launching a 'common foreign energy security strategy' (European Parliament 2006b) and '[focusing] not only on closer cooperation with Russia, but also [stepping up] cooperation with other energy exporters' (European Parliament 2006b, point 65).

However, concerns about an excessive dependence *vis-à-vis* Russia were not shared by all EU actors. Some of the largest Member States – Germany, France and Italy – were proponents of a sustained energy dialogue with Russia, albeit with new mechanisms for preventing disruptions of supplies. In its discourse before the Munich Security Conference a few weeks after the Russian-Ukrainian dispute, the German Minister for Foreign Affairs thus called for an enhanced cooperation between consuming, transit and producing countries (Steinmeier 2006). As far as Russia is concerned, the report prepared on energy security for the French Presidency of the European Union took opposite views from those expressed by some Central European states and by the European Commission. The idea of an excessive dependence on Russia[18] was rejected in favour of an assessment of Russia as a very reliable supplier over the last thirty years, including periods of tense relations with the USSR. Claude Mandil, the report's author, further called on the Union to refrain from lecturing Russia on energy market liberalisation and ratification of the Energy Charter Treaty and to recognise the country's sovereignty.

This brief overview has highlighted different concerns and definitions of threats among EU actors in a sector increasingly crucial for its security interests and in which Member States, reluctant to give up sovereignty, have pursued national strategies in recent years (Delcour 2008a, Natorski and Herranz Surrallés 2008). Whereas internal measures were adopted in 2007–2008,[19] the external dimension of EU energy policy remained scanty owing to such divergences (Natorski and Herranz Surrallés 2008: 83), which are also clearly visible in EU energy strategies in the former USSR.

Recently, the perception by some EU actors of an excessive dependence *vis-à-vis* Russia has pushed forward the objective of diversifying both the EU's suppliers and transportation routes. The post-Soviet area plays a crucial role in both objectives. In particular, the Caspian region is considered as the most desirable alternative supplier to Russia. Three republics of Central Asia, Kazakhstan,

---

18   Russia's share in EU natural gas imports is 40 per cent, but only 25 per cent of EU natural gas consumption. See Mandil 2008: 16.

19   Including progress towards an Internal Energy Market and the package on energy and climate adopted in December 2008 during the French Presidency of the EU (Delcour 2008a).

Turkmenistan and Uzbekistan, possess significant natural gas resources;[20] Kazakhstan, like Azerbaijan, also has huge petroleum resources. Central Asia is viewed as a strategic region by the EU in light of the EU's increasing dependence on imports, especially on natural gas imports.[21] Energy security is therefore a core topic in the Strategy for a New Partnership with Central Asia initiated by the EU in 2007. The EU–Central Asia energy cooperation aims at increasing the role of Central Asian countries as EU energy trade partners: 'The dependency of the EU on external energy sources and the need for a diversified energy supply policy in order to increase energy security open further perspectives for cooperation between the EU and Central Asia' (Council of the European Union 2007: 2).

To reach this objective, the Strategy envisages an enhanced energy dialogue in the framework of the Baku initiative, a policy dialogue launched in 2004 with Black Sea and Caspian Sea countries as part of the INOGATE and TRACECA programmes.[22] The EU's approach attempts to bring Central Asian energy markets closer to the Union's by promoting a 'market-based approach to investment and procurement and transparent, stable and non-discriminatory regulatory Frameworks' (Council of the European Union 2007: 20). The EU also signed bilateral memoranda of understanding with countries of the Caspian Sea region: Azerbaijan, Kazakhstan, Uzbekistan and Turkmenistan.[23] These memoranda provide for an enhanced cooperation on energy security through exchange of information, consultations on energy scenarios and collaboration for upgrading existing infrastructure or facilitating the development of new transportation infrastructure.[24] The cornerstone of the EU approach *vis-à-vis* Central Asia is indeed the creation of a major new transportation route: the Southern corridor, which was singled out by the European Commission as 'one of the EU's highest energy security priorities' (European Commission 2008d: 5). This initiative includes several projects (the White Stream, Trans-Caspian and Nabucco pipelines) to transport natural gas from Central Asia to the EU, thus increasing EU imports from the region while bypassing Russia.[25] As

---

20 All three of them rank among top twenty countries for natural gas reserves. According to Feklyunina (2008: 133) Kazakhstan's proven reserves are estimated at 1.9 trillion cubic metres, Turkmenistan at 2.67 trillion cubic metres and Uzbekistan at 1.74 trillion cubic metres. Stoupnikova (2008a) gives slightly higher figures for the three of them (3 for Kazakhstan, 2.86 for Turkmenistan and 1.87 for Uzbekistan).

21 The EU's dependence on energy imports is estimated at 65 per cent in 2030, yet the figure is much higher (80 per cent) for natural gas only.

22 The Baku initiative was launched as part of the EU INOGATE and TRACECA programmes to foster the harmonisation of participating countries' standards and legal framework with those of the EU, with a view to integrating energy markets.

23 The Council of the EU endorsed in June 2010 the text of a similar memorandum with Uzbekistan. Cf. 3023rd Council Meeting, Press release, Luxembourg, 14 June 2010. Available at: http://www.consilium.europa.eu/uedocs/cms_Data/docs/pressdata/EN/foraff/115185.pdf

24 See for example, the EU-Kazakhstan memorandum (2006: 3).

25 The European Commission, the European Investment Bank and the World Bank are also investigating the feasibility and possible structure of a mechanism for the purchase

far as they will favour the modernisation of the Central Asian energy sector and give access to the large EU market for their natural gas, the initiatives put forward by the EU meet the interests of the countries concerned (Kassenova 2008: 132).

The EU objectives for diversification are to be facilitated by the close involvement of transit countries, that is, EU neighbours.[26] Energy is a priority under all the Action Plans signed with Western NIS and South Caucasus countries under the European Neighbourhood Policy. Convergence with the EU's rules and its market is the main pillar of the EU energy strategy *vis-à-vis* Eastern neighbours.[27] The EU envisages the integration of neighbouring countries in the Energy Community, a legally binding framework created in 2005 which provides a stable investment environment by extending the EU energy market abroad.[28] While Georgia is currently an observer, negotiations for full membership were concluded in 2009 with Ukraine and with Moldova, two countries who have declared their intent to join the Union. The EU energy policy in its Eastern neighbourhood therefore follows the logic of the ENP based on an 'asymmetrical interdependence' (Barbé et al. 2009b: 388) and approximation with the EU *acquis*. Additionally, the South Caucasus countries, which collectively constitute a major route for transit of Centrasiatic natural gas and oil to Europe,[29] also participate in the INOGATE programme and the Baku initiative. Finally, transit countries contribute to the EU's objectives of diversification by participating in new transport infrastructures, for example, the South corridor for Georgia and Azerbaijan (a supplier under the Nabucco project) and the Odessa-Brody-Poland pipeline for Ukraine.

At the same time, the EU has not turned away from Russia as its main supplier. The overall objective of the energy dialogue is still 'to enhance the energy security of the European continent by binding Russia and the EU into a closer relationship.'[30] Compared to EU energy initiatives in the neighbourhood and in Central Asia, however, the EU–Russia energy dialogue is conducted on quite a different basis. This dialogue is shaped jointly and not after EU market rules, especially since

---

of Caspian natural gas, a 'Caspian Development Corporation.' See European Commission 2008d.

26   See for example the objectives mentioned in the EU–Georgia ENP Action Plan 'enhancing co-operation in the fields of energy, transport and environment contributing to energy security and supply diversification needs for the EU.' See EU–Georgia ENP AP, 2006: 3.

27   For instance, the EU–Ukraine ENP Action Plan sets as the first objective in the energy sector the gradual convergence towards principles of EU internal electricity and gas markets. See EU–Ukraine ENP AP 2005: 33. Under the ENPI, Ukraine also benefits from budget support in the energy sector. Furthermore, a monitoring system is being developed to check on the implementation of ENPAP provisions in the energy sector.

28   When the Treaty establishing the Energy Community was signed in October 2005, the extension primarily targeted Southeast Europe.

29   As argued by Melvin (2008: 12) 'Steps to draw the South Caucasus closer to Europe will therefore serve to move Central Asia and Europe that much closer.'

30   *EU–Russia Energy Dialogue*, MEMO/09/121, Brussels, 19 March 2009.

Russian authorities definitely rejected in 2009 the ratification of the Energy Charter Treaty; instead, cooperation takes place in areas of joint interest,[31] and monitoring is carried out by both parties. In other words, convergence between the parties is not unilaterally established by the EU but bilaterally agreed upon (Barbé et al. 2009b). Such a specific pattern cannot be primarily explained by 'Russian dominance in the field of energy', a factor which Barbé puts forward (Barbé et al. 2009b: 388), since Russia and the EU are in fact mutually interdependent when it comes to energy.[32] Rather, this specific pattern is connected to the increasingly different paths taken by the EU and Russia in energy sector management. This is a *de facto* limitation on the scope of the EU–Russia dialogue, which initially sought to improve investment opportunities in Russia's energy sector and to encourage the liberalisation of energy markets based upon the regulatory framework provided by the Energy Charter Treaty. While energy sector management is a major stumbling block in the EU–Russia partnership, EU projects of diversification are also negatively perceived in Russia. The competition for energy resources[33] is identified as a serious challenge in the country's latest National Security Strategy issued in May 2009 (National Security Council of the Russian Federation 2009). This document indeed establishes a strong linkage between energy resources and Russian national security. In this context, EU attempts to reduce its dependence on Russian imports are clearly interpreted as a threat (Feklyunina 2008: 131), even more so as the EU is the largest export market for Russia's oil and natural gas. To mitigate the effects of the EU's diversification policy and to promote its own interests, Russia pursues three interconnected objectives.[34]

First, Russia has on several occasions stated its intention to diversify its own energy exports (Feklyunina 2008: 135), even though it denies any consequences for the EU market.[35] The Energy Strategy of the Russian Federation foresees a

31   The energy dialogue includes 'all issues of mutual concern in the energy sector' (EU–Russia Energy Dialogue, MEMO/09/121, Brussels, 19 March 2009). For instance, the thematic groups under the energy dialogue are subject to revision in connection with the parties' interests. As decided by the Permanent Partnership Council in December 2008, they were recently restructured around topics of joint interest such as energy strategies, forecast and scenarios, and energy efficiency.

32   The EU is Russia's main energy export market, together with CIS countries, yet, owing to different prices, the EU is a much more lucrative market for Russia than the New Independent States.

33   Among the areas mentioned by the National Security Strategy as regions in which competition for the control over energy resources will be particularly fierce, three out of four are located within the post-Soviet area or at its borders (the Arctic Ocean, the Caspian Sea and Central Asia).

34   As far as those are bilateral and do not concern other post-Soviet countries, this chapter will deal with neither Russian companies' activities on the EU market nor the EU's response.

35   'The Russian Party stresses that diversification of oil and natural gas exports by increasing the deliveries to Asia is in no way connected to the stability of the long-term

greater focus on Asian markets, especially on China, which is considered to be a promising market due to its sustained growth and high energy demand. This strategy could reflect long term plans, however, as the construction of new pipelines (for example, the Altai pipeline, the East Siberia Pacific Ocean pipeline) is needed. As a result, the share of EU and CIS countries in the Russian export market is expected to decrease while that of Asian countries will increase up to approximately 20 per cent from the current 6 per cent for oil and 0 per cent for natural gas (Piebalgs and Shmatko 2009: 5).

Second, Russia intends to defend its natural gas exports to the EU by diversifying transport routes to Europe; more specifically, by avoiding Ukraine, which has been presented by Russia in recent years as an unreliable transit country siphoning Russian natural gas transiting to Europe. To bypass Ukraine, Russia has launched major alternative transport routes targeting those EU Member States which are also Moscow's major partners within the EU, primarily Germany, Italy and France. For instance, the Nord Stream[36] gas pipeline directly links Russia to Northern Germany across the Baltic Sea, thus bypassing Poland and the Baltic states who protested against the project.[37] The South Stream project announced in 2007 is considered a direct competitor to the EU-supported Nabucco pipeline; yet, it involves a number of EU Member States (primarily Italy but also Austria, Bulgaria, Greece and Hungary) and EU candidate or potential candidate countries (for example, Turkey, Serbia, Croatia).

The third objective pursued by Russia pertains to its role as a transit country for oil and natural gas from Central Asia to Europe. Whereas the EU has sought to diversify not only its suppliers but also its transportation routes, Russia has so far managed to control Centrasiatic natural gas exports[38] and to remain by far the major transportation route of Centrasiatic natural gas and oil.[39] The memorandum of understanding signed in May 2007 with leaders from Kazakhstan and Turkmenistan[40]

---

contracts of oil and natural gas supply to the EU countries' (Piebalgs and Shmatko 2008: 3).

36   Construction was launched in April 2010 with the first deliveries of natural gas expected by the end of 2011.

37   Shareholders of the company operating the pipeline, Nord Stream AG, include primarily *Gazprom*, the German companies BASF and EON, the Dutch *Nederlandse Gasunie* and the French *Gaz de France,* which acquired a 9 per cent share on 1 March 2010.

38   This can be explained by economic factors, mainly the different prices between Russian and Turkmen natural gas. As indicated by both Denison (2008: 93) and Feklyunina (2008: 134), 'the purchase and exportation of Turkmen natural gas to the EU is more profitable for Moscow in the short-term compared with developing new gas fields in Russia'; they also allow Russia to meet domestic demand. Yet, Russia agreed in March 2008 to significantly raise the price it pays for Centrasiatic natural gas in order to maintain its *de facto* monopoly over its export and transportation (Stoupnikova 2008a).

39   Transit through Russia also generates substantial revenues for Moscow (Feklyunina 2008: 134).

40   In December 2006, the death of Turkmenistan's longstanding President Saparmurat Niyazov had been analysed as presaging a possible shift in the country's energy export

has been a crucial step in this respect: it provides for the modernisation of the Central Asia-Centre pipeline and for the creation of a Pre-Caspian gas pipeline which is meant to increase Turkmenistan's export capacity to Russia.[41] These projects initiated by Russia strongly undermine the feasibility of the alternative transportation pipelines supported by the EU, that is, the Southern corridor initiative. The Pre-Caspian pipeline *de facto* rules out the construction of the Trans-Caspian gas pipeline, which was backed by the EU with a view to increasing imports of Turkmen natural gas. As a result, Azerbaijan natural gas would remain the major source for the Nabucco pipeline intended to reduce EU dependence on Russian natural gas and to connect the EU to Caspian Sea resources.[42]

While there is indeed a thematic coherence in EU policies across the post-Soviet area with respect to energy market management, EU policies do not form a coherent whole when it comes to other aspects of energy security such as diversification of supply and of transport routes. This can be explained both by insufficient EU interstate coherence (that is, divergent policy options favoured by EU Member States) and by Russia's iron grip on post-Soviet countries' energy sectors, especially on Central Asia. Those two factors are tightly interwoven: the diversification attempts pushed forward by some EU actors are perceived by Russia as a threat to its own interests, which in turn results in further strengthening of its efforts to maintain its hegemony over Centrasiatic natural gas exports. In other words, as far as energy is concerned, the geographical coherence of the EU's energy policies in the former Soviet Union is undermined by the decoupling of its growing engagement in Central Asia from its partnership with Russia. However, as convincingly put by Kassenova, 'a certain accommodation of Russian interests' in Central Asia would enable the EU to develop a more favourable cooperative framework in the region, enabling it to fulfil its own objectives and to enhance its energy security.

Visa Regimes: Gaining Coherence?

Whereas EU borders have continually changed, together with various waves of enlargement, the accession of Central and East European countries to the EU marked a major break when it comes to external borders. As explained by Comelli, Greco and Tocci (2006: 5–7), this is connected both to the changing signification of borders after the fall of the Iron Curtain and to the unprecedented scope of

---

markets. Under Niyazov's rule, a 'symbiotic' Russian–Turkmen relationship had indeed developed in the energy sector, especially when it comes to natural gas, with Gazprom providing much needed technology and expertise in exchange for long-term natural gas supply contracts (Denison 2008: 93–4).

41   The final agreement on this pipeline was signed in December 2007.

42   Yet, there are doubts as to the planned Azerbaijani's resource capacities to deliver the requested quantity of natural gas.

the last waves of enlargement, which raised the issue of the final borders of EU integration. Arguably, the EU's perception of its new borders is underpinned by a dual logic within its premises, especially as far as the Eastern neighbours are concerned. On the one hand, as shown in Chapter 3, the new EU periphery was considered to be a source of potential threats, a perception which prompted a vision of the common border not only as a line of demarcation,[43] but also as a line of protection from those countries. On the other hand, this new vicinity was also considered to be an opportunity for the EU to enhance its relations with its Southern and Eastern neighbours in order to avoid new dividing lines across the continent. In this context, visa regimes have become, together with border management measures, major instruments in EU policies *vis-à-vis* the post-Soviet area. These instruments indicate the signification the EU intends to give to its borders, either as a separating or as a connecting line (Comelli, Greco and Tocci 2006: 3).

The main tools used by the EU at its periphery are the visa facilitation and readmission agreements concluded so far with Russia, Ukraine and Moldova.[44] On the one hand, the visa facilitation side is meant to offer neighbours a reward in exchange for signing readmission agreements. Before visa facilitation agreements were concluded, Russia and Eastern neighbours had repeatedly expressed their dissatisfaction with the costly and cumbersome procedures imposed by EU Member States on their citizens; at the same time, the EU was concerned with the damage to its image and to economic and scientific cooperation with these countries. Visa facilitation agreements entail a number of advantages for partner countries, for example, simplified visa procedures, reduced visa fees for short stays and simplified criteria for multiple entry visas for specific categories of persons. The coupling of visa facilitation with readmission agreements, on the other hand, is modelled after the EU–Russia partnership: it was first requested by Russia when negotiating with the EU as a trade-off for accepting readmission (Trauner and Kruse 2008: 4; Barbé et al. 2009). Readmission agreements set out clear obligations and procedures for the authorities of partner countries as to when and how to take back people who are illegally residing in EU territory. Partner countries thus bear the administrative and financial burden for taking back illegal immigrants (either nationals of the contracting party or third country nationals) from the EU border to their homelands.

---

43   Comelli, Greco and Tocci (2006: 3) point out that 'the border can be an area of division and demarcation or alternatively of contact, exchange and integration.'

44   There are, however, a number of other instruments to enhance border management and border control, for example, technical assistance programmes, border assistance missions such as the EU Border Assistance Mission (EUBAM) with Moldova and Ukraine, and cooperation agreements between the European Agency for the Management of Operational Cooperation at the External Borders of the Member States of the European Union (Frontex) and post-Soviet countries (such as those signed with Russia in 2006 and with Ukraine in 2007). For a detailed analysis see Wichmann 2007.

Yet, there are obvious limits to the incentives offered under the visa facilitation side, which do not apply to the population at large but are limited to specific categories of persons. The rewards proposed under these agreements remain below partner countries' preferences for a visa-free regime. More specifically, they are not sufficient to mitigate the negative effects stemming from new EU Member States' accession to the Schengen area. This accession implied a full adherence to Schengen rules and thus put an end to the cheaper visa fees and simpler procedures applied by Central European States *vis-à-vis* their neighbours since they had joined the EU.[45] The full implementation of Schengen rules by Central European countries had a negative impact on regions with strong historical and economic ties, for instance between Poland and Ukraine; at the same time, the local border regimes set up to facilitate contacts across the border apply only to a small number of citizens (Boratynski, Gromadzki, Susho and Szymborska 2006: 3; Trauner and Kruse 2008: 22). In other words, while visa facilitation agreements are presented by the EU as a reward for Eastern partners,[46] the simultaneous accession of new Member States to the Schengen area *de facto* resulted in creating a new cleavage across the continent, which is exactly what the EU wanted to avoid by promoting its 'Wider Europe' initiative (later, the European Neighbourhood Policy). Visa issues are thus at the core of tensions inherent to the ENP between incentives proposed to neighbours and EU security objectives.

Furthermore, the implementation of visa facilitation agreements has also highlighted disruptive effects across the post-Soviet area as a result of time intervals in their conclusion with countries bordering the Union. As a result, implementation processes have been affected by political developments within the post-Soviet area. For instance, the entry into force of the visa facilitation and readmission agreement with Russia in June 2007 was assessed negatively in Georgia (which has not yet concluded such an agreement with the EU), owing to its disruptive (yet unintended) effects on unresolved conflicts (Delcour 2008). As a consequence of Russia's policy of *pasportizatsiya*,[47] prior to the 2008 conflict over 80 per cent of Abkhazians and South Ossetians already possessed a Russian passport. As a consequence, while the EU has recognised neither Abkhazia nor South Ossetia, inhabitants of the two secessionist Republics could theoretically

---

45   During the transitional period, that is, from 1 May 2004 (EU membership) until 21 December 2007 (accession to the Schengen area) there was some flexibility left to new Member States with respect to visa policies. For instance, visa fees then fell within the national competencies. Estonia delivered visas free of charge to Russian citizens having family ties in Estonia, while Poland decided to remove visa fees for Ukrainian citizens after the Orange revolution, in order to foster people-to-people contacts as part of its support for the democratisation process.

46   'The European Union may also consider possibilities for visa facilitation. Facilitation by one side will need to be matched by effective actions by the other' (European Commission 2004: 17).

47   This consisted in delivering Russian passports to the citizens of the two breakaway regions of Georgia, Abkhazia and South Ossetia.

travel to the EU more easily than their fellow Georgian citizens.[48] The delay in negotiations for a visa facilitation and readmission agreement with Georgia was *inter alia* justified by insufficient border control or lack of accommodation centres for readmitted persons. Nevertheless, coherence in EU migration policy diminishes the influence and consistency of EU policies in the former Soviet Union. It was only after the 2008 conflict that the EU announced negotiations for a visa facilitation agreement with Georgia with a view to providing 'facilitations for Georgian citizens equivalent to those granted to Russian citizens.'[49] Negotiations were concluded in November 2009, and the European Commission proposed the conclusion of visa facilitation and readmission agreements at the end of April 2010.[50]

The latest developments in relations with Georgia are an indication that EU visa policies have increasingly gained coherence and effectiveness in the post-Soviet area over the past two years. This is tightly connected to developments within the internal integration process, in particular the entry into force in April 2010 of the EU visa code, which lays down common rules on conditions and procedures for issuing visas.[51] Indeed, differences persisted between Member States regarding the pace of visa deliveries and the flexibility in issuing Schengen visas. The code will put an end to these differences by specifying the rules determining the Member State responsible for a visa application and harmonising provisions on processing of applications and decisions.[52] When it comes to the post-Soviet area, further progress towards visa liberalisation is foreseen with all six countries included in the ENP as well as with Russia. A visa-free regime with the EU is undoubtedly a major incentive for all these countries and hence a strong leverage point for the Union. Further steps proposed by the EU to Eastern neighbours include the 'Mobility and Security Pacts' concluded in 2008 with Moldova and in 2009 with Georgia. Under these agreements, partner countries are offered the prospect of visa liberalisation in line with the EU Global Approach to Migration. Yet, a visa-free regime is only a long-term prospect which is subject to conditionality,

---

48   Caution is needed insofar as no statistics are available on this issue and EU consulates in Moscow also pay attention to applicants' place of residence when they deliver Schengen visas. However, there are reported cases of Abkhazians/South Ossetians getting their visas to the EU through Russia.

49   The decision was announced at the Extraordinary European Council held on 1 September 2008 in the aftermath of the conflict in Georgia. Cf. European Commission, 'Commission recommends the negotiation of Visa Facilitation and Readmission Agreements with Georgia', IP/08/1406, 25 September 2008.

50   European Commission, 'The EU strengthens visa cooperation with Georgia', IP/10/472, Brussels, 27 April 2010.

51   Visa issues were brought under the Community pillar with the entry into force of the Amsterdam Treaty in 1999, which also included the Schengen *acquis* as an annex.

52   The Visa Code was adopted in June 2009 by the European Parliament and by the EU Council. European Commission, 'A step forward for the common visa policy', IP/10/387, Brussels, 30 March 2010.

that is, to neighbours' progress towards fulfilling specific conditions to ensure a 'secure environment' (European Commission 2008) at EU borders. These include 'fighting illegal migration, upgrading the asylum systems to EU standards, setting up integrated border management structures aligned to the EU *acquis*, as well as enhancing the abilities of police and judiciary in particular in the fight against corruption and organised crime' (European Commission 2008: 6). The Mobility and Security Pacts are undoubtedly a watershed in EU security policy in that they attempt to include neighbours' preferences while also pursuing possession goals and protecting EU security interests (Tocci 2007: 29–30). Visa liberalisation is also foreseen with Russia, albeit over a longer term due to potential increase in traffics to the EU in connection to the loose character of the Russia–Kazakhstan border. Temporary specific arrangements are foreseen, however, in order to further facilitate Russian citizens' mobility to the EU.[53]

The final picture which may result from developments in EU visa policies across the former Soviet Union is that of a two-zone area: on the one hand, neighbouring countries, including Russia, which may benefit from a visa-free regime in exchange for increased cooperation with the EU, especially with FRONTEX and the European Police Office (EUROPOL) in fighting transnational threats, and on the other hand, Central Asian countries, from which these threats originate. The underlying EU logic is therefore to move towards a more inclusive conception of a border with neighbouring countries (using internal EU methods and rules) while ensuring that these countries in turn promote a more exclusive conception of the boundary they share with their Eastern neighbours. The example of visa regimes thus confirms that EU policies do have region-building effects across the former Soviet Union.

Changes in visa regimes are also another illustration of the need for the EU to pursue coherent policies in a geographical area. Developments in the post-Soviet space, especially the deteriorating relationship between Georgia and Russia, do also affect EU policies. They were not sufficiently taken into account by the Union when it started devising new frameworks to regulate freedom of movement with its neighbours and the Russia–Georgia conflict served as a wake-up call to EU actors (principally Member States) of the need to harmonise visa regimes. Visa regimes are thus probably the best illustration of the way in which bilateral EU policies can be undermined by the EU's neglecting the regional framework of relations.

Conclusion

The analysis of visa and energy policies pursued by the Union in the post-Soviet area highlights very similar features. First, those issue areas are perceived by

---

53 Visa liberalisation for Russian citizens is advocated by several EU leaders, for example, from Italy, France and Finland.

the EU as vectors of potential threats to its security. Even though its leverage is different in the two issue areas, the EU has used a similar logic to tackle these threats, that is, bringing partner countries closer to its interests, principles and rules. Second, in the two cases, both the internal and the external dimensions of EU policies are under construction. Energy and visas are still crucial areas for Member States which are reluctant to cede further a part of their sovereignty. As a result, both examples display a lack of vertical and sometimes horizontal coherence. Third, the EU has often overlooked or underestimated the influence of interactions between post-Soviet countries and of the regional hegemon (Russia). As a result, the Union has not always pursued coherent policies across the post-Soviet Union. This has undermined the effectiveness of its actions, even at a bilateral level. In other words, the EU's 'extraterritorialising' (Wichmann 2007) security threats also makes its policies more vulnerable to external developments and therefore in need of coherence across a single area.[54] At the same time, by highlighting gaps undermining the effectiveness of EU policies, such vulnerability to external developments also prompts progress towards common policies in specific issue areas.

---

54   Sectoral (or transversal) agreements concluded between countries otherwise included in different EU policy frameworks could provide a basis for increased coherence. Yet this presupposes a convergence of interests between partner countries, which is difficult to reach in the case of the former Soviet Union.

Chapter 8

The EU and Subregional Multilateralism[1] with Post-Soviet Countries: The Northern Dimension, Black Sea Synergy and the Limits of the Functional Approach

Over the past two decades, the EU has promoted framework policies at its borders encompassing both EU Member States and neighbouring countries with a view to addressing common challenges. Although defining subregions is problematic (as noted by Cottey) in the present case of the Eurasian continent, these policies pertain to 'subregional multilateralism', which itself refers to multilateral policy frameworks within 'geographical-political spaces which are sub-sets of a larger regional space' (Cottey 2009: 5). Cottey further distinguishes between five regional sub-groups across the continent: Northern Europe, Central Europe, the Black Sea, the Mediterranean and the former Soviet Union. Within each of those, a number of organisations and initiatives favouring cooperation among member countries have emerged since the end of the Cold War. As mentioned by Hanna Smith (2008: 29), this proliferation justifies the application of the expression 'new regionalism', which was originally coined to refer to the new regional organisations (mostly in the Asia–Pacific region, but also in Europe) created in the 1990s. In this context, the EU plays a key role in promoting '(sub)regional cooperation among close neighbours' (Lannon and Van Elsuwege 2004: 6) as a foreign policy priority. The EU is therefore a major catalyst for the new regionalism across the European continent.

Under the present chapter, subregional multilateralism will be analysed in light of the initiatives promoted by the European Union at its periphery and involving the EU, its Member States, third countries and subregional organisations. The chapter will examine the way in which the EU has tried to shape its periphery by sustaining subregional links between its Member States and neighbours which are not part of the Union; it will also look at the role devoted to subregional organisations in this process. The broad definition of subregional multilateralism mentioned above indeed applies to at least three policies launched by the Union: the Euro-Mediterranean Partnership launched in 1995 (and subsequent initiatives

---

1   The term is borrowed from the EU4seas project, a collaborative research project on multilateral cooperation in four maritime basins: the Mediterranean, the Caspian Sea, the Black Sea and the Baltic Sea, http://www.eu4seas.eu

vis-à-vis the Southern Mediterranean, such as the Union for the Mediterranean introduced in 2008); the Northern Dimension initiated in 1997; and Black Sea Synergy, set up in 2007. All three of them were initiated by the EU and are organised around sea basins. As noted by Lannon and Van Elsuwege (2004: 6), they also share similar objectives for promoting stability and prosperity. In other words, they are central 'to the EU's foreign policy ambition to have greater say and sway over countries bordering its territory' (Johansson-Nogués 2009b: 26). These common features have led scholars to conduct comparative analyses of the EU subregional cooperation initiatives, mainly between the Euro-Med Partnership and the Northern Dimension, both introduced in the mid-1990s (Lannon and Van Elsuwege 2004; Johansson-Nogués 2009a and b). At the same time, these initiatives display important differences, *inter alia* in the context of their creation and in their policy framework. Only the Northern Dimension and Black Sea Synergy include post-Soviet countries and, as such, will be examined in the framework of the present book.

However, before starting the analysis a major difference should be pointed out between those two initiatives and the Euro-Med Partnership. The latter is an overarching umbrella encompassing both bilateral and multilateral aspects of the partnership between the EU and the Southern Mediterranean countries. In other words, regional aspects both support and complement the bilateral relationship between the Union and each Mediterranean partner, which in turns reflects the overall principles of the Barcelona Process. Such strong articulation does not exist in the subregional initiatives launched by the Union in the north and in the east. Both the Northern Dimension and Black Sea Synergy are to some extent disconnected from the bilateral relations developed by the EU with each post-Soviet country. Such a scheme can be explained in light of the variety of statuses enjoyed by the countries concerned in EU foreign policy, whereas a similar contractual framework based upon association agreements and the ENP is being used with Southern Mediterranean partners. When the Northern Dimension was launched, it targeted EU Member States (Finland, Sweden, Denmark and Germany), candidate countries (Poland, Latvia, Lithuania and Estonia) and non-member countries with different statuses (Norway and Iceland being part of the European Economic Area, and Russia). After the EU 2004 enlargement, it gathered the EU, a potential candidate country (Iceland[2]), Norway[3] and Russia. The same heterogeneity can be found around the Black Sea basin when it comes to the contractual framework of coastal countries with the EU. Apart from EU Member States (Romania and Bulgaria being coastal countries), Black Sea Synergy involves five partner countries included in the European Neighbourhood Policy (Ukraine, Moldova, Georgia, Armenia and Azerbaijan), one candidate country (Turkey) and a strategic partner (Russia). In other words, both the Northern Dimension and Black Sea Synergy

---

2   Iceland submitted an application for EU membership in July 2009.
3   Like Iceland, Norway is closely integrated with the EU in the framework of the European Economic Area.

overstep the contractual framework of cooperation worked out by the Union with its vicinity and centre on a geographical area which is confronted with similar policy challenges. Unlike the Eastern Partnership, whose geographical framework is defined by an EU policy (the ENP) and which draws upon 'transformative regionalism',[4] these initiatives reflect a functional, issue-based approach and an inclusive geographical framework gathering all countries bordering the sea basin – whatever their status *vis-à-vis* the EU may be – and, beyond them, all countries involved in regional challenges (Delcour 2008b).

The present chapter will compare the Northern Dimension and Black Sea Synergy by focusing on region-building. What is the respective role played by the EU, by partner countries and by other regional organisations in these initiatives? How do the Northern Dimension and Black Sea Synergy relate to the bilateral policies developed by the EU *vis-à-vis* the post-Soviet countries concerned? What is their added value and to what extent are they effective in dealing with subregional challenges and promoting subregional cooperation?

Three elements will be examined to answer these questions: first, the rationale behind the launch of these initiatives; second, the policy framework, understood as the institutional arrangements and the toolbox, with specific attention being paid to cooperation and possible overlaps with other regional partners and organisations; and third, the scope of activities within each initiative and their implementation record in dealing with regional challenges.

At the Union's Northern and South-eastern Edges: Subregional Cooperation at the Intersection of Enlargement, Neighbourhood and Foreign Policies

This section will analyse the processes which led the European Union to launch, within ten years of each other, two regional initiatives at its outer edges. To do so, it will look at two different sets of factors. The first explanation is located within the EU itself and relates to the foreign policy priorities put forward by specific EU actors in the particular context of enlargement. The second set of explanations is connected to developments within the regions concerned and specifically to the growing security concerns around the Baltic Sea and the Black Sea. The section argues that both factors do matter when accounting for the design of new subregional initiatives and that they are tightly interwoven. Based upon an analysis of the EU's policy discourse, the section also highlights a process of regional construction by EU actors to justify the design of new initiatives.

The Northern Dimension is to some extent an exception in the picture of EU foreign policy initiatives, which as shown under the previous chapters often result

---

4   Michael Emerson defines transformative regionalism as 'regional cooperation as a means of working towards the 'Europeanisation' of the region' (Emerson 2008: 2), a definition which, as shown in Chapter 5, certainly applies to the multilateral dimension of the Eastern Partnership.

from compromises among major EU Member States and EU institutions.[5] In this case, the new initiative originates neither in a coalition of interests from large Member States nor in a compromise among them. It was initially proposed by a small Member State, Finland, and its Prime Minister Paavo Lipponen in September 1997, less than three years after the country joined the Union. Finland was able to play such a major role in the agenda-setting process because it put together a convincing proposal (Romsloe 2005) for a region which was poorly known to the bulk of EU-12 Member States and, as a consequence, had been neglected within EU foreign policy. A year after Finland's and Sweden's accession to the Union, the European Commission put forward a proposal for a Union approach around the Baltic region (European Commission 1996) in which the Council of the Baltic Sea States (CBSS) was considered a major partner for promoting regional cooperation. However, this communication received a lukewarm reception among other EU actors, for example, the Committee of Regions. Consequently, a window of opportunity opened for EU Northern Member States to 'shape the EU's northern agenda' (Joenniemi 2007: 25). This was especially the case for Finland, which had just acceded the Union and which, unlike other Northern countries, had not played a major role in pushing forward new regional cooperation organisations.[6]

Two years after the launch of the Barcelona process paved the way for an ambitious EU Mediterranean policy,[7] the Finnish proposal added another geographical dimension to the manifold array of EU foreign policy. In spite of initial criticism from some Member States, the proposal became part of the EU's agenda and was regularly discussed within the Council (Romsloe 2005: 3). This did not come as the result of a bargain between EU actors, but rather as the result of a deliberation process in which Finland tried to include other Member States and institutions and relied upon arguing (and presenting the best argument) rather than upon bargaining (Romsloe 2005). The European Commission's proposal was mainly built upon Finland's suggestions (Lannon and Van Elsuwege 2004: 24). Yet, Finland's role was not limited to drawing EU attention to the Baltic Sea region and to pushing it to the top of the Union's agenda. The country then sought to use its Presidency of the EU Council (1999) to specify its earlier proposals (Tallberg

---

5 See, for instance, the role of Poland in the creation of the Eastern Partnership (Chapter 5), the influence of Germany on the design of EU strategy for Central Asia (Chapter 6) and the resonance given by France to its project of a Union for the Mediterranean (Liberti 2008).

6 As indicated by Lannon and Van Elsuwege (2004: 8), the CBSS resulted from a joint Danish–German initiative whereas Norway had been a major actor in promoting cooperation around the Barents Euro-Arctic Region.

7 Lannon and Van Elsuwege (2004: 8) point to the inspiration taken from the Barcelona Process in the Northern Dimension initiative. The Euro-Med Partnership was explicitly referred to as an example of effective policy by Finnish Prime Minister Livonen in his speech calling for the launching of a Northern Dimension before the Barents Region Today conference in 1997.

2003: 7).[8] Arguably, even though the policy content was later specified during the Swedish Presidency of the EU, Finland shaped the policy approach to a considerable extent, based upon its own experience of interdependence with Russia. The Finnish proposal for a Northern initiative indeed stemmed from developments around the Baltic Sea since the early 1990s, that is, primarily the end of the Cold War and the collapse of the USSR, on the one hand, and the expansion of the EU on the other.

More specifically, the new vicinity between the EU and Russia born of Finland's accession to the Union and the forthcoming EU enlargement to four Baltic countries was crucial for explaining the design of a new EU initiative focused on fostering stability and managing this new interdependence. Specific challenges to be addressed by this new initiative included disparities in the level of economic development, nuclear safety, environmental policy and the fight against organised crime. The new policy's guiding principle, reflecting Finland's approach, was to turn this new proximity into a positive interdependence by fostering cross-border and regional links in order to avoid Russia's isolation (Joenniemi 2007: 30). The creation of the Northern Dimension thus lies at the intersection of Finland's foreign policy priorities, competences and experience; perceptions of regional challenges and, finally, EU's relationship to its neighbourhood. As argued by Browning (2001b) and Joenniemi (2007: 29–31), the North (principally via the Northern Dimension) has thus contributed to Europe-making in that it established the template for framing the EU's relations with its neighbours and shaping the continent's political space. The Northern Dimension was indeed instrumental in shifting the attention onto borders and regions and considering them as the basic entities for overcoming dividing lines across the continent.

The Black Sea Synergy finds its roots in both the enlargement and the neighbourhood contexts.[9] It primarily stems from the need (according to some EU actors) to give an impetus to the European Neighbourhood Policy in light of its meagre record on security issues. On the one hand, as early as July 2006, the German Minister of Foreign Affairs, Frank-Walter Steinmeier, disclosed his plans for a new EU Eastern policy (*Neue Ostpolitik*) to be proposed under the forthcoming EU Presidency[10] (Kempe 2007). This included, among others, proposals for an 'ENP Plus' aimed at counterbalancing the Eastern and Southern components of the ENP by enhancing relations between the Union and its Eastern neighbours. On

---

8   The Helsinki European Council of December 1999 invited the Commission to prepare a Northern Dimension Action which was then adopted under the Portuguese Presidency by the Feira European Council in June 2000.

9   At the end of the 1990s the European Commission had drafted a first communication on regional cooperation in the Black Sea region (European Commission 1997) which was the basis for the Council conclusions regarding the region's strategic importance to the EU. Yet, this did not result in any concrete initiative enhancing the EU's engagement in the region or its interaction with existing regional institutions.

10   Germany presided over the Council of the European Union from 1 January to 30 June 2007.

the other hand, the European Commission issued at the end of 2006 a lukewarm assessment of the European Neighbourhood Policy's record, especially when it comes to conflict resolution in the South Caucasus or in Transnistria (European Commission 2006c). In this context, regional cooperation was considered necessary to complement the predominant bilateral dimension.

Due to both the Commission's and Southern Member States' reluctance, the German Presidency was unable to push for a stronger orientation of the ENP towards the East as compared to the Southern Mediterranean (Kempe 2007: 4), but the idea of strengthening the ENP through the addition of a regional cooperation initiative in the East appeared more consensual. The European Commission played a pivotal role in pushing the idea forward and designing the policy; the proposal issued in April 2007 for Black Sea Synergy was embraced by the German Presidency[11] and endorsed by the Council in June. The Black Sea also emerged as a framework for regional cooperation on the EU foreign policy agenda in light of the EU's 2007 wave of enlargement, with the accession of Bulgaria and Romania bringing the Union to its shores. Whereas the Black Sea basin is undoubtedly a major foreign policy priority for these countries (Pantev 2003, Micu 2007), they were not, however, the most important actors in pushing the new initiative to the top of the EU agenda. Such a role has partially been fulfilled by Greece, which was mandated by the Organisation of the Black Sea Economic Cooperation (often referred to as BSEC) to conduct exploratory consultations with the EU on the subject of BSEC–EU cooperation. From this position, Greece prepared a working paper on an EU regional dimension in the Black Sea region which was presented at the Council's working group on Eastern Europe and Central Asia (COEST) in January 2006. The paper advocated for a greater EU involvement in the region and suggested that the Commission draft a communication to that purpose (Ministry of Foreign Affairs of the Hellenic Republic 2006).

Against that background, Bulgaria's and Romania's accession was rather considered by other EU stakeholders as a window of opportunity to fill, as put by Michael Emerson, 'an obvious gap in [the EU's] vision of the regions to its periphery' (Emerson 2008: 1). The Black Sea region had indeed been kept in the background of EU foreign policy, with the sum of bilateral policies resulting in the EU's having a 'partial picture' of the region and lacking a 'holistic approach' (Tassinari 2006: 2). In other words, as put clearly by Benita Ferrero-Waldner, the then Commissioner for External Relations and the Neighbourhood Policy, Black Sea Synergy originates in a shift in the EU's foreign policy agenda as a result of new waves of accession:

---

11 While Black Sea Synergy was not among its initial proposals, the German Presidency also stressed that it was a natural link to its proposed Central Asia Strategy (GAERC 2007). The two proposals were adopted by the Council simultaneously in June 2007.

> The proposals we tabled in April this year – for what we call Black Sea Synergy
> – were designed to focus political attention on this region and to capitalise on
> the new opportunities we gained from Bulgaria and Romania's membership ...
> The Black Sea Synergy's genesis and development are very much a result of
> the new perspective Bulgaria brings to the EU and its relations with the outside
> world (Ferrero-Waldner 2007).

The EU sixth enlargement thus shifted the Union's attention onto a sea basin
around which security challenges (whether at a regional, bilateral or national
level) raised increasing concerns among EU policymakers and institutions.
The stability of the whole region is threatened by unresolved conflicts in the
former Soviet Union, more specifically in the South Caucasus. Apart from these,
interstate tensions often flare up quite dramatically, though some of them have
been gradually abating (for instance, between Turkey and Armenia, or between
Russia and Ukraine in the wake of the agreement on the Black Sea Fleet). Another
challenge is energy security, which is 'central to extra-regional perceptions' of the
Black Sea basin (Lesser 2007: 29). The area includes vital routes for transporting
energy resources. More specifically, energy security in the Black Sea region
emerged as a major issue for the EU in the wake of the dispute between Ukraine
and Russia over gas. This dispute highlighted the major role played by transit
countries in bringing natural gas and oil from Central Asia, Russia or Iran to
Europe. Finally, poor governance and pervasive corruption corroded a number
of states around the Black Sea. The area is a patchwork of political trajectories,
with few democracies and volatility being a major feature in many countries. It
is also confronted with disparities in economic development and uneven levels
of regional trade integration among coastal countries (Ban 2006).

In the EU's discourse (European Commission 2007a), the selection of this sea
basin as the geographical framework for a new policy is presented as a rational
and self-evident choice stemming from the combination of several factors.
The Commission justifies the Synergy through the Black Sea's specificity as a
'distinct geographical area rich in natural resources and strategically located at
the junction of Europe, Central Asia and the Middle East' (European Commission
2007a: 2), which therefore cannot be neglected by the EU and whose challenges
are a threat to the stability of the whole continent.

It can be argued, however, that the selection of the Black Sea to launch a
new regional initiative was far from being obvious. As put by Manoli (2010: 7),
'the concept of the Black Sea as a region is by no means unambiguous.' When
compared to other sea basins, the Black Sea area appears more fragmented, with
common historical legacies but also considerable political, economic, social and
cultural differences between coastal states. Whereas the Mediterranean Sea has
been analysed as a unifying factor by historians (for example, Fernand Braudel)
in specific periods and whereas at present southern Mediterranean countries
undoubtedly display common features which justify a regional EU approach,
the definition of the Black Sea as a region can be questioned. Owing to its

geographical situation and its historical legacy, the basin is a major crossroads between Asia and Europe. At the same time, it is a highly diverse area with 'clashing identities' (Grotzky and Isic 2008) and vivid nationalisms. In other words, the Black Sea basin presents a dual picture of unity and diversity (Manoli 2010: 7).

Therefore, it is argued that the identification of the Black Sea as a regional framework for a new policy also reflects a construction by the European Union. This construction is connected both to the EU's perception of facing similar threats in the region and to the responsibility it intends to take for tackling them. The role of region-builder which the EU adopts around the Black Sea is made explicit in a few policy documents, for instance in the European Parliament's resolution, which calls for 'gradually creating a feeling among the Black Sea countries of shared responsibility' (European Parliament 2008a). Several elements clearly indicate that the initiative responds to a constructed political logic as opposed to a strict geographical approach. For example, the Synergy includes non-coastal countries such as Armenia, Azerbaijan and Moldova. To some extent, this approach follows the BSEC definition of the Wider Black Sea region. However, by encompassing all Eastern neighbours, the Black Sea Synergy also partly coincides with the ENP policy framework, thus increasing its consistency, especially with respect to assistance programmes.

This inclusion also reflects the EU's perception of challenges in the Eastern periphery. These are analysed as presenting common features and requiring a single approach. For example, according to the Commission's analysis, overcoming conflicts in the South Caucasus and in Transnistria require a comprehensive approach involving all parties. A regional framework is considered even more indispensable since the ENP's record in tackling 'frozen conflicts' was assessed as poor by the Commission itself (European Commission 2006c). The regional dimension was therefore introduced with two objectives: first, to provide an added-value on transversal issues which could not be dealt with on a bilateral basis and second, to foster links among Eastern neighbours with a view to promoting stability over the long-term.

Overall, the launching of these two initiatives stems from a number of factors and connects several levels of action. Both the Northern Dimension and the Black Sea Synergy should first be analysed from the general context of EU foreign policy, as each are examples of the Union's becoming a global actor and taking new responsibilities abroad (as analysed by the EU security strategy) (Council of the European Union 2003: 2). Following this analysis grid, within ten years of each other the North of Europe and the Black Sea region have appeared as 'blanks to be filled' in the picture of an expanding EU foreign policy which had largely neglected them prior to the aforementioned initiatives. Yet, this aspect cannot be dissociated from another crucial perspective, that is, the 'enlargement/ neighbourhood' angle. EU attention was drawn toward these areas precisely because the Union was brought closer to them by successive enlargements, a process which also made it more urgent for the EU to tackle regional threats.[12] Thus, as put by Haukkala, 'dimensionalism is a by-product of the successive rounds of EU enlargements' (Haukkala 2003: 2). Since the mid-1990s, acceding Member States have often (although not always, as shown in the case of the Black Sea Synergy) shifted EU foreign policy attention toward new peripheries, thus weaving around the enlarged Union a patchwork of initiatives aimed at managing interdependence with its vicinity and at the same time feeding back into the picture of the EU as an emergent global actor.

Subregional Cooperation as an Illustration of Network Governance?

This section will examine the policy and institutional frameworks of both the Northern Dimension and the Black Sea Synergy in order to grasp their underlying logic from the angle of region-building. As shown in Chapter 5, the European Neighbourhood Policy demonstrates that the EU has chosen to stabilise and secure its vicinity mainly through the enhancement of bilateral relations with each partner country. How does it pursue similar objectives within subregional initiatives, and how do those relate to the bilateral links developed by the Union with the countries concerned?

Both the EU discourse and the institutional framework of the two initiatives suggest that the Northern Dimension and the Black Sea Synergy are based upon a EU 'network governance strategy' (Filtenborg, Gänzle and Johansson 2002: 393) which seeks to closely involve non-EU actors in the policy process. In their definition of network governance, Filtenborg, Gänzle and Johansson (2002: 395) emphasise two elements: the 'externalisation of the EU internal governance patterns' and the EU's attempts to build 'an inclusive, but loosely constructed policy space with international organisations and candidate and non-candidate countries' with a view to solving problems at its periphery. In other words, whereas the external governance approach broadly used to analyse the ENP[13] departs from the asymmetrical relationship between the EU and its neighbours to explain the transfer of EU rules to its periphery, the network governance approach focuses on transgovernmental cooperation between different types of actors (for example, regulators, experts, bureaucracies).[14]

---

12   See in particular Benita Ferrero-Waldner (2007) about conflicts in the Black Sea area: 'It is unacceptable that the European Union of the twenty-first century should turn a blind eye to this suffering on its doorstep. We can and must play a role in finding sustainable solutions to these blackholes of despair.'

13   See Chapter 5 for a brief overview of this literature.

14   The intention here is not to oppose strictly external governance and network governance, which would be misleading, but to highlight different *foci*. As shown by Lavenex and Wichmann, network governance can be used as an alternative form of external governance (Lavenex and Wichmann 2009).

In the case of the Northern Dimension, this approach grants a greater role to local actors, non-EU partner countries and regional organisations in the implementation of subregional initiatives. Following the definition given by Filtenborg, Gänzle and Johansson, these actors are supposed to take an active part, together with the EU, in the creation of an area of governance. Furthermore, this approach sheds light on the interactions between those actors and the EU by studying the way in which network governance in turn affects the EU modes of governance (Filtenborg, Gänzle and Johansson 2002: 395). Such processes have been examined in-depth by Browning and Joenniemi (see for example, Browning 2001b, Joennimi 2007). According to Browning, a possible interpretation of the Northern Dimension is to consider it as an 'inherently democratising move, decentralising[15] power in the EU' (Browning 2001b); to that extent, regionalisation in Europe's North is also 'Europe-making' (Joenniemi 2007). To avoid new dividing lines across the continent and to foster peace and stability, the Northern Dimension indeed breaks down borders between insiders and outsiders and produces a complementary and partially overlapping framework for governance, which several authors (see in particular Browning 2001b) refer to as the 'Olympic Rings.'

Two interwoven elements feed this interpretation. The first one is the absence – both in the Northern Dimension and in the Black Sea Synergy – of any new, overarching institution responsible for implementing the policies. The same is true, however, of the ENP, in which the EU acts as the centre of the policy. Yet, in the case of the two subregional initiatives examined here, the lack of a new institution stems both from the existence of a number of EU instruments and policies around the two sea basins and from the involvement of a number of actors in these areas, which is the second important element in the design of these initiatives. These actors include non-member countries, some of which are also major regional powers, such as Russia around the both the Baltic and the Black Seas and Turkey around the Black Sea; sub-state or local actors within the countries covered by those initiatives; and organisations supporting regional cooperation in these areas. All of those display different levels of institutionalisation, with the CBSS[16] and BSEC[17] having well-developed institutions.[18] The EU has also developed different

---

15   Decentralising means not only moving EU policies to the margins of Europe but also engaging local actors, *inter alia* through cross-border cooperation (Browning 2001b).

16   The Members of the Council include the eleven states of the Baltic Sea Region: Denmark, Estonia, Finland, Germany, Iceland, Latvia, Lithuania, Norway, Poland, Russia and Sweden, as well as the European Commission.

17   The 12 BSEC Member States include Bulgaria, Georgia, Romania, the Russian Federation, Turkey and Ukraine which are coastal countries, as well as Albania, Armenia, Azerbaijan, Greece, Moldova and Serbia.

18   The Council of the Baltic Sea States consists of the Ministers for Foreign Affairs from each Member State and a member of the European Commission. The Presidency of the Council rotates among the Member States on an annual basis. The CBSS also has a permanent secretariat located in Stockholm and three specific working groups. A Committee of Senior Officials serves as the main discussion forum and decision-making

degrees of interaction with these organisations. Whereas it is actively involved in the CBSS and in the Barents Euro Arctic Council (BEAC),[19] it had, until the mid-2000s, much looser ties with the main institution promoting regional cooperation around the Black Sea region[20] and it is not involved as such either in the Nordic Council or in the Baltic Council. Interaction with BSEC developed, however, in the wake of the Black Sea Synergy, when the Commission was granted observer status in June 2007. As far as EU instruments are concerned, they include cross-border cooperation programmes, external assistance programmes[21] and the institutional configurations foreseen under the bilateral contractual frameworks.[22]

The fact that there already was a rich institutional environmental around both sea basins prior to the creation of EU initiatives explains that those initiatives are not designed as additional frameworks, but rather are provided with a coordination role. The Northern Dimension and the Black Sea Synergy are conceived as flexible umbrella policies to create bridges between various EU instruments and to foster cooperation between regional actors with a view to strengthening regional stability. Such an approach is reflected in the EU's picking the terms 'dimension' and 'synergy' rather than policy. The underlying idea is to make the most of existing cooperation schemes rather than adding new ones. The Commission proposal for a Northern Dimension even rejected the vision of a new regional initiative and explained it was considered unnecessary (European Commission 1998: 2); instead, it indicated that the 'further promotion of a Northern Dimension

body for matters related to the work of the Council between Ministerial Sessions; it is also responsible for supervising the implementation of activities. As far as BSEC is concerned, the organisation is chaired by each Member State for a six-month period and has its permanent secretariat based in Istanbul. The Council of Ministers of Foreign Affairs is the main decision-making authority, meeting every six months to debate policy issues and to adopt resolutions which are binding for Member States. Its meetings are prepared by a Committee of Senior Officials. The organisation is chaired by each Member State for a six-month period. Summits can also be convened on an ad hoc basis. BSEC also includes a number of working groups and subsidiary organs such as a parliamentary assembly (PABSEC), a Business Council, a Trade and Development Bank and a think-tank, the International Centre for Black Sea Studies.

19 As noted by Lannon and Van Elsuwege (2004: 6–7), the EU played an active role in their creation, especially through the European Commission which is a founding member, although the legal basis of such a role for the Commission is not clear in the Treaties.

20 As indicated by BSEC, following the 1997 communication of the Commission on the Black Sea and the subsequent Council conclusions, contacts developed to identify possible areas of interaction but remained inconclusive for several years.

21 PHARE and TACIS when the Northern Dimension was launched, and currently the ENPI with neighbouring countries and Russia, and the Instrument for Pre-Accession (IPA) with Turkey.

22 For example, basically the Cooperation Council, committees and subcommittees under countries which have signed a Partnership and Cooperation Agreement with the EU; but also various mechanisms of dialogue set up over the past few years, for instance with EU agencies in the area of liberty, security and justice (Frontex, Eurojust, Europol).

concept should take place when there is clear added value, within the existing instruments and frameworks.' The Second Action Plan adopted under the Northern Dimension further emphasises 'subsidiarity and synergy between the different Northern Dimension actors' as major policy concepts (European Commission 2005: 5). This discourse confirms the Olympic Rings interpretation mentioned by Browning (2001b). Such an approach, however, raises major questions when it comes to implementation. What is the actual role devoted to non-EU countries and to regional organisations in the policy process and how is the articulation between various actors and levels of interactions conceived?

The policy process displays a gap with EU discourse, which emphasises the contribution of non-EU actors, as far as both the initial version of the Northern Dimension and the Black Sea Synergy appear as EU-framed initiatives, especially when it comes to the agenda-setting process and the definition of priorities. In the initial documents on the Northern Dimension (European Commission 1998b), the European Commission was given a key role for coordinating EU instruments and activities in the region and for defining further priorities for the EU and for the Northern Dimension as a whole, *inter alia* through Action Plans.[23] These provided for a set of objectives and actions to be implemented by the Northern Dimension under EU policies and instruments, but also under other stakeholders' projects. Consequently, the coordination role taken over by the EU with the Northern Dimension allowed it to frame the overall agenda in Europe's North. Interaction with regional organisations was limited to consultations through the participation of the Commission in CBSS and BSEAC. The involvement of partner countries in the policy making process was also initially restricted to consultation and participation in meetings. In other words, in the Northern Dimension as originally implemented, instruments were shaped at the EU level and applied at the subregional level, with subregional organisations acting as interfaces (Lannon and Van Elsuwege 2004: 26).

The Northern Dimension triggered sharp criticism from Russian authorities as early as the end of the 1990s, mostly for inequality among partners in policy formulation, for not taking Russian views into consideration (Aalto, Blakkisrud and Smith 2008: 8) and, consequently, the inadequacy and ineffectiveness of projects implemented at a regional level (see also Joenniemi and Sergounin 2003). These criticisms were similar to those put forward by the Russian government in the broader framework of its relationship with the EU[24] and prompted an in-depth review of the policy framework in 2005–2006. As a result of that review, 'equal partnership' is a major policy principle in the revised framework, interwoven with

---

23   In the first version of the Northern Dimension two Action Plans were implemented (2001–2003 and 2004–2006). Under the second Action Plan, priorities included economy, business and infrastructure, social issues (including education, training and public health), environment, nuclear safety and natural resources, justice and home affairs and cross-border cooperation.

24   See Chapter 4.

the 'common responsibility' shared by the four partners (the EU, Russia, Norway and Iceland) for Europe's North (Political Declaration on the Northern Dimension Policy 2006). In addition, EU enlargement led to a revised policy framework that is, more tightly connected to the EU–Russia partnership, and the revised Northern Dimension is intended to become 'a regional expression of the four EU–Russia common spaces' (Political Declaration on the Northern Dimension Policy 2006), using the objectives and methods developed under the EU–Russia strategic partnership for regional purposes (for example, environmental, indigenous people or health issues) with full participation of Iceland and Norway. The institutional arrangements under the revised framework focus on intergovernmental meetings between all four partners (either at ministerial, senior official or expert levels), with provisions providing for the participation of regional organisations and other actors (Northern Dimension Policy Framework Document 2006: 6).

Whereas the Northern Dimension has been revised with a view to enhancing the participation of partner countries in the policy process, the role of the EU is quite central in the case of the Black Sea Synergy, which is clearly described as an initiative of the Union: 'The moment has ... come for increased European Union involvement in further defining cooperation priorities and mechanisms at the regional level. In the present Communication, the Commission puts forward Black Sea Synergy as a new regional cooperation initiative of the EU' (European Commission 2007a).

The progress report drafted by the European Commission in the first year of implementation also highlights its central role in implementing the tasks it had prioritised in the policy formulation process (European Commission 2008c). In the EU's discourse, this is connected to the EU's experience and influence (in other words to its 'added-value') and therefore implicitly accepted by partners.[25] Yet at the same time the EU stresses that the Black Sea Synergy is a 'collective endeavour' (European Commission 2008c: 2) involving all partners around the sea basin. True, since the Synergy was launched the EU has stepped up the level of interaction with the main regional organisation, BSEC.[26] However, partners' involvement has been limited to participation in discussions and consultations with the EU Council and the Commission. The major event in this respect is the Kyiv meeting of February 2008, which gathered Foreign Ministers of the countries involved with the Black Sea Synergy. Yet, this meeting also points to the ambiguities of the Black Sea Synergy policy process. As explained by Michael Emerson (Emerson 2008: 9), it in fact encompassed two overlapping, yet different

---

25 For an example of such discourse, the European Commission summarises as follows the Kyiv Foreign Ministers' Meeting's Joint Statement: 'It states that greater involvement by the European Union can increase the potential of Black Sea regional cooperation' (European Commission 2008c: 6).

26 Interactions have mainly taken the form of meetings of the BSEC *troïka*, with the EU Council working group and of participation of European Commission's representatives in BSEC meetings (European Commission 2008c).

sessions, one gathering BSEC ministers (also attended by EU representatives) and the other the ministers of the EU and the Wider Black Sea area; this resulted in two different statements being adopted. Such duality is significant as far as it reflects different positions on institutional arrangements and, beyond these, on the role of the EU in the Black Sea area. More specifically, a strong articulation with BSEC has been pushed forward by the two regional powers, Turkey and (principally) Russia, as a means to retain their influence in the region (Alexandrova-Arbatova 2008: 36) and to control the EU's emergence as a regional power in the Black Sea region, *inter alia* through BSEC's consensus decision-making rule (Emerson 2008). Russia thus refused to sign the second statement which provides for the possibility of EU activities outside BSEC. As far as it is concerned, the EU is reluctant to give a central role to BSEC due in part to Russia's role in the organisation (Emerson 2008), but also to BSEC's wide agenda and mitigated record. As a result, the Black Sea Synergy formally overlaps with other regulatory frameworks, but as far as non-EU partners are concerned interaction is mainly characterised by information exchanges and consultations rather than joint decision-making processes. To a certain extent, such a pattern contradicts the picture of Olympic rings in that decision-making is centralised within the EU.

To sum up, while the latter was explicitly modelled after the former (Ministry of Foreign Affairs of the Hellenic Republic 2007), the revised Northern Dimension and the Black Sea Synergy offer contrasting illustrations of the way in which the EU promotes regional cooperation at its outer edges. The Northern Dimension now better reflects the notion of partnership between participants, a notion which is widely used in EU policy discourse but which is seldom put into practice, as noted by Korosteleva in the case of the neighbourhood policy (Korosteleva 2010). This entails that non-EU participants, Russia in particular, are closely involved in the policy drafting process, in the implementation, monitoring and funding processes, the latter also being a major difference with the initial version of the Northern Dimension.[27] Moreover, the fact that Russia can shape the policy process indicates additional coherence with the EU-Russia strategic partnership which, as shown in Chapter 4, was revised along similar lines in the period 2003–2005. The principle of equal partnership embedded into the revised version of the policy as a result of Russian pressures thus emphasises 'a move away from a hierarchically ordered Europe centred on Brussels to a more equitable one where governance, authority and decision-making is dispersed and brought closer to the people' (Browning 2001b: 10).

By contrast, the Black Sea Synergy highlights a different EU attitude to other actors and instead illustrates a new EU presence in the Black Sea regional

---

27   The Northern Dimension was initially funded under TACIS, which was managed directly from European Commission's headquarters in Brussels until the early 2000s, when management was devolved to the European Commission's delegations in the field; yet, even by that time the participation of partner countries in the programme cycle remained limited (Delcour 2002 and 2003).

constellation with a view to 'bringing stability and prosperity' to the area (European Commission 2007a). the Black Sea Synergy modes of governance thus confirm the picture of an expanding EU foreign policy where the EU projects its solutions and therefore its influence onto its periphery. However, rather representing a post-Westphalian state, the EU initiative around the Black Sea would corroborate the metaphor of an emerging or neo-medieval Empire, a metaphor used by scholars to describe the untidy process of EU development as an international actor (see in particular Browning 2001b; Zielonka 2007 and 2008). At the same time, it is worth pointing out that in both cases the policy processes producing either partnership or EU-led policies are framed by interaction with regional powers, most of all with Russia. In the Black Sea region, the EU's engagement has been particularly constrained by both Russia's reluctance to accept the Union's new presence around the sea basin, the region's fragmentation and the poor record in regional cooperation, including under regional institutions such as BSEC.

Subregional Cooperation as a Tool For Filling The Gaps Between EU Policies in the Former Soviet Area?

As explained in the previous chapters, the EU has developed increasingly differentiated and compartmentalised policy frameworks in the former Soviet Union. Chapter 7, in particular, has highlighted the need for the EU to build bridges between its various policies in order to enhance coherence and to tackle more effectively transnational challenges. Subregional cooperation initiatives have been conceived to fulfil these objectives (among others). Based upon an overview of their activities, this section holds that the degree of inclusion of regional partners in the policy processes significantly affects the implementation of Northern Dimension and Black Sea Synergy cooperation activities and their effectiveness in linking different EU frameworks. The Northern Dimension will mainly be used as a reference for comparison here, as far as it includes only one post-Soviet country and is therefore not expected to deliver additional coherence between EU initiatives in the former Soviet Union, as opposed to Black Sea Synergy, which is expected to play a pivotal role in this respect.

The European Commission identified for the Black Sea Synergy the following priorities rooted in transnational challenges: democracy, respect for human rights and good governance; managing movement and improving security; 'frozen conflicts'; energy; transports; environment; maritime policy and fisheries; trade; research and education networks (European Commission 2007a). Arguably, the new EU initiative's record is poor for most of these priorities. While the possibility of European Community accession to the Convention to protect the Black Sea against pollution would increase the EU's regional involvement in the environment sector, environmental issues are still primarily dealt with at a bilateral level, for instance under ENP Action Plans and EU assistance programmes (see for example, the case of Georgia, European Commission 2009c: 44). When it comes to energy, a highly sensitive issue for Russia (Alexandrova-Arbatova 2008: 26–7), the progress report on the implementation of the Black Sea Synergy published by the European Commission in 2008 only mentions those instruments meant to strengthen convergence with EU standards (for example, the European Energy Community)[28] – a method which has been repeatedly discarded by Russia – or those aimed at reducing EU dependence on Russian natural gas (for example, the TransCaspian–Black Sea corridor). This suggests that Black Sea Synergy does not bring any substantial added value at a regional level, and activities implemented so far in the energy sector do not allow for the closing of gaps noted in Chapter 7.

As far as unresolved conflicts are concerned, the Black Sea Synergy has not resulted in an enhanced EU engagement nor yielded any decisive progress in their resolution, as clearly evidenced by the Russian–Georgian conflict which broke out in August 2008. While the EU indeed played an important role in this crisis, its intervention was channelled outside the Black Sea Synergy's (and, for that matter, the European Neighbourhood Policy's) framework. What is more, the Russian–Georgian conflict has considerably hindered the implementation of other regional activities under the Synergy. In the aftermath of the conflict, due to the sharp deterioration of regional links, it appeared impossible for the EU to undertake what was initially foreseen under the European Commission's proposal (European Commission 2007a), that is, to promote any measure to foster confidence among the regions and countries concerned, especially between Georgia and Russia. It is also noteworthy that plans or initiatives for regional security were introduced at that time without EU participation. The Turkish–Armenian rapprochement, with all its limitations, developed on a bilateral basis. Talks and meetings between Armenian and Azerbaijani authorities to discuss the Nagorno-Karabakh conflict continued to be conducted under Russia's auspices. Finally, the Platform for Stability and Cooperation in the South Caucasus, proposed by Turkey as part of its 'zero-problems-with neighbours policy' (Fotiou 2009), does not include the EU, but only those countries which are perceived as legitimate players in the region, that is, the three South Caucasus countries and Russia.

To sum up, the Black Sea Synergy seems to be stalling, as suggested by the lack of a European Commission annual progress report in 2009 and 2010. Regional diversity and other players strongly constrain the EU's action around the Black Sea. In particular, the role played by Russia as an obstacle comes in sharp contrast to its preferences and attitudes as a partner under the revised Northern Dimension. While the EU's actions within the Black Sea Synergy is perceived by Moscow as an intrusion around the Black Sea, the Northern Dimension is considered an

---

28   These are negotiated bilaterally, a framework which enhances the EU's leeway as implicitly acknowledged in the EU's policy discourse: 'The Republic of Moldova, Turkey and Ukraine have confirmed their intention to engage in formal negotiations to join the Energy Community Treaty, which provides for the implementation of the Community *acquis* in the electricity and gas sectors. Georgia was accepted as an observer in December 2007' (European Commission 2008c: 4).

opportunity to tackle regional challenges around the Baltic Sea. Such differences in Russian perceptions are tightly connected to regional configurations and to the country's participation in the policy process. Around the Baltic Sea, Russia does not feel (or no longer feels) threatened by any regional security or political arrangements which would exclude her; the current regional configuration gives a *de facto* central role to the EU–Russia relationship. The situation is different around the Black Sea, where Russia had to face the emergence in the 1990s of other regional powers (for example, Turkey) and external actors (for example, the US and NATO) prone to increase their influence in the post-Soviet space (Alexandrova-Arbatova 2008: 25). While Russia has strengthened its positions over the past few years, particularly after the 2008 conflict and even more so after the agreement concluded with Ukraine on the Black Sea Fleet in April 2010, its major policy objective – retaining its influence – has not changed in the region, and it is therefore reticent to accept any new initiative in which it does not play a central role. As far as the policy process is concerned, the principle of 'equal partnership' enshrined in the Northern Dimension is acceptable as it coincides with Russia's preferences, while the country is not willing to accept an EU-led regional initiative (the Black Sea Synergy) in its backyard.

As a consequence of these different policy processes, the scope of activities differs between the two initiatives. Both the grassroots or project-based approach and the de-politicised angle at the core of the new Northern Dimension fit with Russian preferences (Busygina and Filippov 2008). This approach facilitated easy agreements and some results in sectors of common interest such as health (in the framework of the Northern Dimension Partnership in Public Health and Social Well-Being) (see Aasland 2008). By contrast, the Black Sea Synergy initial priority sectors included highly politicised issues (for example, conflicts, democracy, security) which the EU had already failed to tackle either under its strategic partnership with Russia or under the Neighbourhood Policy owing to Russia's influence. The first years of implementation suggest that the Black Sea Synergy does not bring any substantial added value when compared to other EU policies in addressing these issues. However, concentration on a smaller number of priorities, especially on depoliticised issues of common interest such as environment, may change the situation and yield more significant results (Delcour and Manoli 2010). The launch of an environmental partnership in 2010 looks promising in this respect.

Conclusion

Both the Northern Dimension and the Black Sea Synergy are inspired by the approach and methods upon which the European integration process was grounded[29] in that

---

29   On the influence of neo-functionalism and the Jean Monnet method upon EU regional initiatives, see the research conducted by Elisabeth Johansson-Nogués on the

they favour the development of grassroots cooperation in specific policy sectors to create a *de facto* solidarity between partner countries involving a number of participants at a regional, national and subnational level. The revised version of the Northern Dimension, in particular, puts a greater emphasis on cooperation in low policy areas and therefore gives a push to actors such as local authorities, business communities, universities and civil society organisations (Johansson-Nogués 2009a). Such emphasis is certainly constrained both by the weak capacities of Russian counterparts and the restoration of the verticality of power between the centre and the subjects of the Russian Federation since the early 2000s (see Raviot 2008, Daucé 2008). However, this approach has yielded results in sectors such as health, the management of which is rather decentralised in Russia (Aasland 2009). At the same time, a major difference with the neo-functionalist approach in the Northern Dimension is the lack of supranational institutions and the role played by national government to give flesh to the principle of co-equality.

As far as the Black Sea Synergy is concerned, the institutional situation differs in that it is mainly shaped by EU institutions and limits the role of other organisations, such as BSEC.[30] While this should in principle be a factor for advancing cooperation, the EU has not succeeded in giving a substantial impetus to regional cooperation in a fragmented area. Tensions also derive from the fact that, unlike the new Northern Dimension, the Black Sea Synergy initially intended to address high policy areas as well, that is, areas which have highlighted the limits of the Monnet method in the European integration process.[31] Issues such as democracy, human rights and, more specifically, unresolved conflicts and energy hampered the whole cooperation agenda at a regional level. In other words, subregional cooperation around the Black Sea is undermined by factors similar to those hindering the effectiveness of EU bilateral policies. As a result, it has not contributed to closing the gaps between EU policies in the former Soviet Union.

---

initiatives around the Mediterranean Sea and the Baltic Sea (Johansson-Nogués 2009a). As far as the Northern Dimension is concerned, as noted by Johansson-Nogués, this approach is combined with the experience of post-war Nordic cooperation.

30   BSEC functions according to consensual decision-making, thus granting an important role to other players such as Russia while limiting policy effectiveness.

31   Interestingly, high policy areas which ranked first in the list of priorities included in the EC Communication on Black Sea Synergy are last mentioned in the 2008 report, a clear indication of the lack of progress in these sectors.

Conclusion:
Shaping or Shaped by the Post-Soviet Area?

This volume has analysed the extent to which the EU channels its policies at the regional level and interacts with other regional institutions in the post-Soviet space, as well as the degree to which it acts as a driving force for regional cooperation in this area. Since the European Community was launched, the place of regions as objects of EU external action/foreign policy has indeed been central in light of its own experience of integration and even more so in the context of a new regionalism flourishing in the international arena at the end of the 1980s and into the early 1990s. In the post-Cold War context, the EU's support for region-building seems to be natural (De Lombaerde and Schulz 2009: 2), taking into account both its successful internal model and international developments. Yet this book started from an opposite hypothesis, singling out the post-Soviet area as an exception to the picture of EU foreign policy as promoting regional and inter-regional links worldwide.

Overall, this central assumption has been validated. The EU's policies have only conveyed a message promoting regional cooperation and interregionalism in the post-Soviet area to a limited extent. At the same time, the empirical analysis of the various policies, programmes and initiatives developed by the Union over the past two decades brings important nuances to this assumption and suggests major evolutions in the EU's foreign policy *vis-à-vis* the former Soviet Union, including instances of support for regional integration. The concluding section of this volume will characterise this evolution, assess the respective weight of the three independent variables selected in the analytical framework to account for the EU's support for regionalisation and examine the hypotheses formulated at the beginning of the book in light of empirical findings.

Strong evidence suggests that, in manner and degree, the EU's development of interregional links and preference for regional integration across the post-Soviet area closely corresponds to its influence in the countries concerned and to its overall policy objectives; in other words, to the evolution of the EU's foreign policy *vis-à-vis* the New Independent States.

Over the past two decades, the EU's policy has undergone drastic changes when it comes to the objectives pursued and the tools utilised in the former Soviet Union, as well as to the overall EU presence and influence. When the Soviet Union collapsed, the European Community was a newcomer in the region. It only recently had established official links with the COMECON after thirty years of mutual ignorance; it had signed an economic cooperation agreement with the USSR two years before its demise and it had just set up its technical assistance programme for the Soviet Union. In sharp contrast to the early 1990s, the EU is now both present and influential in all parts of the former Soviet Union. It has deployed a broad network of instruments and agreements and it is attractive to most post-Soviet countries, either as a political project and as an organisation to join (in the case of Ukraine, Moldova and, to a lesser extent, Georgia) or as a partner countervailing the influence of other players in the area (in the case of Kazakhstan and some other Central Asian republics, as well as of Azerbaijan). While the EU has undoubtedly stepped in as an important political player in the post-Soviet area, this evolution has been incremental. Throughout the 1990s the EU kept a low profile in the post-Soviet area, which was clearly not a priority for a Union concentrating on its own internal integration project and on the enlargement process on the one hand, and more concerned with its foreign policy in other parts of the world on the other hand. As a consequence, the EU *de facto* relied upon technical assistance which served as a major socialisation tool to familiarise the Union with the New Independent States. Together with the prospect of EU enlargement to Central and Eastern European countries, the rise of security issues on the EU political agenda and the increasing blurring of boundaries between EU internal and external security were instrumental in shifting the EU's attention to the post-Soviet area and revisiting its policy framework, a process which started at the end of the 1990s with Russia and Ukraine, which developed gradually and which is not over. A major consequence of this process is the EU's increased engagement and visibility in the former Soviet Union since the mid-2000s; however, as shown by the recent introduction of new initiatives (the Eastern Partnership and the Partnership for Modernisation with Russia agreed upon in 2010), EU policies in the former Soviet area are still a moving target.

In a nutshell, the post-Soviet space, more than any other area in the world, mirrors the whole range of changes which have affected European foreign policy since the early 1990s. Over the past decade, it has emerged as a major test altogether for the EU's capacity to define and implement its external action objectives, to deal with its vicinity and to address security issues – in other words, for the EU's capacity to act in the international arena. As such, the EU's activities in the post-Soviet space raise a number of important questions: What is the character of the EU stance which has underpinned regional cooperation in the overall dynamics of European foreign policy? To what extent has this traditional EU-promoted norm and foreign policy objective been at the root of changes made in EU policies developed in the post-Soviet area? Conversely, to what extent has the objective of regional cooperation been shaped and transformed by the evolving external action framework and tools in the former Soviet Union?

Examination of the EU's support for regional cooperation and interregionalism in the post-Soviet area reveals a discontinuous, differentiated and contrasted use of these norms and foreign policy objectives by the Union. To account for the EU's support for regionalisation, the analytical framework presented in Chapter 1 featured three independent variables, the first one pertaining to EU institutional processes for foreign policy, the second one focusing on the existence of endogenous regional initiatives, mechanisms and structures fostering cooperation among former Soviet countries, and the third one connected to the role played by other region-builders in the area, primarily by Russia.

The findings of this book confirm that all three variables help explain the lack of EU support for regionalisation, although not to the same degree. The empirical analysis has led to *three main conclusions* which are discussed hereafter:

- exogenous factors are salient to account for the predominance of bilateralism in EU policies in the former Soviet Union while endogenous factors do matter to explain the introduction of a regional or multilateral approach;
- EU attempts and initiatives to foster region-building have been strongly constrained by the existence of other regional players in the post-Soviet area (primarily by Russia);
- at the same time, bilateral policies developed by the EU *vis-à-vis* post-Soviet countries do have transversal effects and thus affect region-building processes in the post-Soviet area.

Undoubtedly, the post-Soviet area was not a favourable field for the EU's support of regional cooperation in that disintegration dynamics prevailed in the aftermath of the USSR's collapse. To some extent, the lack of regional cooperation schemes among Soviet republics indicates that the former USSR was nothing but an imposed federation among entities which had little in common. Following this argument, many existing links among republics were therefore doomed to fail once communist ideology, a centralised economy and the whole Soviet bloc had fallen to pieces. However, economic, cultural, political and military relations among former Soviet republics were still strong after the demise of the Soviet Union and could possibly form the basis for new forms of cooperation. This was clearly the opinion reflected in the EU discourse in 1991–1992.

Arguably, what lacked above all in various attempts to develop regional cooperation schemes in the former Soviet Union in the 1990s and in the early 2000s was a *core*. Due mainly to its focus on its internal reform process and partially to its foreign policy stance in the aftermath of the USSR's collapse, Russia was not able to act as a catalyst for regional cooperation. While it has conducted an interventionist policy in the post-Soviet area since the early 2000s, it has never emerged as a pole of attraction around which post-Soviet countries could gather (de Tinguy 2007). At a subregional level, no other post-Soviet country has been able to act as a catalyst for regional integration either, be it Kazakhstan in Central Asia or even more obviously Ukraine around the Black Sea.

Furthermore, the economic, political, social and international transformation processes which have taken place over the past two decades, especially in the 2000s, have moved the post-Soviet countries away from one another. Apart from their common Soviet legacy, which includes to some degree preserved economic, cultural and people-to-people links (and hence, apart from facing common problems in addressing this legacy), it is difficult to find anything in common between, for example, 'sultanic' Central Asian republics and a country like Ukraine, which has made huge progress on its path towards being a democracy. As a result of these twofold dynamics (the lack of an attracting leader and divergent trajectories), regional cooperation schemes in the post-Soviet area have ultimately failed whatever the reason which led to their creation may be – whether the preservation of links among former Soviet republics (for example, the Commonwealth of Independent States), the need to address regional challenges (for example, the various regional cooperation initiatives introduced by Kazakhstan in Central Asia), or the desire to group countries by political affinities (for example, the Community of Democratic Choice). In other words, the post-Soviet space cannot be considered a region anymore and it has not been replaced by any alternative arrangements.

At the same time, the lack of endogenous regional initiatives (or, more exactly, the lack of any successful regional or subregional cooperation schemes initiated from the inside) does not appear *per se* as a sufficient reason to account for the limited extent of EU support for regional cooperation. In other parts of the world, the EU has supported cooperation among countries which shared less in common than the post-Soviet republics; it has backed schemes of integration which had poorer records than in the former USSR. The latter example can be found in Africa, for example, in Central Africa. The former is illustrated by the example of the Southern Mediterranean area, where the EU has actively promoted regional cooperation since the mid-1990s while trade between Southern Mediterranean partners remains limited and political tensions hinder cooperation between these countries. Even though to a limited extent, the EU has contributed to regionalisation in the Southern Mediterranean area, *inter alia* through constructing regional practices (Bojinović Fenko 2009: 200). The comparison with the Southern Mediterranean highlights the existence, in the post-Soviet area, of a major factor which is lacking around the Mediterranean basin: other influential regional players. Arguably, Russia has not been able (or willing) to act as a locomotive for regional cooperation, much less integration; at the same time, it has considered with much reticence the growing involvement of external players in the former Soviet Union and it has tried as much as possible to limit their influence and to thwart their strategies, including those designed with region-building purposes. In other words, the EU's attempts to support regional cooperation or to contribute to region-building have been strongly constrained by the existence of other region-builders in the former Soviet Union, more specifically by the regional hegemon.

In many respects the post-Soviet area is indeed considered by Russia as its backyard or its *chasse gardée*. Russia has a number of instruments and assets at its disposal for maintaining an overpowering influence in the former Soviet Union, though these have also changed over time. Russia combines its bilateral policies *vis-à-vis* the New Independent States with regional cooperation initiatives (for example, Customs Unions) and activities in the framework of regional organisations which de facto serve its interests in the post-Soviet area. Moreover,

Russia can rely not only upon political and military influence inherited from the Soviet Empire, but also economic links (which it has fostered in the 2000s around new strategic sectors such as energy) and, finally, cultural ties which have only recently emerged as a foreign policy tool (Delcour 2007b). The fact that the post-Soviet area was unknown to the European Community resulted in the latter's difficult and often inaccurate assessment of Russia's role. In the aftermath of the Soviet Union's collapse, Russia was deemed capable of being the core of post-Soviet regional integration initiatives. By the end of the 1990s and into the early 2000s, the EU's assessment of both the failure of regional cooperation and of increasingly divergent trajectories in the former USSR resulted in an opposite (and also inaccurate) conclusion that Russia had lost its status as a regional power. Yet, as shown by recent development and tensions in the common neighbourhood, the current situation rather validates the hypothesis of a dual influence in Western NIS. This book has also shown the EU's difficulty in accounting for the role played by Russia and for existing relations between post-Soviet countries when defining its sectoral policy objectives and designing regional initiatives meant to complement its bilateral policies. This holds especially true in the case of energy, in which the EU's strategies have so far been adversely affected by Russia's own policies in the post-Soviet area. Overall, the effectiveness of EU policies in the post-Soviet area is undermined by its failure to take sufficiently in consideration the interactions between partner countries and the regional framework of its bilateral policies.

Yet, it is argued that to whatever extent the lack of endogenous cooperation schemes among post-Soviet countries and the absence of an integration pole able to aggregate these countries around itself affect the EU's decision-making in the region, the main factor explaining the lack of EU support for regional cooperation lies with the EU itself, more specifically with the evolution of its external action. A major conclusion of this volume is that the way in which the EU has envisioned regional cooperation in the post-Soviet area and its role in supporting this process have been considerably altered by the evolution of its global foreign policy objectives in the region.

On the one hand, support for regional cooperation as a traditional objective of EU external action has been limited to specific cases in the former USSR. The empirical analysis conducted in the post-Soviet area has shown that over the past two decades, the EU has adopted a regional approach or launched regional initiatives when its presence in the area concerned was new or weak. Three examples are salient here. The first one relates obviously to the European Community's initial reactions after the collapse of the Soviet Union, when the EU advocated for the preservation of regional links among the New Independent States (apart from the three Baltic countries) and when it designed a similar contractual framework for all twelve countries. The second one coincides with the creation of Black Sea Synergy, a sea basin to which, as acknowledged in the EU's discourse, the Union had not paid specific attention and around which it had not previously developed any dedicated initiative. The third example corresponds to the regional dimension which prevailed in the EU's initial proposals for the new partnership with Central Asia.

These examples confirm the validity of historical institutionalist approaches for analysing the EU's attempts to support to regional cooperation in the former Soviet Union. They indeed illustrate the EU's tendency to apply well-known policy patterns in similar situations. In other words, the EU has reproduced its traditional approach favouring regional cooperation as a point of departure for developing its relations with countries in which it previously had no policy framework. The recurrence of this policy pattern can be explained by the traditional EU conception of regions and is tightly connected to the institutional balance among EU actors. Arguably, regions have been considered both as desirable developments in international relations and as appropriate levels for action since the early stages of the EU integration process. Regions are seen in a positive way, as protections from war and from nationalism and they are also viewed as gateways to the global stage, a global stage which is ideally viewed as a world of connected and interacting regions. Although political *par excellence*, since it provides regions with a stabilisation function in the international arena, this vision has historically found expression in EU external action though the utilisation of economic tools, managed by the European Commission in the framework of the Community's economic relations. Within the post-Soviet area, this applies for instance to the similar policy framework proposed by the Commission for the twelve NIS in the early 1990s in which the European Commission plays a central role for policy formulation and management. At the same time, this vision has been overwhelmingly supported by EU Member States. Support to regional cooperation is a non-controversial issue between Member States in that it connects them to a crucial part of their recent history.

On the other hand, with the reframing of its policies in the early 2000s the EU has shifted is role from traditional supporter of regional cooperation to region-builder, that is, a more proactive stance. This is related to both the new proximity with the Western parts of the post-Soviet area and the rise of security issues on its political agenda. Yet, while new regional initiatives have been launched, the EU's contribution to region-building has primarily been achieved through its bilateral policies favouring convergence with its own model. This indicates that in parallel to this traditional conception supporting regional cooperation as a positive development in international relations, the EU has developed a significantly different, more sceptical vision of regions at its periphery. In a world in which threats are to a large extent transnational, regions as envisioned by the EU are not necessarily adequately equipped or sufficiently institutionalised to become the appropriate actors to address security issues which in turn may threaten the Union. Rather, experiences with other parts of the Southern Mediterranean, to take one example, show that regions can be gangrened by conflicts and other security issues. As a consequence of its proximity with 'turbulent neighbours' (European Commission 1998, quoted in Gänzle 2008), the EU increasingly envisions regions as nascent security communities (Adler 1997) needing a core to foster convergent understandings of security issues and shared practices. This entails that the EU no longer relies upon local players to foster regional links across a geographical area; rather, as evidenced by its discourse on the neighbourhood (Bengtsson 2008), it takes over a role of security-community builder in areas which are deemed crucial for its security and for the continent's stability. The neighbourhood policy is an obvious example of such assertiveness of the EU's self-image as the core of a regional security complex and of the tensions implied by such a process. Even though it relies mainly upon bilateral instruments, the ENP can thus be analysed as an EU attempt to 'make' regions (De Lombaerde and Schutz 2009). On the one hand, the ENP gathers countries which have little in common apart from being neighbours of the European Union; on the other hand, through fostering convergence of these countries with EU norms, standards and values as vectors of stabilisation and security, it endorses to some extent a region-building role. The ENP example, and more specifically the Eastern Partnership, thus confirms the validity of constructivist approaches to analyse the shift from a role of regional cooperation supporter to region-builder.

Overall, EU policies and approaches to region-building in the post Soviet area are guided and moulded by interactions and tensions: at an internal level between EU actors' preferences and between the EU's various modes of governance and at an external level between the EU's position reached as the result of compromises and partner countries' expectations and interests. As perfectly illustrated by the post-Soviet area, another level is the interaction between the internal project and EU foreign policy, with EU integration also being advanced or affected by its external activities, as evidenced for instance in the energy area. The resulting picture is of not only an international actor advancing through dialectics, proposing solutions based upon its own experience and attempting to project its norms abroad in an inside-out dynamic, but of an actor being shaped by outsiders as well.

References

Aalto, P. (ed.) 2008. *The EU–Russian Energy Dialogue: Europe's Future Energy Security*. Aldershot: Ashgate.

Aalto, P., Blakkisrud, H. and Smith, H. 2009. *The New Northern Dimension of the European Neighbourhood*. CEPS Paperbacks, January.

Aasland, A. 2009. 'Assessing the Northern Dimension Partnership in Public Health and Social Well-being', in: Aalto, P., Blakkisrud, H. and Smith, H. (eds), *The New Northern Dimension of the European Neighbourhood*. Brussels: CEPS Paperbacks, 91–107.

Adler, E. 1997. 'Imagined (Security) Communities: Cognitive Regions in International Relations', *Millennium*, (26)2, 249–77.

Adler, E. and Barnett, M. 1998. *Security Communities*. Cambridge: Cambridge University Press.

Adler, E. 2002. 'Constructivism and International Relations', in: Carlsnaes, W., Risse, T. and Simmons, B. (eds), *Handbook of International Relations*. London: Sage, 95–118.

Adler, E. and Crawford, B. 2002. *Constructing a Mediterranean Region: A Cultural Approach*. Paper presented at the conference on 'The Convergence of Civilizations? Constructing a Mediterranean Region.' Fundação Oriente, Lisbon, Portugal, June.

Adomeit, H. 1979. 'Soviet Perceptions of Western European Integration: Ideological Distortion or Realistic Assessment?', *Millennium – Journal of International Studies*, 8(1), 1–24.

Alexandrova-Arbatova, N. 2008. 'Regional Cooperation in the Black Sea Area in the Context of EU–Russia Relations', *Xenophon*, Paper No. 5.

Alieva, L. 2009. 'The EU Policies and Sub-regional Multilateralism in the Caspian Basin.' *EU4seas Papers*. Available at: http://www.eu4seas.eu/images/stories/projects/publications/barcelona/eu4seas_leila_alieva.pdf

Allison, R., Light, M. and White, S. 2006. *Putin's Russia and the Enlarged Europe*. London: Chatham House Papers; Oxford: Blackwell.

Antonenko, O. and Pinnick, K. (eds), 2005. *Russia and the European Union: Prospects for a New Relationship*. London and New York: Routledge and IISS.

Antonenko, O. 2005. 'Russia and EU Enlargement: From Insecure Neighbour to a Common Space of Security, Justice and Home Affairs', in: Antonenko, O. and Pinnick, K. (eds), *Russia and the European Union: Prospects for a New Relationship*. London/New York: Routledge and IISS, 67–101.

Antonenko, O. 2007. 'The EU should not ignore the Shanghai Cooperation Organisation', *CER Policy Brief*, May, available at: http://www.cer.org.uk/pdf/policybrief_sco_web_11may07.pdf

Arbatova, N. 2006. 'Stanut li strany SNG 'yablokom razdora' v otnosheniyakh Rossii I ES?', *Mirovaya Èkonomika i Mezhdunarodnye Otnoshenya*, No. 6.

Armbruster, C. 2008. 'Discerning the Global in the European Revolutions of 1989', paper presented at the workshop 'Global 1989', London School of Economics and Political Science, 29 May, available at http://papers.ssrn.com/sol3/papers.cfm?abstract_id=1261202

Atnachev, T. 2001. 'Les nouvelles frontières de la civilisation russe', *Raisons politiques*, n°2, May, 153–73.

Attinà, F. 2003. 'The Euro-Mediterranean Partnership Assessed: The Realist and Liberal Views', *European Foreign Affairs Review*, 8, 181–200.

Averre, D. 2005. 'Russia and the European Union: Convergence or Divergence?', *European Security*, 14(2), 175–202.

Averre, D. 2009. 'Competing Rationalities: Russia, the EU and the "Shared Neighbourhood"', *Europe–Asia Studies*, 61(10), 1689–1713.

Aydin, M. 2004. 'Europe's Next Shore: the Black Sea Region after EU Enlargement', *Occasional Paper No. 53*, European Institute for Security Studies, June.

Balzacq, T. 2007. 'La politique européenne de voisinage, un complexe de sécurité à géométrie variable', *Cultures et conflits*, 66.

Ban, I. 2006. *The Black Sea Region and the European Neighbourhood Policy*. Budapest: Central European University, Centre for Enlargement Studies.

Barbé, E., Costa, O., Herranz, A. and Natorski, M. 2009a. 'Which Rules Shape EU External Governance? Patterns of Rule Selection in Foreign and Security Policies', *Journal of European Public Policy*, 16(6), 834–52.

Barbé, E., Costa, O., Herranz, A., Johansson-Nogués, E., Natorski, M. and Sabiota, M. 2009b. 'Drawing the Neighbours Closer ... to What ? Explaining Emerging Patterns of Policy Convergence between the EU and its Neighbours', *Cooperation and Conflict*, 44(4), 378–99.

Bechev, D. 2006. 'Constructing South East Europe: The Politics of Regional Identity in the Balkans', RAMSES Working Paper. Oxford: European Studies Centre.

Bengtsson, R. 2008. 'Constructing Interfaces: The Neighbourhood Discourse in EU Policy', *European Integration*, (30)5, 595–616.

Bicchi, F. 2006. 'Our Size Fits All: Normative Power Europe and the Mediterranean', *Journal of European Public Policy*, 13(2), 286–303.

Bigo, D. 2001. 'Internal and External Security(ies), the Möbius Ribbon', in: Albert, M., Bigo, D., Heisler, M., Kratochwil, F., Jacobson, D. and Lapid, F., *Identities, Borders and Orders, Borderlines*. Minneapolis: University of Minnesota Press.

Biscop, S. 2004. 'The European Security Strategy. Implementing a Distinctive Approach to Security', *Sécurité & Stratégie*, Paper No. 82.

Biscop, S. 2005. *The European Security Strategy: A Global Agenda for Positive Power*. Aldershot: Ashgate.

Bojinovic Fenko, A. 2009. 'An Evaluation of the EU–Mediterranean Region-Building from the Perspective of the Regionalization Process in the Mediterranean', in: De Lombaerde, P. and Schulz, M. (eds), *The EU and World Regionalism: The Makability of Regions in the 21st Century*. Farnham: Ashgate.

Boratynski, J., Gromadzki, G., Sushko, O. and Szymborska, A. 2006. *Questionable Achievement: EU–Ukraine Visa Facilitation Agreement*. Warsaw: Batory Foundation.

Bordachev, T. 2010. 'Georgia, Obama, Economic Crisis: Shifting Ground in EU–Russia Relations', *IFRI Russie NEI-Visions* No. 46.

Borko, Y. 1997. 'The New Intra-European Relations and Russia', in: Maresceau, M. (ed.) 1997. *Enlarging the European Union: Relations between the EU and Central and Eastern Europe*. London: Longman.

Borko, Y. 1998. 'D'un partenariat virtuel à un partenariat effectif?', in: Raux, J. and Korovkine, V. (eds), *Le partenariat entre l' Union européenne et la Fédération de Russie*, 111–30.

Borko, Y. 2002. 'Russia and the EU: The Kaliningrad Dilemma', *CEPS Policy Brief* No. 15, March.

Borko, Y. 2004. 'Rethinking EU–Russia Relations', *Russia in Global Affairs*, No. 8, August.

Bosse, G. and Korostoleva-Polglase, E. 2009. 'Changing Belarus? The Limits of EU Governance in Eastern Europe and the Promise of Partnership', *Cooperation and Conflict*, 44(2), 143–65.

Bretherton, C. and Vogler, J. 1999. *The European Union as a Global Actor*. London: Routledge.

Browning, C. 2001a. 'The Region-Building Approach Revisited: The Continued Othering of Russia in Discourses of Region-Building in the European North', *Working Paper No. 6*, Copenhagen: Copenhagen Peace Research Institute.

Browning, C. 2001b. 'The Construction of Europe in the Northern Dimension', COPRI Working Paper No. 39/2001.

Browning, C. and Joennimi, P. 2003. 'The European Union's Two Dimensions: The Eastern and the Northern', *Security Dialogue*, 34(4), 463–78.

Browning, C. (ed.) 2005. *Remaking Europe in the Margins: Northern Europe after the Enlargements*. Aldershot: Ashgate.

Browning, C. and Joennimi, P. 2007. 'Geostrategies of the European Neighbourhood Policy', *DIIS Working Paper No. 2007/9*.

Bruter, M. 1999. 'Diplomacy Without a State: the external delegations of the European Commission', *Journal of European Public Policy*, (6)2, 183–205.

BSEC (no date). BSEC–EU interaction: the BSEC Approach, prepared by the International Centre for Black Sea Studies, available at: http://icbss.org/index.php?option=com_content&task=view&id=25&Itemid=39

Busygina, I. and Filippov, M. 2009. 'End Comment: EU–Russian Relations and the Limits of the Northern Dimension', in: Aalto, P. Blakkisrud, H. and Smith, H. *The New Northern Dimension of the European Neighbourhood*, 204–19.

Buzan, B. 1991. *People, State and Fear: An Agenda for International Security Studies in the Post-Cold War Era*. Boulder: Lynne Rienner Publishers.

Buzan, B. 1997. 'Rethinking Security after the Cold War', *Cooperation and Conflict*, 32(1), 5–28.

Buzan, B., Wæver, O. and de Wilde, J. 1998. *Security: a New Framework for Analysis*. Boulder: Lynne Rienner Publishers.

Buzan, B. and Wæver, O. 2003. *Regions and Powers: The Structure of International Security*. Cambridge: Cambridge University Press.

Brzezinski, Z. and Sullivan, P. 1997. *Russia and the Commonwealth of Independent States*. Armonk/London: M.E. Sharpe.

Carlsnaes, W., Risse, T. and Simmons, B. (eds) 2002. *Handbook of International Relations*. London: Sage.

Carlsnaes, W., Sjursen, H. and White, B. (eds) 2004. *Contemporary European Foreign Policy*. London: Sage.

Carlsnaes, W. 2004. 'Introduction', in: Carlsnaes, W., Sjursen, H. and White, B., (eds), *Contemporary European Foreign Policy*. London: Sage.

Centre for Social and Economic Research (CASE). 2008. 'The Economic Aspects of the Energy Sector in CIS Countries', *Economic Papers No. 327*, June.

Charillon, F. 2004. 'Sovereignty and Intervention: EU's Interventionism in its Near Abroad', in: Carlsnaes, W., Sjursen, H. and White, B. (eds), *Contemporary European Foreign Policy*. London: Sage, 252–64.

Checkel, J. 1999. 'Social Construction and Integration', *Journal of European Public Policy*, 6(4), 545–60.

Checkel, J. 2001. 'A Constructivist Research Programme in EU Studies', *European Union Politics*, 2(2), 219–49.

Christiansen, T. 2001. 'Intra-Institutional Politics and Inter-Institutional Relations in the EU: Towards Coherent Governance?', *Journal of European Public Policy*, 8, 747–69.

Cianciara, A. 2008. '"Eastern Partnership" – Opening a New Chapter of Polish Eastern Policy and the European Neighbourhood Policy?', *Analyses and Opinions*, No. 4. Warsaw: The Institute of Public Affairs, June.

Chuvin, P., Létolle, R. and Peyrouse, S. 2008. *Histoire de l'Asie centrale contemporaine*. Paris: Fayard.

Comelli, M., Greco, E. and Tocci, N. 2006. *From Boundary to the Border Land: Transforming the Meaning of Borders in Europe through the European Neighbourhood Policy*, Working Paper EU – Consent Constructing European Network.

Committee of Independent Experts. 1999. *First Report on Allegations Regarding Fraud, Mismanagement and Nepotism in the European Commission*, 15 March.

Coppieters, B., Emerson, M., Kovziridse, T., Noutcheva, G., Tocci, N. and M. Vahl. 2004. *Europeanisation and Conflict Resolution: Case Studies from the European Periphery*. Ghent: Academia Press.

Copsey, N. 2007. 'The Member States and the European Neighbourhood Policy.' *European Research Working Papers Series No. 20*. European Research Institute: University of Birmingham.

Copsey, N. and Pomorska, K. 2010. 'Poland's Power and Influence in the European Union: The Case of its Eastern Policy', *Comparative European Politics*, 8(3), 281–303.

Cornell, S.E. and Starr, S.F. (eds). 2009. *The Guns of August 2008: Russia's War in Georgia*. Armonk/London: M.E. Sharpe.

Cottey, A. 2009. 'Sub-regional multilateralism in Europe: an Assessment', *EU4Seas papers*. Available at: http://www.eu4seas.eu/images/stories/projects/publications/barcelona/eu4seas_andrew_cottey.pdf

Council of the European Community. 1988. Decision 8/345/CEE 22 June 1988, on the Conclusion of the Joint Declaration on the Establishment of Official Relations between the European Economic Community and the Council of Mutual Economic Assistance, *Official Journal of the European Communities* no. L157/35, 24 June.

Council of the European Union. 1999. 'Common Strategy of the European Union of 4 June 1999 on Russia', 1999/414/CFSP, *Official Journal of the European Communities* No. L157/1, 24 June.

Council of the European Union. 2003. *A Secure Europe in a Better World: European Security Strategy*, Brussels, 12 December, available at: http://ue.eu.int/uedocs/cmsUpload/78367.pdf

Council of the European Union. 2005 15th EU–Russia Summit. Press release, No. 8799/05 (Presse 110) Moscow, 10 May.

Council of the European Union, General Secretariat. 2007b. *The EU and Central Asia: Strategy for a New Partnership*, October. Available at: http://ue.eu.int/uedocs/cmsUpload/EU_CtrlAsia_EN-RU.pdf

Council of the European Union 2008a. *Consolidated Versions of the Treaty on European Union and the Treaty on the Functioning of the European Union*, 6655/1/08, 30 April, available at: http://www.consilium.europa.eu/uedocs/cmsUpload/st06655-re01.en08.pdf

Council of the European Union 2008b. *Brussels European Council 19–20 June 2008, Presidency Conclusions*, 17 July, available at: http:/www.consilium.europa.eu/uedocs/cms_data/docs/pressdata/en/ec/101346.pdf

Council of the European Union 2008c. *Report on the Implementation of the EU Security Strategy: Providing Security in a Changing World*, 11 December, S407/08, available at: http://www.consilium.europa.eu/ueDocs/cms_Data/docs/pressdata/EN/reports/104630.pdf

Council of the European Union. 2009. Joint Declaration of the Prague Eastern Partnership Summit, 7 May, 8435/09.

Council of the European Union. 2010. *Joint Progress Report by the Council and the European Commission to the European Council on the implementation of the EU Strategy for Central Asia*, 11402/10 COEST 194, 28 June.

Court of Auditors of the European Union, 'Rapport n°25/98 relatif aux opérations engagées par l'Union européenne dans le domaine de la sûreté nucléaire dans les pays d'Europe centrale et orientale et les Nouveaux États Indépendants (1990–1997)' (consulted in French), *Journal officiel des Communautés européennes* n° C35, 9 February.

Cremona, M. 2004. 'The European Neighbourhood Policy: Legal and Institutional Issues', *CDDRL Working Papers* no. 25, November.

Cremona, M. and Hillion, C. 2006. 'The Potentials and Limits of the European Neighbourhood Policy', in: Mayhew, A. and Copsey, N. (eds), 'The European Neighbourhood Policy: The Case of Ukraine', Sussex: University of Sussex, *SEI Seminar Papers No. 1*: 20–44.

Cremona, M. and Hillion, C. 2006. 'L'Union fait la force? Potential and Limits of the European Neighbourhood Policy as an integrated EU Foreign and Security Policy', *EUI Working Paper* LAW No. 2006/39.

Cremona, M. and Meloni, G. 2007. 'The European Neighbourhood Policy: A Framework for Modernisation?', *EUI Working Paper* LAW No. 21/2007.

Cremona, M. 2008. 'Coherence through Law: What Difference will the Treaty of Lisbon Make?', in: Portela, C. and Raube, K. (eds), 2008. 'Revisiting Coherence in EU Foreign Policy'. *Hamburg Review of Social Sciences*, 3(1), 11–36.

Dave, B. 2008. 'The EU and Kazakhstan: is the pursuit of energy and security cooperation compatible with the promotion of human rights and democratic reforms?', in: Melvin, N.J. (ed.), *Engaging Central Asia*. Brussels: Centre for European Policy Studies, 43–68.

Daucé, F. 2008. *La Russie post-soviétique*. Paris: La Découverte.

Delcour, L. 2002. *La politique de l'Union européenne en Russie, 1990–2000: de l'assistance au partenariat?* Paris: L'Harmattan.

Delcour, L. 2003.'La refonte de l'aide européenne à la Russie', *Revue d'études comparatives Est-Ouest*, No. 4.

Delcour, L. 2005. 'EC Delegations in the Former USSR: Towards a New Political Assertiveness?', paper presented at the conference 'The EU as an External Actor', Université libre de Bruxelles, Brussels, May.

Delcour, L. 2006. 'La politique de voisinage et les relations russo-européennes: partenariat stratégique ou lutte d'influence?', *Etudes européennes* n°9.

Delcour, L. 2007a. 'Does the European Neighbourhood Policy Make a Difference? Policy Patterns and Reception in Ukraine and Russia', *European Political Economy Review* No. 7, 118–55.

Delcour, L. 2007b. 'Comment la Russie voit-elle le monde ? Eléments d'analyse d'une politique étrangère en mutation', *Revue internationale et stratégique* n°68, Winter 2007–2008, 133–41.

Delcour, L. and Ternova, I. 2007. 'Quelle coopération régionale pour les pays d'Asie Centrale?', IRIS, *Actualités Russie CEI*, n°4, October, available at: http://www.iris-france.org/docs/pdf/actu_cei/2007-10-24.pdf

Delcour, L. and Tulmets, E. (eds) 2007. 'Is the European Union an International Actor in the Making? The European Neighbourhood Policy as a Capability Test', *European Political Economy Review*, No. 7, 3–8.

Delcour, L. 2008a. 'L'énergie, un enjeu-clé de la Présidence française de l'Union européenne', *Revue internationale et stratégique*, 69, 37–44.

Delcour, L. 2008b. 'Voisine malgré elle: l'Ukraine et la politique européenne de voisinage', *Revue d'études politiques et constitutionnelles est-européennes*, n° 2, Bruylant, 33–48.

Delcour, L. 2008c. 'A Missing Eastern Dimension ? The ENP and Region-Building in the Post-Soviet Area', in: Delcour, L. and Tulmets, E. *Pioneer Europe? Testing European Foreign Policy in its Neighbourhood*. Baden-Baden: Nomos, 161–76.

Delcour, L. and Tulmets, E. (eds) 2008. *Pioneer Europe ? Testing EU Foreign Policy in the Neighbourhood*. Baden-Baden: Nomos.

Delcour, L. 2010. '1989: Towards a Global Europe?', in: Lawson, G., Armbruster, C. and Cox, M. (eds), *The Global 1989: Continuity and Change in World Politics 1989–2009*. Cambridge: Cambridge University Press.

Delcour, L., Manoli, P. 2010. *The Black Sea Synergy: Results and Possible Ways Forward*, European Parliament, note for the Foreign Affairs Committee.

De Lombaerde, P., Schulz, M. (eds) 2009. *The EU and World Regionalism: The Makability of Regions in the 21st Century*. Farnham: Ashgate.

Delors, J. 1992. *Le nouveau concert européen*. Paris: Odile Jacob.

Denison, M. 2008. 'Turkmenistan and the EU: Contexts and Possibilities for Greater Engagement', in: Melvin, N.J. (ed.), *Engaging Central Asia*. Brussels: Centre for European Policy Studies, 81–104

Diez, T. 1999. 'Speaking "Europe": The Politics of Integration Discourse', *Journal of European Public Policy*, 6(4), 598–613.

Diez, T. 2005. 'Constructing the Self and Changing Others: Reconsidering "Normative Power Europe"', *Millennium*, 33(3), 613–36.

Dijk, T.A. Van. 2001. 'Critical Discourse Analysis', in: Schiffrin, D., Tannen, D. and Hamilton, H.E. (eds), *The Handbook of Discourse Analysis*. Oxford: Blackwell, 352–71.

Dijk, T.A. van (ed.). 2007. *Discourse Studies*. London: Sage.

Di Maggio, P. and Powell, P. 1983. 'The Iron Cage Revisited: Institutional Isomorphism and Collective Rationality in Organizational Fields', *American Sociological Review*, 48(2), 147–60.

Di Puppo, L. 2009. 'The Externalization of JHA Policies in Georgia: Partner or Hotbed of Threats?', *Journal of European Integration*, (31)1, 103–18.

Dmitrova, A. and Dragneva, R. 2009. 'Constraining External Governance: Interdependence with Russia and the CIS as Limits to the EU's Rule Transfer in the Ukraine', *Journal of European Public Policy*, (16)6, 853–72.

Duchêne, F. 1973. 'The European Communities and the Uncertainties of Interdependence', in: Kohnstamm, M. and Hager, W. (eds), *A Nation Writ*

Large? Foreign Policy Problems before the European Community, London: Macmillan, 1–73.

Duchêne, G. 1994. 'Intégration ou désintégration économique dans l'ex-URSS', *Revue économique*, n°3, 574–85.

Edwards, G. and Regelsberger, E. 1990. *Europe's Global Links*, London: Pinter.

Eisemann P.-M. and Koskenniemi, M. (eds). 2000. *State Succession: Codification Tested Against the Facts*. The Hague: Academy of International Law.

Ellner, A. 2008. 'Regional Security in a Global Context: A Critical Appraisal of European Approaches to Security', *European Security*, 17(1), 9–31.

Emerson, M. 2004. 'European Neighbourhood Policy: Strategy or Placebo?', *CEPS Working Document No. 215*, November.

Emerson, M. (ed.) 2005. 'EU–Russia: Four Common Spaces and the Proliferation of the Fuzzy', *CEPS Policy Brief No. 71*, May.

Emerson, M., Aydin, S., Noutcheva, G. Tocci, N., Vahl, M. and Youngs, R. 2005. 'The Reluctant Debutante – The EU as Promoter of Democracy in its Neighbourhood', in: Emerson, M. (ed.), *Democratisation in the European Neighbourhood*. Brussels: CEPS, 169–230.

Emerson, M., Noutcheva, G. and Popescu, N. 2007. 'European Neighbourhood Policy Two Years on: Time indeed for an "ENP Plus"', in: *CEPS Policy Brief No. 126*, March.

Emerson, M. 2008. 'The EU's New Black Sea Policy: What Kind of Regionalism is This?', *CEPS Working Document No. 297*, July.

Emerson, M., Boonstra, J., Hasanova, N., Laruelle, M. and Peyrouse, S. 2010. *Into EurAsia. Monitoring the EU's Central Asia Strategy*, report of the EUCAM project, Brussels/Madrid: CEPS/FRIDE.

Engelen, H., 2004. 'The Construction of a Region in the Baltic Sea Area', paper presented at the Fifth Pan-European Conference, The Hague.

EU–Georgia European Neighbourhood Policy Action Plan. 2006. Available at: http://ec.europa.eu/world/enp/pdf/action_plans/georgia_enp_ap_final_en.pdf

EU–Ukraine European Neighbourhood Policy Action Plan. 2005. Available at: http://ec.europa.eu/world/enp/pdf/action_plans/ukraine_enp_ap_final_en.pdf

EU–Kazakhstan Memorandum of Understanding on Cooperation in the Field of Energy. 2006. Brussels, 4 December.

EU–Russia Memorandum on an Early Warning Mechanism in the Energy Sector within the Framework of the EU–Russia Energy Dialogue. 2009. Moscow, 16 November.

European Commission. 1991. 'Proposal for a Council Regulation (EEC, EURATOM) concerning aid to assist economic reform and recovery in the Union of Soviet Socialist Republics', COM (91) 172 final, 8/05/1991, *Official Journal of the European Communities* no. C140, 30 May.

European Commission. 1992a. *Communication to the Council*, SEC (92)39, 9 January.

European Commission. 1992b. *Communication to the Council*, SEC (92)373 final, 26 February.

European Commission. 1992c. Press release (92)226, 19 March.

European Commission, DG IA. 1996a. *TACIS Contract Information. Budget 1995, Part II.* Brussels.

European Commission. 1996b. *The Baltic Sea Region Initiative*, Communication of the Commission, SEC (96)608 final. Brussels, 10 April.

European Commission. 1997. Regional Co-operation in the Black Sea area: State of Play, Perspectives for EU action Encouraging its Further Development, Communication of the Commission COM(97)597 final. Brussels, 14 November.

European Commission, DG IA. 1998a. *Contract Information. Budget 1996 and 1996–1997.* Brussels.

European Commission. 1998b. *A Northern Dimension for the Policies of the Union*, Communication of the Commission COM(98)589 final. Brussels, 25 November.

European Commission, DGIA. 1999a. *TACIS annual report 1998*, COM(99)380. Brussels, 23 July.

European Commission, DG Energy. 1999b. *European Energy Outlook to 2020.*

European Commission. 2000. *TACIS Annual Report 1999*, COM (2000) 835 final. Brussels, 20 December.

European Commission. 2003. *Wider Europe Neighbourhood. A New Framework for Relations with our Eastern and Southern Neighbours.* COM(2003) 104 final, 11 March.

European Commission. 2004a. *European Neighbourhood Policy. Strategy Paper*, COM (2004) 373 final. Brussels, 12 May.

European Commission. 2004b. *The Energy Dialogue Between The European Union and the Russian Federation between 2000 and 2004*, Communication to the Council and the Parliament, COM (2004) 777 final, 13 December.

European Commission 2005. *2004 Annual Progress Report on the Implementation of the Northern Dimension Action Plan.* Commission Staff Working Document, SEC(2005) 688. Brussels, 20 May.

European Commission. 2006a. *Green Paper. A European Strategy for Sustainable, Competitive and Secure Energy.* Brussels, 8 March.

European Commission. 2006b. *An External Policy to Serve Europe's Energy Interests.* Paper from Commission SG/HR for the European Council, S160/06.

European Commission. 2006c. *Strengthening the European Neighbourhood Policy*, Communication to the Council and to the European Parliament, COM 2006 (726) final, 4 December.

European Commission. 2007a. *Black Sea Synergy, A New Regional Cooperation Initiative*, communication to the Council and the Parliament, COM (2007) 160 final, 11 April.

European Commission, 2007b. *Non-Paper Expanding on the Proposals Contained in the Communication to the Council and to the European Parliament on 'Strengthening the ENP' – COM 2006 (726) final, of 4 December*, available at: http://ec.europa.eu/world/enp/documents_en.htm.

European Commission. 2007c. *A Strong Neighbourhood Policy.* Communication to the Council and to the European Parliament, COM 2007 (774) final, 5 December.

European Commission. 2008a. *Implementation of the Neighbourhood Policy in 2007. Communication to the Council and to the European Parliament*, COM (2008) 164, 3 April.

European Commission. 2008b. *EU Russia Common Spaces. Progress Report 2007*, 11 April. Available at: http://ec.europa.eu/external_relations/russia/docs/commonspaces_prog_report2007.pdf

European Commission. 2008c. *Report on the First Year of Implementation of the Black Sea Synergy*, Communication to the Council and to the European Parliament, COM (2008) 391 final, 19 June.

European Commission. 2008d. *Second Strategic Energy Review. An EU Energy Security and Solidarity Action Plan.* Communication to the European Parliament, the Council, the European Economic and Social Committee and the Committee of the Regions, COM (2008) 781 final, 13 November.

European Commission. 2008e. *Eastern Partnership.* Communication to the Council and to the European Parliament, COM (2008) 823 final, 3 December.

European Commission. 2009a. *Implementation of the Neighbourhood Policy in 2008.* Communication to the Council and to the European Parliament, COM (2009)188/3, 23 April.

European Commission. 2009b. *EU Russia Common Spaces. Progress Report 2008.* 24 April. Available at: http://ec.europa.eu/external_relations/russia/docs/commonspaces_prog_report_2008_en.pdf

European Commission. 2009c. ENPI National Indicative Programme 2011–2013 Georgia. Available at: http://ec.europa.eu/world/enp/pdf/country/2011_enpi_nip_georgia_en.pdf

European Commission. 2010. *Taking stock of the European Neighbourhood Policy.* Communication to the Council and to the European Parliament, COM (2010)207, 12 May.

European Commission and Council of the European Union. 2008. *Joint Progress Report by the Council and the European Commission to the European Council on the implementation of the EU Central Asia Strategy*, Available at http://ec.europa.eu/external_relations/central_asia/docs/progress_report_0608_en.pdf.

European Communities. 1990. 'Agreement between the European Economic Community and the European Atomic Energy Community, and the Union of Soviet Socialist Republics on Trade and Economic Cooperation', *Official Journal of the European Communities* no. L68, 15 March.

European Community. 2007. *Regional Strategy Paper for Assistance to Central Asia 2007–2013.* Available at: http://ec.europa.eu/external_relations/central_asia/rsp/07_13_en.pdf

European Council. 1991. Presidency Conclusions, Maastricht European Council, *Bulletin* 16/12/1991, available at: http://www.europarl.europa.eu/summits/maastricht/ma1_en.pdf

European Council. 1998. Conclusions of the Presidency, *Bulletin of the European Union*, No. 12.

European Council. 1999a. Common Strategy of the European Union on Russia, adopted on 4 June, 1999/414/PESC.

European Council. 1999b. Common Strategy of the European Union on Ukraine, adopted on 11 December, 1999/877/CFSP.

European Parliament. 2006a. European Parliament resolution on security of energy supply in the European Union. P6 TA(2006)0110, 23 March, available at: http://www.europarl.europa.eu/sides/getDoc.do?type=TA&reference=P6-TA-2006 0110&language=EN&ring=B6-2006-0192.

European Parliament. 2006b. European Parliament resolution on a European strategy for sustainable, competitive and secure energy – Green paper. P6 TA(2006)0603, 14 December. Available at: http://www.europarl.europa.eu/sides/getDoc.do?pubRef=-//EP//TEXT+TA+P6-TA-2006-0603+0+DOC+XML+V0//EN&language=EN

European Parliament. 2007. Resolution of 15 November 2007 on strengthening the European Neighbourhood Policy, including the proposal of a EURONEST Parliamentary Assembly, A6-0414/2007, available at: http://www.europarl.europa.eu/sides/getDoc.do?type=TA&language=EN&reference=P6-TA-2007-0538

European Parliament. 2008a. *Resolution of 17 January 2008 on a Black Sea Regional Policy Approach*, P6_TA-PROV(2008)0017. Available at: http://www.europarl.europa.eu/sides/getDoc.do?type=TA&reference=P6-TA-2008-0017&language=EN

European Parliament. 2008b. *Resolution of 3 September 2008 on the situation in Georgia*, P6_TA(2008)0396. Available at: http://www.europarl.europa.eu/sides/getDoc.do?pubRef=-//EP//TEXT+TA+P6-TA-2008-0396+0+DOC+XML+V0//EN

European Political Cooperation. 1991. 'Déclaration sur les lignes directrices sur la reconnaissance de nouveaux États en Europe orientale et en Union soviétique' (consulted in French). Extraordinary Ministerial Meeting, 16/12/1991, *Press Release P. 128/01.*

European Political Cooperation. 1992. 'Déclaration sur la reconnaissance des Républiques de la Communauté d'États Indépendants' (consulted in French), *Press Release P8/92*, 15 January.

Farrell, M. 2005. 'EU External Relations: Exporting the EU Model of Governance?', *European Foreign Affairs Review*, 10, 451–62.

Farrell, M. 2009. 'EU policy towards other regions: policy learning in the external promotion of regional integration', *Journal of European Public Policy*, 16(8), 1165–84.

Fawcett, L. 2003. 'The evolving architecture of regionalization', in: Pugh, M.P. and Sidho, W.P.S., *The United Nations and Regional Security: Europe and Beyond*. Boulder: Lynne Rienner, 11–30.

Fawcett, L. 2004. 'Exploring Regional Domains: A Comparative History of Regionalism', *International Affairs*, 3, 429–40.

Feklyunina, V. 2008. 'The "Great Diversification Game": Russia's Vision of the European Union's Energy Projects in the Shared Neighbourhood', *Journal of Contemporary European Research*, 4(2), 130–48.

Ferrero-Waldner, B. 2007. 'The European Neighbourhood Policy and Black Sea Synergy – new opportunities for Bulgaria', SPEECH/07/538, Public Lecture, Aula Maxima, Sofia University, Sofia, 17 September.

Ferrero-Waldner, B. 2008. 'Black Sea Synergy: The EU's Approach to the Black Sea Region.' Black Sea Synergy Ministerial Meeting, Kyiv, 14 February.

Filippov, M. 2009. 'Diversionary Role of the Georgia–Russia Conflict: International Constraints and Domestic Appeal', *Europe–Asia Studies*, 61(10), 1825–47.

Filtenborg, M., Gänzle, S. and Johansson, E. 2002. 'An Alternative Theoretical Approach to EU Foreign Policy: "Network Governance" and the Case of the Northern Dimension Initiative', *Cooperation and Conflict*, 37(10), 387–407.

Fischer, S. 2006a. 'Russia and EU: New Developments in a Difficult Partnership', in: Friedrich Ebert Stiftung, *Partnership with Russia in Europe Scenarios for a Future Partnership and Cooperation Agreement*, 23–32.

Fischer, S. 2006b. 'Die EU und Russland. Konflikte und Potentiale einer schwierigen Partnerschaft', Stiftung Wissenschaft und Politik, *Studie*, 34, December.

Fischer, S. (ed.) 2008. 'Ukraine: Quo Vadis', *Chaillot Paper No. 108*, EU Institute for Security Studies.

Fischer, S. (ed.) 2009. 'Back from the Cold? The EU and Belarus in 2009', *Chaillot Paper No. 119*, EU Institute for Security Studies.

Fotiou, E. 2009. '"Caucasus Stability and Cooperation Platform": What is at Stake for Regional Cooperation?', *ICBSS Policy Brief*, No. 16.

Friedrich Ebert Stiftung. 2006. *Partnership with Russia in Europe Scenarios for a Future Partnership and Cooperation Agreement*.

Gänzle, S. 2008. 'Externalizing EU Governance and the European Neighbourhood Policy: a Framework for Analysis.' Presentation prepared for 'The EU as a Global Actor' Conference at Dalhousie University EU Centre of Excellence, May.

Gaspers, J. 2008. 'The Quest for European Foreign Policy Consistency and the Treaty of Lisbon', *Humanitas Journal of European Studies*.

Gautron, J.-C. 1997. 'Otnosheniya mezhdu Evropeiskim Soyuzom i Rossiei: istoricheskii i teoreticheskii aspekty' [Relations between the European Union and Russia: historical and theoretical aspects], paper presented at the International conference '40 Years of Rome Treaties', St.Petersburg, available at: http://www.edc.spb.ru/activities/conferences/40years/gotron.html

Gauttier, P. 2004. 'Horizontal Coherence and the External Competencies of the European Union', *European Law Journal*, 10(1), 23–41. Available at: http://papers.ssrn.com/sol3/papers.cfm?abstract_id=513548

General Affairs and External Relations Council 2007. *Strengthening the European Neighbourhood Policy*, Presidency Progress Report, 18/19 June.

Gordadze, T. 2009. 'Georgian–Russian Relations in the 1990s', in: Cornell, S.E, and Starr, S.F. (eds). *The Guns of August 2008: Russia's War in Georgia*. Armonk/London: M.E. Sharpe, 28–48.

Goujon, A. 2005. 'L'Europe élargie en quête d'identité: légitimation et politisation de la politique européenne de voisinage', *Politique européenne*, n° 5, 137–63.

Goujon, A. 2009. *Révolutions politiques et identitaires en Ukraine et en Biélorussie (1988–2008)*. Paris: Belin.

Grant, C. and Barysch, K. 2003. 'The EU–Russia Energy Dialogue', *CER Briefing Note*, May.

Grevi, G. and Vasconcelos A. (eds) 2008. 'Partnerships for Effective Multilateralism. EU Relations with Brazil, China, India and Russia', *Chaillot Paper*, n°109, May.

Gromadzki, G. 2009. 'Belarusian Foreign Policy – Change or Continuity?', in Fischer, S. (ed.), 2009. 'Back from the Cold? The EU and Belarus in 2009', *Chaillot Paper No. 119*, EU Institute for Security Studies, 93–104.

Grotzky, D. and Isic, M. 2008. 'The Black Sea Region: Clashing Identities and Risks to European Stability', *CAP Policy Analysis No. 4*, October.

Haas, E.B. 1964. *Beyond the Nation-State: Functionalism and International Organization*. Stanford: Stanford University Press.

Haas, E.B. 1968. *The Uniting of Europe: Political, Social and Economic Forces 1950–1957*. Stanford: Stanford University Press.

Hall, M. 2008. 'The EU and Uzbekistan: Where To Go From Here?', in: Melvin, N.J. (ed.), *Engaging Central Asia*. Brussels: Centre for European Policy Studies, 68–80.

Hamant, H. 2008. *Démembrement de l'URSS et problèmes de succession d'Etats*, Brussels: Bruylant.

Hänggi, H., Roloff, R. and Rüland, J. (eds), 2006. *Interregionalism and International Relations*. London/New York: Routledge.

Haukkala, H. 2000. 'The Making of the European Union's Common Strategy on Russia', *UPI Working Papers No. 28*.

Haukkala, H. 2003. 'A Hole in the Wall? Dimensionalism and the EU's New Neighbourhood Policy', *UPI Working Papers No. 41*.

Haukkala, H. 2005a. 'The Relevance of Norms and Values in the EU's Russia Policy', *FIIA Working Papers No. 52*.

Haukkala, H. 2005b. 'The Northern Dimension of EU Foreign Policy', in: Antonenko, O. and Pinnick, K. (eds), *Russia and the European Union: Prospects for a New Relationship*. London/New York: Routledge and IISS.

Haukkala, H. 2008a. 'The Russian Challenge to EU Normative Power: The Case of European Neighbourhood Policy', *The International Spectator*, 43(2), June, 35–47.

Haukkala, H. 2008b. 'The European Union as a Regional Normative Hegemon: The Case of European Neighbourhood Policy', *Europe–Asia Studies*, 60(9), November, 1601–22.

Haukkala, H. 2009. 'Lost in Translation? Why the EU has Failed to Influence Russia's Development', *Europe–Asia Studies*, 61(10), 1757–75.

Haukkala, H. 2010. *The EU–Russia Strategic Partnership: The Limits of Post-Sovereignty in International Relations*. London: Routledge.

Helly, D. 2006. 'EUJUST THEMIS in Georgia: An ambitious bet on Rule of Law', in: Nowak, A. (ed.), 'Civilian Crisis Management: The EU Way', *Chaillot Paper*, Institute for Security Studies of the European Union, available at: www.eu-iss.org

Hettne, B., Inotai, A. and Sunkel, O. (eds), 1999. *The New Regionalism. 1. Globalism and the New Regionalism*. Basingstoke: Macmillan/New York: Saint Martin's Press,

Hettne, B., Inotai, A. and Sunkel, O. (eds), 2001. 'Regionalism, Security and Development: A Comparative Perspective', in *Comparing Regionalism: Implications for Global Development*. London: Palgrave.

Hettne, B. and Söderbaum, F. 2005. 'Civilian Power or Soft Imperialism? The EU as a Global Actor and the Role of Interregionalism', *European Foreign Affairs Review*, 10, 2005, 535–52.

Hill, C. and Smith, M.(eds). 2005. *International Relations and the European Union*. Oxford: Oxford University Press.

Hillion, C. 1998. 'Partnership and Cooperation Agreements Between the European Union and the New Independent States of the ex-Soviet Union', *European Foreign Affairs Review*, 3(3), 399–420.

Hillion, C. 2000. 'Partnership between the European Union and the Newly Independent States', *Georgian Law Review*, 3rd and 4th quarters, 3–18.

Hillion, C. 2008. 'Tous pour un, un pour tous! Coherence in the External Relations of the European Union', in: Cremona, M. *Developments in EU External Relations Law*. Oxford: Oxford University Press, 10–36.

Hillion, C. and Mayhew, A. 2009. 'The Eastern Partnership – something new or window-dressing', *Sussex European Institute Working Paper No. 109*.

Hohmann, S. 2006. 'Le narcotrafic en Asie Centrale: enjeux géopolitiques et répercussions sociales', *Revue internationale et stratégique*, n°64, Winter 2006–2007, 110–19.

Illarionov, A. 2009. 'The Russian Leadership's Preparation for War, 1999–2008', in: Cornell, S.E and Starr, S.F. (eds). 2009. *The Guns of August 2008: Russia's War in Georgia*. Armonk/London: M.E. Sharpe, 49–84.

International Crisis Group 2006. 'Central Asia: What Role for the European Union?', *Asia Report No. 113*, 10 April.

Jeandesboz, J. 2007. 'Définir le voisin. La genèse de la politique européenne de voisinage'. *Cultures et conflits*, 66.

Joenniemi, P. 2002. 'Can Europe Be Told From The North? Tapping into the EU's. Northern Dimension', *Working Paper No. 12*, COPRI.

Joenniemi, P. and Sergounin, A. 2003. *Russia and EU's Northern Dimension: Encounter or Clash of Civilizations?* Nizhny Novgorod: Linguistic University Press.

Joenniemi, P. 2007. 'Regionalisation as Europe-Making: The Case of Europe's North', in: Hayashi, T. and Fukuda, H. (eds), *Regions in Central and Eastern Europe: Past and Present*. Slavic Research Centre, Hokkaido University, 21–48.

Joenniemi, P. 2009a. 'The EU Strategy for the Baltic Sea Region: a Catalyst for What?', *DIIS Brief*, August.

Joenniemi, P. 2009b. 'Europe's North: A Model Region?', *EU4Seas papers*. http://www.eu4seas.eu/images/stories/projects/publications/barcelona/eu4seas_pertti_joenniemi.pdf

Johansson-Nogués, E. 2009a. 'Cooperation in the Baltic and the Mediterranean: The Jean Monnet method at work ?', *EU4Seas Paper*.

Johansson-Nogués, E. 2009b. 'Is the EU's Foreign Policy Identity an Obstacle? The European Union, the Northern Dimension and the Union for the Mediterranean'. *European Political Economy Review*, 9, Autumn, 24–48.

Kalyuzhnova, Y. and Lynch, D. (eds). 2000. *The Euro-Asian World: A Period of Transition*. Basingstoke: Macmillan.

Karaganov, S. (ed.) 2005a. *Russia–EU Relations. The Present Situation and Prospects*. Brussels: CEPS Working Document No. 225, July.

Karaganov, S. (ed.) 2005b. 'Russia's European: Strategy: A New Start', *Russia in Global Affairs*, No. 3, July–September.

Kassenova, N. 2008. 'A View from the Region', in: Melvin, N.J. (ed.), *Engaging Central Asia*. Brussels: CEPS, 137–50.

Kassenova, N. 2009. 'The Gas Crisis and the Financial Crisis: the Impact on EU – Central Asia Relations in the Energy Sphere', *ISS Opinion*, European Institute for Security Studies, April.

Kelley, J. 2006. 'New Wine in Old Wineskins: Policy Adaptation in the European Neighborhood Policy', *Journal of Common Market Studies*, 44(1), March, 29–55.

Kempe, I. and Smith, H. 2006. *A Decade of Partnership and Cooperation in Russia–EU Relations*. Munich: Centre for Applied Policy.

Kempe, I. 2007. 'A New Ostpolitik? Priorities and Realities of Germany's EU Council Presidency', *CAP Policy Analysis No. 4*, August.

Kempe, I. and Grotzky, D. 2007. 'Crossroads of Cooperation: The Future of EU–Russia relations and the Impact of the Baltic States', *Lithuanian Foreign Policy Review*, 19, available at: http://www.lfpr.lt/uploads/File/2007-19/Kempe_ENG.pdf

Khalib, A. 2006. 'L'islam et l'Etat post-soviétique en Asie centrale', *Revue internationale et stratégique*, n°64, Winter 2006–2007, 101–9.

Kimmage, D. 2008. 'Security Challenges in Central Asia: Implications for the EU's Engagement Strategy', in: Melvin, N.J. (ed.), *Engaging Central Asia*. Brussels: Centre for European Policy Studies, 9–19.

Koblandin, K.I. 2008. 'Integratsionnye processy v Centralnoj Asii', [Integration Processes in Central Asia], VI Annual Almaty Conference 'Central Asia: Current Status and Prospects of Regional Interaction', Almaty: KISI/Friedrich Ebert Stiftung/ Fund of the First President of the Republic of Kazakhstan.

Koopmann, M. and Lequesne, C. (eds) 2007. *Partner oder Beitrittskandidaten?: die Nachbarschaftspolitik der Europäischen Union auf dem Prüfstand*. Baden-Baden: Nomos.

Kobrinskaya, I. 2008. 'The Black Sea Region in Russia's Current Foreign Policy Paradigm', PONARS Eurasia Policy Memo No. 41.

Korostoleva, E. 2010. 'Rocking the Boat? Security Dilemmas for the Contested Neighbourhood' (forthcoming), manuscript made available to author.

Kratochvíl, P. 2006. 'The European Neighbourhood Policy: A Clash of Incompatible Interpretations', in: Kratochvíl, Petr (ed.) *The European Union and its Neighbourhood: Policies, Problems, Priorities*. Prague: Institute of International Relations, 13–28.

Kratochvíl, P. 2008. 'Constructing the EU's External Roles: Friend in the South, Teacher in the East?', in: Delcour, L. and Tulmets, E., *Pioneer Europe? Testing European Foreign Policy in the Neighbourhood*. Baden-Baden: Nomos, 230–9.

Kratochvíl, P. 2009. 'Discursive Constructions of the EU's Identity in the Neighbourhood: An Equal Among Equals or the Power Centre?', *European Political Economy Review*, 9, 5–23.

Kratochvíl, P. and Tulmets, E. 2010. *Constructivism and Rationalism in EU External Relations*. Baden-Baden: Nomos.

Korovkin, V.Y. 1992. 'Opyt ES dlya ekonomicheskogoy soobshchestva suverennykh respublik' [The European Community's experience for the Economic Community of sovereign republics], *Mirovaya Èkonomika i Mezhdunarodnye Otnoshenya*, no. 1, 95–105.

Kushkumbayev, S. 2008. 'Regional'noe vzaimodejstvie v Central'noj Asii: opyt i problemy', [Regional interaction in Central Asia: experience and problems], VI Annual Almaty Conference 'Central Asia: Current Status and Prospects of Regional Interaction', Almaty: KISI/Friedrich Ebert Stiftung/Fund of the First President of the Republic of Kazakhstan.

Laïdi, Z (ed.), 2008. *EU Foreign Policy in a Globalized World: Normative Power and Social Preferences*. London: Routledge.

Lankina, T. 2005, 'Explaining European Aid to Russia', *Post-Soviet Affairs*, 21(4) October–December, 309–334.

Laruelle, M. 2006. 'Le nouveau rôle de la Russie en Asie centrale: les migrations de travail des Centre-Asiatiques vers la Fédération russe', *Revue internationale et stratégique*, n°64, Winter 2006–2007, 132–141.

Laruelle, M. and Peyrouse, S. 2006. *Asie centrale, la dérive autoritaire. Cinq républiques entre héritage soviétique, dictature et islam.* Paris: CERI-Autrement.

Laruelle, M. and Vinatier, L. 2007. 'Le Kazakhstan, porte d'entrée' de l'Union européenne en Asie Centrale?', *Tribune No. 14*, Institut Thomas More, November.

Lavenex, S. 2004. 'EU External Governance in "Wider Europe"', *Journal of European Public Policy*, 11(4) August, 680–700.

Lavenex, S. 2007. 'A Governance Perspective', paper presented at the UACES conference 'The Study of the European Neighbourhood Policy: Methodological, Theoretical and Empirical Challenges', University of Nottingham, October.

Lavenex, S. and Wichmann, N. 2009. 'The External Governance of EU Internal Security', *Journal of European Integration*, (31)1, 83–102.

Lavenex, S., Lehmkuhl, D. and Wichmann, N. 2009. 'Modes of External Governance: a Crossnational and Cross-Sectoral Comparison', *Journal of European Public Policy*, (16)6, 813–33.

Lavenex, S. and Schimmelfennig, F. 2009. 'EU Rules beyond EU Borders: Theorizing External Governance in European Politics', *Journal of European Public Policy*, (16) 6, 791–812.

Leonard, M. and Popescu, N. 2007. 'A Power Audit of EU–Russia relations', *ECFR Policy Paper*.

Lesser, I. 2007. 'Global Trends, Regional Consequences: Wider Strategic Influences on the Black Sea', *Xenophon Paper No. 4*.

Liberti, F. 2008. 'The European Union and the Southern Mediterranean: L'Union pour la Méditerranée, a French Attempt to Refocus the EU Engagement Toward the South', in: Delcour, L. and Tulmets, E., *Pioneer Europe? Testing European Foreign Policy in the Neighbourhood*. Baden-Baden: Nomos, 93–101.

Light, M. 1988. *The Soviet Theory of International Relations*. Brighton: Wheatsheaf.

Light, M., White, S. and Löwenhardt, J. 2000. 'A Wider Europe: The View From Moscow and Kyiv', *International Affairs*, 76(1), 77–88.

Light, M. 2006. 'The Place of Europe in Russian Foreign Policy', in: Allison, R., Light M. and White S., *Putin's Russia and the Enlarged Europe*. London: Chatham House Papers, Oxford: Blackwell.

Lipkin, M. 2006. 'The Soviet Union, CMEA and the Question of First EEC Enlargement', XIV International Economic History Congress, Helsinki, available at: http://www.helsinki.fi/iehc2006/papers3/Lipkin.pdf

Lippert, B. 1990. 'EC-CMEA Relations: Normalization and Beyond', in: Edwards, G. and Regelsberger, E., *Europe's Global Links*, 119–40.

Lippert, B. 1993. 'Questions and Scenarios on EC-CIS Republics Relations. An Outline on the Political Dimension', in: Ehrahrt, H.-G., Kreikemeyer, A. and

Zagorski A. (eds), *The Former Soviet Union and European Security: Between Integration and Re-Nationalization*. Baden-Baden: Nomos.

Lussac, S. 2010. *Géopolitique du Caucase. Au carrefour énergétique de l'Europe de l'Ouest*, Paris: éditions Technip.

Lukyanov, F. 2008. 'Russia–EU: the Partnership that Went Astray', *Europe–Asia Studies*, 60(6).

Lukyanov, F. 2009. *The Future of EU–Russia Relations: A View From Russia*, European Parliament, Policy Department External Policies, Briefing Paper, February.

Lynch, D. (ed.) 2003a. 'La Russie face à l'Europe', *Cahiers de Chaillot* n°60.

Lynch. D. 2003b. 'The New Eastern Dimension of the Enlarged EU', *Cahiers de Chaillot* n°64.

Lynch, D. (ed.) 2005a. 'What Russia Sees', *Cahiers de Chaillot* n°74.

Lynch. D. 2005b. 'The Security Dimension of the European Neighbourhood Policy', *The International Spectator*, (XL) 1, January–March, 33–43.

Lytvynyuk, A. 2007. 'Is Bilateralism a Solution? The Case of Ukraine', in: Cremona, M. and Meloni, G. 'The European Neighbourhood Policy: a Framework for Modernisation?', *EUI Working Paper*, LAW 21/2007, 137–46.

Mahoney, J. 2000. 'Path Dependence in Historical Sociology', *Theory and Society*, 29(4), 507–48.

Makachyrev, A. 2003. 'Europe's Eastern Dimension Russia's Reaction to Poland's Initiative', *PONARS Policy Memo 30.1.*

Makarychev, A. 2008. 'Securitization and Identity: The Black Sea Region as a "Conflict Formation"', *PONARS Eurasia Policy Memo No. 43.*

Makarychev, A. 2009. 'Russia and its 'New Security Architecture' in Europe: A Critical Examination of the Concept', *CEPS Working Document No. 310*, February.

Malfliet, K., Verpoest, L. and Vinokurov, E. (eds), 2007, *The CIS, the EU, and Russia: Challenges of Integration*. London: Palgrave.

Mandil, C. 2008. *Energy Security and the European Union. Proposals for the French Presidency*, Report to the Prime Minister, 21 April.

Manners, I. 2002. 'Normative Power Europe: A Contradiction in Terms', *Journal of Common Market Studies*, 40(2), 235–58.

Manners, I. 2006. 'Normative Power Europe Reconsidered: Beyond the Crossroads', *Journal of European Public Policy*, 13(2), March, 182–99.

Manoli, P. 2009. 'The Dynamics of Sub–Regional Cooperation Around the Black Sea: Continuity and Change', *EU4Seas Papers*, http://www.eu4seas.eu/images/stories/projects/publications/barcelona/eu4seas_panagiota_manoli.pdf

Manoli, P. 2010. *Reinvigorating Black Sea Cooperation: A Policy Discussion*, Policy Report 3, Commission on the Black Sea/Bertelsmann Stiftung.

Maresceau, M. 1989. *The Political and Legal Framework of Trade Relations between the European Community and Eastern Europe*. Dordrecht: Kluwer Academic Publishers.

Maresceau, M. (ed.) 1997. *Enlarging the European Union: Relations between the EU and Central and Eastern Europe*, London: Longman.

Maresceau, M. 1998. 'Les relations entre l'Union européenne et la Russie à un tournant de leur histoire?', in: Raux, J. and Korovkine, V. (eds), *Le partenariat entre l'Union européenne et la Fédération de Russie*, 161–8.

Matveeva, A. 2006. 'EU Stakes in Central Asia', *Chaillot Papers No. 91*, July, special issue.

Mayhew, A. and Copsey, N. (eds), 2006. 'The European Neighbourhood Policy: The Case of Ukraine', Sussex: University of Sussex, *SEI Seminar Papers No. 1*.

Melvin, N.J. 2008. *Engaging Central Asia: The European Union's New Strategy in the Heart of Eurasia*. Brussels: Centre for European Policy Studies.

Meloni, G. 2007. 'Is the Same Toolkit Used During Enlargement Still Applicable to Countries of the New Neighbourhood? A problem of Mismatching Between Objectives and Instruments', in: Cremona, M. and Meloni, G. 'The European Neighbourhood Policy: a Framework for Modernisation?', *EUI Working Paper* LAW No. 21/2007, 97–111.

Meloni, G. 2008. 'Who is my Neighbour?', in: Delcour, L. and Tulmets, E., *Pioneer Europe? Testing European Foreign Policy in the Neighbourhood*. Baden-Baden: Nomos, 35–42.

Mendras, M. 2008. *Russie: l'envers du pouvoir*. Paris: Odile Jacob.

Mény, Y. and Thoenig, J.-C. 1989. *Politiques publiques*. Paris: Presses Universitaires de France.

Micu, N. 2007. 'The Policy of Romania Towards the BSEC and the Black Sea Region', *Xenophon Paper No. 2*, 101–10.

Mikhelidze, N. 2009. *The Eastern Partnership and Conflicts in the South Caucasus: Old Wine in New Skins?*, Istituto d'Affari Internazionale, IAI No. 0923, available at: http://www.iai.it/pdf/DocIAI/IAI0923.pdf

Ministry of Foreign Affairs of the Hellenic Republic. 2006. *Towards an EU Regional Dimension in the Wider Black Sea Area*, working paper, available at: http://www.photius.com/bsec/EU_regional_dimention.pdf

Ministry of Foreign Affairs of the Republic of Poland. 2003. 'Non-Paper with Polish proposals concerning policy towards new Eastern neighbours after EU enlargement', January 2003, in: Stefan Batory Foundation, *EU Enlargement and Neighbourhood Policy*, February.

Ministry of Foreign Affairs of the Russian Federation. 2000a. *Konseptsya inostranoy politiki* (Conception of foreign policy), available at: www.mid.ru

Ministry of Foreign Affairs of the Russian Federation. 2000b. *Mid-term Strategy Towards the European Union 2000–2010*, available at www.mid.ru

Monaghan, A. 2008. '"An Enemy at the Gates" or "From Victory to Victory?" Russian Foreign Policy', *International Affairs*, 4(4), 717–33.

Moravcsik, A. 1993. 'Preferences and Power in the European Community: A Liberal Intergovernmentalist Approach', *Journal of Common Market Studies*, 31(4), December, 473–524.

Moravcsik, A. 2005. 'The European Constitutional Compromise and the Neofunctionalist Legacy', *Journal of European Public Policy*, 12(2), 349–86.

National Security Council of the Russian Federation. 2009. *Strategya natsional'noy bezopasnosti Rossiiskoy Federatsii do 2020 goda [Strategy of National Security of the Russian Federation until 2020]*, adopted by decree No. 537, 12 May. Available at: http://www.scrf.gov.ru/documents/99.html

Natorski, M. 2008. 'National Concerns in the EU Neighbourhood: Spanish and Polish policies on the Southern and Eastern Dimensions', in: Delcour, L. and Tulmets, E., *Pioneer Europe? Testing European Foreign Policy in the Neighbourhood*. Baden-Baden: Nomos, 57–76.

Natorski, M. and Herranz Surrallés, A. 2008. 'Securitizing Moves To Nowhere? The Framing of the European Union's Energy Policy', *Journal of Contemporary European Research*, 4(2), 71–89.

Neumann, I.B. 1994. 'A Region-Building Approach to Northern Europe', *Review of International Studies*, 20, 53–74.

Neumann, I.B. 1996. *Russia and the Idea of Europe: A Study in Identity and International Relations*. London: Routledge.

Nikolov, K. and Gültekin-Punsmann, B. 2007. *Regional Cooperation in the Black Sea Area: Analysis of the Opportunities to Foster Synergies in the Region*, European Parliament, Policy Department External Policies.

Nilsson, N. 2009. 'Georgia's Rose Revolution: The Break with the Past', in: Cornell, S.E. and Starr, S.F. (eds), *The Guns of August 2008: Russia's War in Georgia*. Armonk/London: M.E. Sharpe, 85–103.

Noël, P. 2008. 'Beyond Dependence: How to Deal with Russian Gas', *ECFR Brief*.

Northern Dimension Policy Framework Document, 2006. Available at: http://ec.europa.eu/external_relations/north_dim/docs/frame_pol_1106_en.pdf

Nowak, A (ed.) 2006. 'Civilian crisis management: the EU way', *Chaillot Papers No. 90*.

Nuttall, S. 2005. 'Coherence and Consistency', in: Hill, C. and Smith, M. (eds), *International Relations and the European Union*. Oxford: Oxford University Press, 91–112.

Nye, J. 1990. *Bound to Lead: The Changing Nature of American Power*. New-York: Basic Books.

Nye, J. 2004. *Soft Power: the Means to Success in World Politics*. New York: Public Affairs.

Parmentier, F. 2008. 'The ENP Facing a De Facto State. Lessons from the Transnistrian Question', in: Delcour, L. and Tulmets, E. *Pioneer Europe? Testing European Foreign Policy in the Neighbourhood*. Baden-Baden: Nomos, 216–29.

Parmentier, F. 2008. 'The Reception of EU Neighbourhood Policy', in: Laïdi, Z. (ed.), *EU Foreign Policy in a Globalized World: Normative Power and Social Preferences*. London: Routledge, 103–17.

Parmentier, F. 2009. 'Normative Power, EU Preferences and Russia. Lessons from the Russian–Georgian War', *European Political Economy Review*, 9, 49–61.

Petiteville, F. 2001. 'La coopération économique de l'Union européenne: entre globalisation et politisation', *Revue française de science politique*, 51(3), 461–58.

Petiteville, F. 2006. *La politique internationale de l'Union européenne*. Paris: Presses de Sciences-Po.

Peyrouse, S. 2006. 'Quinze ans après l'indépendance, quels nouveaux enjeux en Asie centrale ?', *Revue internationale et stratégique*, n°64, Winter 2006–2007, 65–8.

Piebalgs, A. 2006a. *Challenges and perspectives of the EU energy policy*. SPEECH/06/285, Brussels, 10 May. Available at: http://europa.eu/rapid/pressReleasesAction.do?reference=SPEECH/06/285&type=HTML&aged=0&language=FR&guiLanguage=en

Piebalgs, A. 2006b. *Nabucco Pipeline – Searching for Alternative Routes for our Gas Supply*. SPEECH/06/413, Brussels, 26 June. Available at: http://europa.eu/rapid/pressReleasesAction.do?reference=SPEECH/06/413&format=PDF&aged=1&language=EN&guiLanguage=en

Piebalgs, A. 2007. *European Energy Policy and the role of Energy Community*, SPEECH/07/575, Athens, 28 September. Available at: http://europa.eu/rapid/pressReleasesAction.do?reference=SPEECH/07/575&guiLanguage=de

Piebalgs, A. and Shmatko, S. 2008. *EU–Russia Energy Dialogue, Ninth Progress Report*, Paris, October.

Piebalgs, A. and Shmatko, S. 2009. *EU–Russia Energy Dialogue, Tenth Progress Report*, Moscow, November.

Pinder, J. 1991. *The European Community and Eastern Europe*. London: Royal Institute of International Affairs/Pinter.

Pipes, R. 1976. *Soviet Strategy in Europe*. New York: Crane/Russak.

Plantev, P. 2003. 'Bulgaria's role and prospects in the Black Sea region: implications of NATO and EU enlargement', *Research Reports No. 15*, Sofia: Institute for Security and International Studies.

Polish–Swedish Proposal. 2008. *Eastern Partnership*, 23 May. Available at: http://www.tepsa.eu/docs/draft_proposal_eastern_partnership.pdf

Political Declaration on the Northern Dimension Policy. 2006. Available at: http://ec.europa.eu/external_relations/north_dim/docs/pol_dec_1106_en.pdf

Pomfret, R. 2006. 'Coordinating Aid for Regional Cooperation Projects: the Experience of Central Asia', *IIIS Discussion Paper No. 163*, June.

Popescu, N. 2005. 'The EU in Moldova – Settling Conflicts in the Neighbourhood', *EU ISS Occasional Paper No. 60*, October.

Popescu, N. 2006. '"Outsourcing" de facto Statehood: Russia and the Secessionist Entities in Moldova and Georgia', in: *CEPS Policy Brief, No. 109*, July.

Popescu, N. 2007. 'The European Union and conflicts in the South Caucasus'. Caucaz.com, 8 January.

Popescu, N. 2009. 'EU's Borders and Neighbours', EU Observer, http://blogs. euobserver.com/popescu/2009/05/04/eus-borders-and-neighbours, accessed on 10 March 2010.

Portela, C. 2005. 'Where and Why Does the EU Impose Sanctions?', *Politique européenne*, 17, 83–111.

Portela, C. 2007. 'Community Policies with a Security Agenda: The Worldviews of Benita Ferrero-Waldner', *EUI Working Papers*, RSCAS, 2007/10.

Portela, C. and Raube, K. (eds) 2008. 'Revisiting Coherence in EU Foreign Policy.' *Hamburg Review of Social Sciences*, special issue, 3(1).

Portela, C. and Raube, K. 2009. '(In-)Coherence in EU Foreign Policy: Exploring Sources and Remedies', Paper presented at the European Studies Association Bi-Annual Convention, Los Angeles, April. Available at: http://www.unc.edu/ euce/eusa2009/papers/portela_11B.pdf

Poujol, C. 2006. 'L'Asie centrale, bilan: quinze années de discours et de pratiques sur l'intégration dans un espace désintégré', *Revue internationale et stratégique*, n°64, Winter 2006–2007, 69–76.

President of the Russian Federation. 2008. *The Foreign Policy Concept of the Russian Federation*, 12 July, Available at: http://eng.kremlin.ru/text/ docs/2008/07/204750.shtm

President of Ukraine, 1998. 'Strategy of Ukraine's Integration to the European Union', 11 June, No. 615/98, Available at: http://www.mfa.gov.ua/mfa/en/ publication/content/2823.htm

Prozorov, S. 2000. 'The Structure of the EU–Russian Conflict Discourse: Issue and Identity Conflicts in the Narratives of Exclusion and self-Exclusion', *Working Papers Series in EU Border Conflicts Studies*, n°13, April.

Prozorov, S. 2005. 'The Structure of the EU–Russian Conflict Discourse: Issue and Identity Conflicts in the Narratives of Exclusion and Self-exclusion', *Working Paper Series in EU Border Conflicts Studies* n°13, April, University of Birmingham.

Radvanyi, J. 1998. 'Transport et géostratégie au sud de la Russie. Quand les Occidentaux poussent les nouveaux Etats indépendants loin de Moscou', *Le Monde diplomatique*, June.

Rahr, A. 2005. 'How can the EU's Policy Objectives in Relation to its Eastern Neighbourhood be Translated into more Effective EU action?' *European Parliament, Policy Department External Policies, Briefing Paper.*

Raux, J. (ed.), 1998. *Le partenariat entre l'Union européenne et la Fédération de Russie*. Rennes: Apogée.

Raviot, J.-R. 2008. *Démocratie à la russe. Pouvoir et contre-pouvoir en Russie*, Paris: Ellipses.

Robin Hivert, E. 2006. 'L'Europe unie, "idée neuve" ou "bloc agressif?" La naissance d'un discours soviétique sur l'intégration européenne', in: Rücker, K. and Warlouzet, L. (eds), *Quelle(s) Europe(s) ? Nouvelles approches en histoire de l'intégration européenne*. Brussels: Peter Lang, 275–84.

Robin Hivert, E. and Soutou, G.-H. (eds). 2008. *L'URSS et l'Europe de 1941 à 1957*. Paris: PUPS.

Romsloe, B. 2005. 'Finland and the Case of a Northern Dimension for the EU: Inclusion by Bargaining or Arguing?', *Arena Working Paper* 31/2005.

Rose, R. 1993. *Lesson-Drawing in Public Policy: A Guide to Learning Across Time and Space*. London: Chatham House.

Rummel, R. (ed.) 1990. *The Evolution of an International Actor: Western Europe's New Assertiveness*. Boulder: Westview Press.

Rupnik, J. (ed.) 2007. *Les banlieues de l'Europe*, Paris: Presses de Sciences-Po.

Sasse, G. 2008a. 'The European Neighbourhood Policy: Conditionality Revisited for the EU's Eastern Neighbours', *Europe Asia Studies*, 60(2).

Sasse, G. 2008b. 'The ENP Process and the EU's Eastern Neighbours: "Conditionality-lite", Socialisation and "Procedural Entrapment"', *Global Europe Papers* No. 2008/9.

Saurugger, S. 2009. *Théories et concepts de l'intégration européenne*, Paris: Presses de Sciences-Po.

Scott, J. (ed.) 2006. *EU Enlargement, Region Building and Shifting Borders of Inclusion and Exclusion*. Aldershot: Ashgate.

Serrano, S. 2008. *Géorgie: sortie d'Empire*. Paris: éditions du CNRS.

Shapovalova, N. 2009. 'The Eu's Eastern Partnership: Stillborn?', *FRIDE Policy Briefs No. 11*, May.

Shemiatenkov, V. 2002. *EU–Russia: The Sociology of Approximation*. Paper to the 6th ECSA World Conference, Brussels, December.

Shukan, I. 2007. 'Les principaux enjeux de la vie politique en Ukraine depuis la révolution Orange', *Les études du CERI No. 134*.

Sikorski, R. 2009. 'The EU's "Eastern Partnership" with former Soviet states holds the key to relations with Russia', *Europe's World*. Available at: http://www.gees.org/files/documentation/doc_Documen-031.pdf.

Silitski, V. 2009. 'Belarus – a Country in Transition? The State, elections and opposition', in Fischer, S. (ed.), 'Back from the Cold? The EU and Belarus in 2009', *Chaillot Paper No. 119*, EU Institute for Security Studies, 25–36.

Shemiatenkov, V. 1997. 'The relations between Russia and the European Union', *Revue des Affaires Européennes*, n°3, 277–89.

Shishkov, Y.V. 1997. 'Evropeiskaya integratsia i SNG: Zapadnyi obrazets i ego otrazhenie v vostoshnom zerkale' [European integration and the CIS: Western image and its reflect in the eastern mirror], in: *Razvitie integracionnykh processov v Evrope i Rossya* [Development of integration processes in Europe and Russia], Moscow: RAN (Russian Academy of Sciences), 174–200.

Sjursen, H. 2006. 'The EU as a "Normative" Power: How Can This Be?', *Journal of European Public Policy*, 13(2), March, 235–51.

Smith, H. 2009. 'Russian Foreign Policy, Regional Cooperation and Northern Relations', in: Aalto, P. Blakkisrud, H. and Smith, H. *The New Northern Dimension of the European Neighbourhood*, 19–34.

Smith, K.E. 2005a. 'Beyond the Civilian Power EU Debate', *Politique européenne*, 17, 63–82.

Smith, K.E. 2005b. 'The Outsiders: the European Neighbourhood Policy', *International Affairs*, 81(4), 757–73.

Smith, K.E. 2005c. 'The EU and Central and Eastern Europe: The Absence of Interregionalism', *European Integration*, 27(3), 347–64.

Smith, K.E. 2006. 'EU and Central and Eastern Europe: Absence of Interregionalism', in: Söderbaum, F., and van Langenhove, L. *The EU as a Global Player. The Politics of Interregionalism.*

Smith, K.E. 2008. *European Foreign Policy in a Changing World.* Malden: Polity Press, 2nd edition.

Smith, M.S. and Webber, M. 2008. 'Political Dialogue and Security in the European Neighbourhood: The Virtues and Limits of New Partnership Perspectives', *European Foreign Affairs Review No. 13*, 73–95.

Smith, S. 1994. 'Foreign Policy Theory and the New Europe', in: Carlsnaes, W. and Smith, S. *European Foreign Policy. The European Community and Changing Perspectives in Europe.* London: Sage.

Smith, S. 1999. 'Social Constructivisms and European Studies: a Reflectivist Critique', *Journal of European Public Policy*, 6(4), 682–91.

Söderbaum, F. and van Langenhove, L. 2006. *The EU as a Global Player: The Politics of Interregionalism.* London and New York: Routledge.

Steinmeier, F.-W. 2006. 'Russland, Europa und die Welt – Perspektiven der Zusammenarbeit in globalen Sicherheitsfragen', 42nd Munich Conference for Security Politics, Munich, 5 February, available at: http://www.pressrelations. de/new/standard/result_main.cfm?r=220105&sid=&aktion=jour_pm&print=1

Stern, J. 2006. *The Russian–Ukrainian Gas Crisis of January 2006*, Oxford Institute for Energy Studies.

Stoupnikova, L. 2008a. 'L'augmentation du prix du gaz naturel centrasiatique: quelles perspectives pour la Russie?', *Actualités Russie-CEI No. 8*, IRIS, April.

Stoupnikova, L. 2008b. 'Les alliances énergétiques: vers une réorganisation de l'espace eurasiatique?', *Revue internationale et stratégique*, 72, 131–39.

Surovell, J. 1995. 'Western Europe and the Western Alliance: Soviet and Post-Soviet Perspectives', *Journal of Communist Studies and Transition Politics*, 2, June, 155–97.

Sushko, O. 2006. 'EU Initiatives for Border Management in the EU's Eastern Neighbourhood', *The International Spectator*, 4, October–December, 43–53.

Tardieu, J.-P. 2009. 'Russia and the Eastern Partnership After the War in Georgia', *Russie-NEI Visions No. 43*, August.

Tallberg, J. 2003. 'The Agenda-Shaping Powers of the EU Council Presidency', *Journal of European Public Policy*, 10(1), 1–19.

Tassinari, F. 2005. 'Security and Integration in EU's Neighbourhood: The Case for Regionalism', *CEPS Working Document No. 226*, Brussels, July.

Tassinari, F. 2006. 'A Synergy for Black Sea Regional Cooperation: Guidelines for an EU Initiative', *CEPS Policy Brief No. 105*.

Telò, M. 2006. *Europe, A Civilian Power? European Union, Global Governance, World Order*. New York: Palgrave.

Telò, M. (ed.) 2007. *European Union and New Regionalism: Regional Actors and Global Governance in a Post-Hegemonic Era*. Aldershot: Ashgate, 2nd edition.

Tinguy, A. de (ed.) 2007. *Moscou et le monde, L'ambition de la grandeur retrouvée: une illusion?* Paris: Autrement.

Tocci, N.(ed.) 2007a. *The EU and Conflict Resolution: Promoting Peace in the Backyard*. London/New York: Routledge.

Tocci, N. 2007b. 'Can the EU Promore Democracy and Human Rights Through the ENP? The Case for Refocusing on the Rule of Law', in: Cremona, M. and Meloni, G. (eds), *The European Neighbourhood Policy: A Framework for Modernisation?*, EUI Working Papers LAW 2007/21, 24–35.

Trauner, F. and Kruse, I. 2008. 'EC Visa Facilitation and Readmission Agreements: Implementing a New EU Security Approach in the Neighbourhood', *CEPS Working Document No. 290*, April.

Tsygankov, A.P. 2006. 'If Not by Tanks, then by Banks? The Role of Soft Power in Putin's Foreign Policy', *Europe–Asia Studies*, 38(7), 1079–99.

Tulmets, E. 2007. 'Can the Discourse on "Soft Power" Help the EU to Bridge its Capability – Expectations Gap?', *European Political Economy Review No. 7*, 195–226.

Tulmets, E. 2008a. 'The European Neighbourhood Policy: A Flavour of Coherence in the EU's External Relations?', in: Portela, C. and Raube, K. (eds), 'Revisiting Coherence in EU Foreign Policy', *Hamburg Review of Social Sciences*, special issue, 3(1), 107–41.

Tulmets, E. 2008b. 'A "Soft Power" with Civilian Means: Can the EU Bridge its Capabilities-Expectations Gap in the ENP?', in: Delcour, L. and Tulmets, E., *Pioneer Europe: Testing European Foreign Policy in the Neighbourhood*, 138–69.

Vahl, M. 2006. 'A Privileged Partnership? EU–Russia relations in a Comparative Perspective', *DIIS Working Papers No. 3*.

Van Elsuwege, P. 2008. *From Soviet Republics to EU Member States: A Legal and Political Assessment of the Baltic States Accession to the EU*. Leiden/Boston: Martinus Nijhoff Publishers.

Vasconcelos, Á. 2008. '"Multilateralising" multipolarity', *Chaillot Paper No. 109*, 11–32.

Vasconcelos, Á. (ed.), 2009. *The European Security Strategy 2003–2008. Building on Common Interests*. ISS Report No. 5, February.

Vasilyan, S. 2009. 'The EU's Ambitious Regionalization of the South Caucasus', in: De Lombaerde , P. and Schulz, M. (eds). *The EU and World Regionalism: The Makability of Regions in the 21st Century*. Aldershot: Ashgate.

Wæver, O. 1995. 'Securitization and Desecuritization', in: Lipschutz, R. (ed.), *On Security*. New York: Columbia University Press, 46–87.

Wendt, A. 1999. *Social Theory of International Politics*. Cambridge: Cambridge University Press.

Wennersten, P. 1999. 'The Politics of Inclusion: the Case of the Baltic States', *Cooperation and Conflict*, 34(3), 272–96.

Westphal, K. 2006. 'Energy Policy between Multilateral Governance and Geopolitics: Whither Europe?', *Internationale Politik und Gesellschaft*, 4, 44–62.

White, B. 2004. 'Foreign Policy Analysis and the New Europe', in: Carlsnaes, W., Sjursen, H. and White, B. (eds), *Contemporary European Foreign Policy*. London: Sage Publishers, 11–31.

Whitman, R. 1998. *From Civilian Power to Superpower? The International Identity of the European Union*. New York: St. Martin's Press; Basingstoke: Macmillan.

Wichmann, N. 2007. 'The Intersection between Justice and Home Affairs and the European Neighbourhood Policy: Taking Stock of the Logic, Objectives and Practices', *CEPS Working Document No. 275*, October.

de Wilde d'Estmaël, T. 1998. *La dimension politique des relations économiques extérieures de la Communauté Européenne*. Brussels: Bruylant.

Wilson, A., Popescu, N. and Noël, P. 2009. *The Future of EU–Russia Relations: a Way Forward in Solidarity and the Rule of Law*. European Parliament, Policy Department External Policies, Briefing Paper, February.

Wolczuk, K. 2004. 'Integration without Europeanisation: Ukraine and its Policy towards the European Union', *European University Institute Working Paper No. 2004/15*.

Wolczuk, K. 2007. 'Adjectival Europeanisation? The Impact of EU Conditionality on Ukraine under the European Neighbourhood Policy', *European Research Working Paper Series No. 18*.

Wolczuk, K. 2008. 'Ukraine and its Relations With the EU in the Context of the European Neighbourhood Policy', in Fischer, S. (ed.), 'Ukraine: Quo Vadis?', *Chaillot Paper No. 108*, 87–118.

Wolczuk, K. 2010. 'Convergence without Finalité: EU Strategy towards Post-Soviet States in the Wider Black Sea Region', in: Henderson, K. and Weaver, C., *The Black Sea Region and EU Policy: The Challenge of Divergent Agendas*. Farnham: Ashgate.

Young, J.C. and Caporaso, J. 2002. 'Comparative Regional Integration', in Carlsnaes, W., Risse, T., and Simmons, B. (eds), *Handbook of International Relations*. London: Sage.

Zielonka, J. 2002. *Europe Unbound: Enlarging and Reshaping the Boundaries of the European Union*. London: Routledge.

Zielonka, J. 2007. *Europe as Empire: The Nature of the Enlarged EU*. Oxford: Oxford University Press.

Zielonka, J. 2008. 'Europe as a global actor: empire by example?', *International Affairs*, 84(3).

Index